TENACITY

A Vegas Businessman Survives Brooklyn,
the Marines, Corruption and Cancer
to Achieve the American Dream

A True Life Story by Ron Coury

Michael,

Please enjoy my story!

Ron Coury

LAS VEGAS PUBLISHING GROUP, LLC

Las Vegas Publishing Group, LLC
8635 West Sahara Ave., #240
Las Vegas, NV 89117

Hardcover ISBN: 978-1-7327210-0-5
Paperback ISBN: 978-1-7327210-1-2
eBook ISBN: 978-1-7327210-2-9
Audiobook ISBN: 978-1-7327210-3-6

Cover by Tom Coury
Book design by Barbara Aronica

Manufactured in the United States of America

CONTENTS

DISCLOSURE

The author has attempted to re-create events, locales, and conversations from his memories of them. Certain discussions among others that he was not privy to have had to be fictionalized. In order to maintain certain persons' protection and anonymity, in some instances the names of places, individuals, and events have been changed. Identifying characters, conversations, and details such as physical property locations, occupations, and other events outside of the author's first-hand knowledge have had to be created. Every story told in this book is accurate to the best of the author's recollection. Although the author and publisher have made every effort to ensure that the information in this book was correct at press time, the author and publisher do not assume and hereby disclaim any liability to any party for any loss, damage, or disruption caused by errors or omissions, whether such omissions or errors result from negligence, accident, or any other cause.

PREFACE

Las Vegas of the early 1970s was a true dichotomy—a small American city with a base population of under 300,000 that attracted around 10 million annual visitors responding to the lure of wide-open casino gambling. In many ways, Vegas was still the Wild West, where some folks strolled the streets with exposed six-shooters on their hips and the occasional horseback rider clopped along the dusty thoroughfares—all in the glow of the bright lights of the Las Vegas Strip just a mile or two away. In those days, we had a mythically tough sheriff, Ralph Lamb, who ruled the town with an iron fist, drove undesirables out, warned them never to come back, and asked no forgiveness. In his own way, he kept the place safe. In 2012, his story was featured in a TV series on CBS, starring Dennis Quaid as Ralph Lamb. Titled "Vegas," the show lasted only one season.

Later, in the 1970s, '80s, and '90s, I ran my Las Vegas bars much like Sheriff Lamb ran his police department. Troublemakers were asked to settle down and if necessary, to leave. Without exception, when the situation demanded it, they were forcibly removed. In my younger years, I was fortunate to possess the inner drive to set a standard and the military training to back it up. I loved this city and its potential for my businesses and future and I was prepared to ensure that right prevailed over wrong, bullies were defeated, and justice was served.

That's what this book is about—the determination to overcome any unjust obstacles that may stand in the way of one's dreams. In a word: *Tenacity*.

The principle of tenacity applied especially to one instance in the 1980s that threatened to cost me not only my livelihood, but my very freedom. I'd worked long and hard to achieve financial and professional goals I'd set for myself and suddenly, I was faced with the prospect of losing everything.

I had no choice but to fight back—and I did.

I can thank the United States Marine Corps for helping mold me into the person I am today, the one I had to be to overcome what would threaten the life I was building for myself and my family in Las Vegas.

I've found through personal experience that success in business requires many skills and talents, but none more essential than the core belief of the Marine Corps: "Failure is not an option!" This fighting spirit drives a person to take on life's challenges with resolve and a refusal to be defeated. Once again, tenacity! The word exemplifies what overtakes me when someone says "no" or "impossible" to me when I know I'm in the right, or when someone tries to deny me something I'm pursuing, whether it's starting a business, protecting one I already have, or preserving my liberty and rights as an American.

Tenacity, along with my deeply held values and a strong belief in the American Dream, motivated me to start or purchase eight businesses before I turned 35, as I doggedly pursued my entrepreneurial aspirations. I was also blessed with great partners; we shared a trust, respect, and honesty that enabled me to excel and seek each new challenge. Along with those excellent partners, I had the support of many close friends. It was all challenging, fun, and rewarding, but within two short years in the late 1980s, I found that everything I had was in jeopardy.

The absurd circumstances that transpired over a brief four-hour period on a chilly night in November 1989 involved a thieving waiter, a hands-on owner trying to get his business off the ground, the misinformed officials of the City of Opportunity, Nevada, an overly aggressive detective, an eager-to-please district attorney, and an ensuing chain of events that changed the lives of everyone involved. Innocent but presumed guilty, my managers and I found ourselves in the fight of our lives—for being the *victims* of theft!

We like to believe the "system" is designed to protect the innocent and prosecute the guilty. The reality is that under unique circumstances, there can be a faint fine line between the wronged and the wrongdoer, which can be further obscured when the facts are tainted by carelessness or corruption.

When everything you've worked for is in peril and your personal freedom is at stake, you can do one of two things. You can sit by, hoping that the system works as it should, the truth will be revealed, and justice will be served. Or you can fight for what's right. As you'll see within these pages, the latter is the road I chose.

Desperate times called for desperate measures.

I planted my feet and fought tooth and nail to reveal the truth and let the potential consequences be damned. Failure was not an option.

So sit back and enjoy the ride, knowing this story is based on actual events. And with luck, this book will inspire others to stand up for what they know is right, whatever the odds.

CHAPTER 1

City of Opportunity Justice Court

August 1990. I stood next to my attorney, confident silver-haired Chuck Thompson, before a judge in Opportunity Justice Court. It felt like I was having an out-of-body experience.

The City of Opportunity, Nevada, is a small town in the northwest area of the Las Vegas Valley, just on the other side of Lone Mountain. With its own city government and police department, this stand-alone community operated under a city charter providing attractive business opportunities that the City of Las Vegas no longer offered.

"People of the State of Nevada versus Ron Coury, Arthur Coury, Robert Alber, and Arthur Charles. Criminal case numbers 90FH0010 A, B, C & D. The Honorable Judge Arnold Stabinski presiding."

All sights and sounds were surreal, the whole scene like something out of a bad dream. How could four innocent men be standing here accused? And yet, there we were.

"Defendant Ron Coury is charged with: Count One, second degree kidnapping, a felony. Count Two, false imprisonment, a gross misdemeanor. Count Three, coercion, a felony. Count Four, extortion with the use of a deadly weapon, a felony. Count Five, extortion to collect a debt with the use of a deadly weapon, a felony. Count Six, coercion with the use of a deadly weapon, a felony."

As the court clerk droned on, my eyes drifted to Deputy District

Attorney Bryn Baird, her placid features giving no hint of her goal to put me and the managers of my three bars in prison for more than 50 years.

"Mr. Coury, how do you plead?"

For a moment, I didn't realize the judge was speaking to me. A surge of adrenaline snapped me out of the fog. "Not guilty, Your Honor." My voice was unwavering. I hoped the judge took note, perhaps seeing it as evidence of my innocence.

Next up was "Defendant Robert Alber," charged with five counts, the same as mine except for coercion with the use of a deadly weapon. My general manager Bob Alber, who oversaw operations at all three of my bar/restaurant locations, stood tall, befitting a fellow former Marine with nothing to hide. With his attorney, Don Green, by his side and providing directions as needed, Bob stood when his name was announced. "Not guilty, Your Honor," Bob declared, without waiting to be asked how he was pleading.

Then it was on to my brother Artie, eight years my junior and the location manager of Winners Lounge and Restaurant. He'd done it all at my other bars, working as a cook, bartender, server, and bouncer, diligently rising through the ranks before earning his position as manager. And now this.

Charged with three counts, Artie answered, "Not guilty," then calmly sat back down beside noted criminal-defense attorney Richard "Rick" Wright.

My cousin, Art Charles, patiently waited his turn with his attorney, Steve Stein beside him. A big man of about 280 pounds and strong as an ox, Art had been a Las Vegan ever since his parents, my Uncle Joe and Aunt Margie, along with his younger brother Doug, moved out from Brooklyn back in the 1950s. Art was head chef and kitchen manager at Winners, a job I'm sure he never thought in a million years could put him in danger of spending the rest of his life behind bars.

"Not guilty!" Arthur thundered, in a deep resonant voice befitting a man his size, to the three counts with which he was charged.

How did it come to this? How did four businessmen working hard to take care of their families and contribute something to the community end up pleading innocence when we were the ones who should have been pressing charges? The answer was a paradox. It was simple, yet much more complex than you might ever imagine.

The Las Vegas Bar Business

The Las Vegas bar business is unlike any other tavern industry in the world. Of course, we offer food and drinks, but we also have a significant differentiating feature—gaming devices, a.k.a. slot machines. Other casino jurisdictions, like Atlantic City, don't allow local bars to engage in gaming, but thankfully, Las Vegas is different.

These devices replicate every major casino game: blackjack, craps, roulette, keno, and poker. The themes of regular slot machines run the gamut, from Rocky, the Beverly Hillbillies, and Playboy to the various signs of the Zodiac, country music, Americana—even machines based on McIlhenny Tabasco Sauce. However, the wide diversity of packaging and marketing all serves the same goal: luring players to wager their money in hopes of hitting a life-changing jackpot. And no device has proven to be better at this than video poker, a revolutionary development in slot machines that began redefining the gaming industry, especially within the Las Vegas bar business, in the 1980s. With the explosive popularity of video poker, Vegas bars that had relied on food and beverage for the majority of their revenue almost overnight experienced a tectonic shift in which over 70 percent now came from gaming. At the same time, these machines require little space and minimal oversight and are fairly incidental in the overall operation of a bar.

Unlike other towns across America, in Las Vegas, bar patrons can play the ultimate bar game, giving them the chance to turn $5 into $5,000. And some of us business owners are a bit gutsier. At my operations, our machines were set to accept $50 per hand with a chance of winning $50,000 by hitting a royal flush.

But these places are so much more than just gambling parlors. They're gathering spots for neighborhood residents to eat, drink, and unwind after work and on their days off, watch a big game, play pool, enjoy a beer while eating great food, and have a few laughs. Many taverns also contribute to their communities by sponsoring Little League and children's soccer teams, adult sports teams, pool leagues, charitable causes—more than just about any other neighborhood business you can name. And most Vegas bars serve their neighborhoods, far removed from the hustle and bustle of downtown and the Strip, relying primarily on residents, not tourists, for revenue.

The tavern business can be quite lucrative, but as in any enterprise, challenges are ongoing. And being a cash business, one of the most significant problems is theft—by armed robbers as well as employees. As someone who's created jobs for hundreds of people, I can tell you that there may be nothing more troubling than to discover that a trusted member of your team, whom you've provided with employment, health insurance, and other benefits, has stolen from you. But it happens. And it was just such an occurrence that ignited the sequence of events that landed me in Judge Stabinski's courtroom on that hot summer day in 1990.

The Defense Team

After Deputy District Attorney Baird introduced herself to the court, Judge Stabinski peered over the wire-rimmed glasses perched on the tip of his aged nose at the defense team I'd assembled and remarked, "It's not often my courtroom sees the likes of this battalion of prominent defense attorneys."

I'd met attorney Chuck Thompson years earlier at my Suburban Lounge West location. A former district attorney in Clark County, he was now in private practice. With a full head of gray hair, Chuck's distinguished appearance, authoritative air and confident manner made him someone you'd tend to remember. When I learned I needed to hire a criminal-defense attorney, which I'd never had to do before, Chuck immediately came to mind. In our first meeting, I knew I'd made the right call.

Chuck suggested we retain a private investigator to do a deep dive into the life of our accuser, who happened to be the employee we'd caught stealing. He also explained that Artie, Bob, and Arthur, while not legally required to retain their own attorneys, should definitely do so.

However, none of my managers could afford lawyers. Dan Hughes, my closest friend and partner in all my businesses at the time, agreed that we should pay for everyone's legal representation.

Chuck knew virtually every criminal-defense lawyer in town and possessed a wealth of information on who would bring the most to the table. We discussed many options before deciding on our dream team. I hoped our first choices would be available. We got very lucky. Each attorney was available and in a position to join us.

Steve Stein, a former federal prosecutor, was now in private practice with impressive experience in criminal-defense work. Steve would represent my cousin Arthur.

A top litigator, Rick Wright, brought a low-key style to the team, while exuding incredible confidence and a commanding presence. He would represent my brother Artie.

The final piece of the puzzle was Don Green, a sharp legal mind and relentless researcher. Chuck convinced me that having a strategist like Don on board was crucial to rounding out the defense team. A successful litigator in his own right, he would represent my general manager, Bob.

Although technically, each defendant hired his own attorney, we each had four attorneys fighting on our behalf. In our first strategy session, we all agreed that we'd win or lose as a team, sticking together through thick and thin. We'd unmask for the court the misguided beliefs of both the lead detective and the Opportunity City Attorney, and the chicanery of a certain Opportunity city councilman whom I believed had a hidden agenda to eliminate me as a business competitor.

I left the meeting energized and alive, as I always am when I feel in charge of a situation. Letting things play out and hoping for the best was never my style, particularly this time, when my liberty, reputation and personal wealth were all at stake. I couldn't rest on the hope that right is might and the truth would win the day. I was ready to fight.

Failure was not an option!

CHAPTER 2

Brooklyn

Before getting into the improbable chain of events that landed me in court, it will be helpful to give you a feel for what it took to get to where I was, before it all appeared to be going up in smoke.

Strangers in a Strange Land

In the early 1900s, people from all over the world immigrated to this great nation. Many of them, like my relatives and those of my childhood friends, came through Ellis Island. My grandparents left the Middle East to escape religious persecution. They looked forward to becoming Americans, earning a decent living, and practicing their religion in safety.

It amazes me how brave those folks were. Driven to find a better life and future for their families, they traveled on ships under deplorable conditions and endured unimaginable hardships to come to a strange country where they didn't know the language or customs. They knew it was all worthwhile as they stood on those decks— shoulder to shoulder—gazing at the welcoming lady in the harbor, the Statue of Liberty. She belongs to each and every one of us, representing what America offered then and does today—an opportunity to practice religion and pursue dreams under the great umbrella of freedom and democracy.

Immigrants spread out all around the country, but my maternal grandparents, Catherine and Thomas Tannous, paternal grandparents Abdoo and Saada "Sadie" Coury, and those of some of my closest friends settled just a couple of miles from Ellis Island, in South Brooklyn near the intersection of Atlantic Avenue and Court Street. They found jobs, opened stores and did whatever they had to do in order to provide for their families. Our parents grew up on those streets, going to school, socializing and later vacationing together. When they married, most of them chose spouses from within the group of friends they'd known all their lives. The list of Middle Eastern surnames on residential mailboxes and storefronts in our area of Brooklyn was seemingly endless. Mansour, Arbeeny, Akel, Shaia, Sahadi, Bistany, Khoury, Jehamy, Ajami, Habib, Hassen, Metres, Aboushanab, Zahralban, Hajjar, Shaheen and Jalinos are just a few names that come to mind. The Kirshy family, which owned a few small businesses in the old neighborhood, was particularly close to mine. One of the younger Kirshy boys, George, has been a friend since childhood. Although his family relocated to Florida to pursue a new business opportunity in 1970, George has remained a close friend and member of our Brooklyn crew to this day. Similarly, Steve Bistany relocated as a teen to New Jersey with his parents, but stayed in touch and joined us in Brooklyn and elsewhere when our group got together for decades to follow.

My friends and I grew up knowing one another's parents and grandparents and out of respect, we prefaced their first names with "Uncle" or "Aunt." We lived on similar streets, went to the same schools and developed a bond of trust and loyalty that have survived the test of time.

I was very lucky to grow up in a terrific family. My early household consisted of me, my mom and dad, my brother Artie, my maternal grandparents, and my Aunt Gloria, my mother's sister, who later married and moved with her husband to Las Vegas.

My grandmother handled the household, since my parents and aunt all worked. She cooked the meals and was there when my brother and I came home from school. She spoke very little English, but I could communicate with her in Arabic, a language that I've lost to a certain extent, after not speaking it much over the past 45 years.

In Brooklyn I had a warm, loving home where we ate dinner together every night to catch up on what we'd been doing, a tradition I tried to continue once I began raising a family of my own. My parents weren't rich by any means, but there was always food on the table, and my initial allowance was 50 cents a week.

My dad lost his own father when he was six, right after the Great Depression. His mother raised four boys and two girls by herself. What a loving and capable dad mine was, especially considering that he grew up without a father of his own. All my friends loved my father as well. When we were little, on occasion, he'd gather up all the kids I was playing with outside, tell them to run and ask their parents if they could go to Coney Island, load us into the car, and treat us to Brooklyn's famous amusement park. We rode the rides, ate Nathan's hot dogs, and had a blast. As we grew older, even old enough to drive, when the phone rang and my friends wanted me to come out, if I said I just wanted to stay home that night, they'd say, "Well, what's your dad doing?" He was so cool, they loved being around him.

My dad always labored very hard to support us. Throughout his career, he drove a cab, worked at the Brooklyn Navy Yard, opened a small business with two friends, and finally settled into a job at a small Wall Street brokerage firm, Fahnestock & Co., where my mom worked as well. Aunt Gloria also worked on Wall Street. There's no doubt in my mind that I got my work ethic and entrepreneurial spirit from my dad.

The Working Life

I spent the first eight years of my academic career at St. Paul Catholic School, the same school my dad attended in the 1930s. Unlike today where kids wear jeans and sneakers, in 1960s Brooklyn, Catholic-school students wore uniforms and black dress shoes. And those shoes were expected to be shined. When I was 12, my parents gave me a wooden shoeshine box for Christmas and for the first time, I was in business. I often got up early and hustled down to the corner subway station, where I shined shoes for a dime a pop. I'd hurry home, drop off my gear, and run the block and a half to school, hoping I wouldn't be late. It was a great feeling to devise a plan and be earning my own money.

Not too long after, a new mid-rise condo building with a health club opened a few blocks from me. Word hit the street that management was paying kids to pass out flyers for the club, so I raced over and before I knew it, I was knocking down 25 cents an hour handing out flyers and placing them in apartment building vestibules and under windshield wipers.

From there, I landed a job at the Near East Bakery, through my Aunt Gloria's friendship with the owner. It was a brick-oven operation in the basement of a brownstone on Atlantic Avenue. They made Syrian pastries and "Syrian bread," which nowadays is called pita bread, a staple for people of Middle Eastern heritage. Working from 5 to 11 a.m., I earned $15—a real score at the time.

Next door to the bakery was Sahadi's Middle Eastern Groceries, a third-generation, family-owned importer of gourmet specialties that were—and still are—in great demand in my old neighborhood. There, I met a lifelong friend and current owner/partner, Bob Sahadi, also a Brooklyn Technical High School (a.k.a. Brooklyn Tech) student in our class of 1970. Bob couldn't hang with us at an early age, as he worked many hours at the family store while attending school. But in later years, his presence was assured whenever we all got together.

Another good friend from Brooklyn Tech, Rich Wieboldt, joined our group in downtown Brooklyn for reunions and came along on several family vacations over the years. He resonated with the preliminary architectural classes taught to all Brooklyn Tech students and later became a Virginia-based architect. When I was old enough for more traditional employment, my parents got me a summer job at Fahnestock & Co, which gave me my first real paycheck, an introduction to Wall Street finance and an entirely new work environment. At Fahnestock, I met Tom Squillante, a.k.a. "Tommy Bear," a co-worker who eventually joined our group of downtown Brooklyn buddies and has remained a close friend for life. While attending high school, I also got a part-time job at a department store called Martin's, on Fulton Street in downtown Brooklyn.

Long before indoor malls, there was Fulton Street—five blocks of stores on both sides of the street. It was a hub of shopping activity, Brooklyn's version of Manhattan's 5th Avenue. Martin's was an upscale store compared to others in the area, much like a Nordstrom's today. I was an after-school "box boy" there, doing anything the floor manager needed done. I stocked shelves, cleaned up messes, tossed trash—whatever I was asked to do. At barely 17, I was earning a net check of about $55 a week and loving it.

One of my co-workers at Martin's was John Metres, another lifelong friend and fellow student at Brooklyn Tech. He was in amazing shape, boxed in the Golden Gloves and, to this day, is a self-avowed basketball junkie. One evening, we were waiting outside a small apartment building for another friend from Brooklyn Tech, Joe Shaia, to come out from visiting a friend who was babysitting upstairs that night. John and I were horsing around and he threw me into some wall lockers lined up beneath an apartment where three guys lived. The lockers tumbled over like dominos and made one hell of a noise. We were laughing and standing them back up when the three guys came down and, out of the blue, started throwing punches at us! I gave as good as I got, but John dropped two of them in seconds, then came for the one I was tangling with. Three fiery rights from John to the third guy's face and the three of them ran upstairs.

Joe Shaia heard the commotion and came flying down. We were standing there talking about how crazy the whole thing was, when suddenly one of those idiots leaned out his apartment window and fired a rifle at us! We scattered and luckily, no one was hit. But we didn't return to that corner for quite a while. And none of us even thought to call the cops. It was just another adventurous night with buddies in Brooklyn.

The Volunteers

My first real stab at making money as an entrepreneur came, as many opportunities do, in a most unexpected way. Although most of my childhood friends were second-generation Middle Eastern like me, a couple of others were part of the crew. Tom "TK" Kennedy and Rocco Giovanniello also attended Brooklyn Tech.

Tom was a very good keyboard player. One day in 1970, a few of us were hanging out on our favorite Brooklyn street corner, Verandah Place and Henry Street, when TK said, "Why don't we start a band?"

Joe Shaia said, "I'll sing." Joe was a great dancer, with a crowd-pleasing, entertaining personality. We knew he'd be perfect as a lead singer and front man.

Richie Habib, a former grade-school classmate of ours, announced he'd play the drums.

I didn't play anything but the radio and couldn't carry a tune in a bucket. So I was either left out or had to find my own way in. I said, "I'll be the manager!"

We learned that another guy we knew from Brooklyn Tech, Sam DiBenedetto, played rhythm guitar. We pitched him on the idea and he agreed to join. Through him we found our bass guitarist, Mousey. To this day, I don't know what Mousey's actual name was, he was just Mousey, but he was in and our group, the Volunteers, was born. I don't know how we landed on the name Volunteers, but it was accurate because in the early days, none of us was making a cent.

The band went from lousy to good quickly, so next on my to-do list was to get us some kind of a real gig. My family's church, Our Lady of Lebanon, was located in Brooklyn Heights. It had a nice large hall and since I knew Monsignor Stephens pretty well from my years as an altar boy, I asked him if we could hold a dance there. To my pleasant surprise, he agreed to let us use the hall—at no charge!

Now we needed to let people know this event was happening. Getting permission from my boss at the Wall Street brokerage house, I ran off 200 flyers and hit the streets. Drawing on my health-club-flyer experience, I blanketed the neighborhood. But what if only a few people showed up and paid admission? How would we earn any real money?

I knew a guy from the neighborhood named Joe Tedeshi, who operated a beverage business. One day after school, I stopped by to see him.

"Hey Joey," I said, adopting my most professional demeanor and handing him a flyer. "Our band is playing a dance at the church hall in two weeks and I want to sell soft drinks and beer." Never mind that we were underage and didn't have a license to sell alcohol, much less on church property. (Ah, the casual nature of things in the early1970s.) "The thing is, Joe, I don't have any money and I was wondering if we could work something out."

Fortunately, Joe knew my parents and me and was aware that I was considered a good kid in the neighborhood. Rather than throwing me out of the place, which I half-expected, he used a term I'd never heard before.

"Just come by that day and take whatever you want on consignment," he said. "Bring back what's left the next day and I'll only charge you ten cents a can for soda and twenty cents a beer for whatever you sell."

Consignment! And paying just 10 cents a can for soda and 20 cents for beer, when I could sell them for a dollar each! The margins were mind-boggling.

The evening of the event rolled around and my dad, Rocco, Tommy Bear, and other friends—Ron Hassen, John Metres, and Joe "Bush" Aboushanab—helped me pick up the beverages and set up the concession stand, while the band got ready to play. Then I thought, "What if people don't buy drinks? I'll have to haul it all back to Joe!" A lot of work for little return. So I ran to the store and bought bags of popcorn, pretzels, and peanuts to put out for free. Surely, all those free salted goodies would make all our wallflowers and dancing guests very thirsty.

My heart was in my throat as it came time to open the doors, but teenagers from all over the neighborhood poured in to see what all the excitement was about. Tommy Bear collected the $2-a-head admission, while the rest of the boys and my dear ol' dad sold soda and beer as fast as they could hand them out. Between beverage sales and the $2 admission charge, we took in over $3,000 that night! That was a lot of money in 1970.

It was one of the greatest nights of my early life and I wish we'd had camcorders back then. But there's no record of it, other than the memories that will be with me forever.

CHAPTER 3

Mean Streets

When I think back on the aspects of my youth that helped instill the ability to pursue my goals, I know adversity played a key role.

Once when I was 12, my mom left me a dollar bill to get a haircut after school. That included 75 cents for the haircut and a 25-cent tip. A kid named Harrison "Harry" Beach and I were killing time hanging out on the steps of St. Paul's rectory, two blocks from the barbershop. I was folding and unfolding the dollar when four kids walked by and as they passed, one of them reached out and tried to snatch it from me. I pulled it back before he could get near it. They continued on their way and I figured that was the end of it. But a few minutes later, as Harry and I headed to the barbershop, the four of them jumped out from behind a parked car and pushed us up against the church fence.

"I want that dollar," demanded the kid who originally tried to grab it.

"I'm not giving it to you," I said, clutching it tightly in my fist.

The words were barely out of my mouth before one kid grabbed me and another started punching me. The other pair were giving Harry the same treatment. I refused to let go of the bill. It was only a dollar, but the idea of someone taking it really pissed me off.

As we were getting worked over, a couple of power-company workers broke up the fight and chased the four boys off. I didn't think much of it afterward. Back then, people in our neighborhood got into fights all the time. But a few days later, I was sitting on the stoop outside my house when the same four kids walked up. Somebody must have told them my name, because the ringleader said, "Hey, Ronnie, remember us?" They laughed and continued on their way to the housing projects, two blocks down.

That night, I was watching TV in the living room when I heard laughter and voices drifting in from outside. I peeked through the Venetian blinds and spied the same guys outside—taunting me.

"Hey, Ronnie, whatcha doin'? Wanna come out and play?"

The fact that they knew my name and where I lived really got my heart pounding. I walked into the kitchen, and maybe it was the look on my face, but immediately my dad sensed something was wrong.

My dad fought in World War II. He'd been stationed in the South Pacific on a small island, defending it against Japanese who were entrenched in tunnels and repeatedly landing on its shores. He never discussed his experiences there with me, despite my inquiries over the years. After his death in 2002, I went through his affairs to assist my mom and found a small metal box tucked away in his closet. Inside were documents listing the medals he was awarded for his bravery. Only then did my mom tell me that his silence was how he tried to forget those fierce battles. After the war ended, he threw his uniforms and gear in the trash, tossed his medals in the ocean, and never spoke about these events again. A peaceful man at heart and truly a member of the greatest generation, who made it possible for us to enjoy the freedoms in the U.S. that so many take for granted today, my dad was a patriot who was moved to enlist after the Pearl Harbor sneak attack and fought when he had to.

"What's wrong, Ronnie?" he asked.

With a quick glance toward the living room windows, I described the fear I was feeling. "Remember those kids I told you about who tried to mug me a few days ago for my haircut dollar? They're out front, calling my name."

I half-expected my dad to be filled with anger, but instead, with a calmness that was even more intimidating, he casually picked up his napkin, wiped his mouth, stood up, and strode to the front door. Taking a moment to compose himself, he threw the door open and ran outside. I don't know what frightened my tormentors more, my dad coming at them or the sight of my four-foot-ten grandmother right behind him, her broomstick raised, with my mom, my aunt, and me right on her heels.

The kids scattered like scared pigeons as my dad vaulted the four-foot-high fence in front of our house and lit out after them. I'd never seen my old man run like that. He chased them for two blocks, right into the projects, crossing a boundary that scared me, but not him. My parents had lived in the projects before I was born and apparently, my dad knew his way around down there.

In the meantime, my mom flagged a passing police car, which stopped just as my dad stomped back toward us, gripping one of the culprits by the collar. The kid was terrified, crying his eyes out. With the same sense of calm he'd shown in the living room, he led the kid to the cop car, opened the door, deposited him inside, leaned in close, and said, "Touch my son again and you're dead."

I never saw those kids after that, even though they lived nearby. I'd always loved and respected my dad, but that night I developed a whole new level of admiration for him—a hero, standing up to bullies, fighting for what was right, and possessing a trait I dreamed I might emulate.

Backing Down Is Not an Option

A freckle-faced Irish kid in the neighborhood, Jimmy Callaghan, was a notorious bully. I tried to steer clear of him, but whenever he was around, I couldn't get past him without a pinch, a punch in the arm, or a slap in the face.

One day I was shooting marbles in the street with friends when Jimmy walked by, grabbed me and gave me a good shaking. Fed up with being picked on, I fought back. As I started throwing punches from all angles, Jimmy gaped at me in surprise, turned me loose and started running.

"Wow," I thought. "Jimmy Callaghan is running away from me."

That was a turning point. I came to learn that if you're confident and resist, bullies don't want any part of you. I discovered this to be true on several subsequent occasions.

After the Jimmy Callaghan experience, I had a newfound confidence. Little did I know I'd be tested in just a few months. I was 16 and walking home from a store on Atlantic Avenue with a bag of groceries for my grandmother. I walked down Clinton Street, a little out of the way, but wanted to see if any friends were out playing one of the many street games Brooklyn was known for. No one was around, but when I turned the corner onto Congress Street, I spotted a commotion on the lawn of Congress Gardens, an upscale apartment complex with a large, well-manicured front lawn—unique to downtown Brooklyn.

I could see that it was a three-on-one situation, three punks pummeling a guy I recognized. It was Timmy Boyd, who lived across the street from me. He was a good guy, a simple sort who kept to himself, never caused anyone grief, and was by no means a fighter. He was on his back, and the more he tried to get up, the more relentless and vicious their attack became.

For a few seconds, I contemplated my involvement and the chance I'd myself catch a beating from these teenage thugs. But I knew I couldn't leave a friend in need, whatever the risk.

I dropped the groceries and ran into the fray with a ferocity that I hoped might compensate for the shortage in numbers on our side.

I shoved the gang off Timmy, swinging lefts and rights as they came back at me. They found a different opponent who didn't just take a beating till they eased up. Instead, I brought the fight to them and kept myself between them and Timmy.

Pretty quickly, they wanted no part of someone who dished it out right back at them and ran up Congress Street. Typical bullies. Before long, they ran away, the true cowards they were. As Timmy and I walked home, he thanked me repeatedly, all the way to Wyckoff Street, a short three blocks away.

It felt good to do the right thing, despite the adverse odds, and to have it work out so well.

This seemingly minor fight helped mold me into a defender of right, an opponent of bullies, and someone who understood the challenge of going against the odds, as long as what I was fighting for was something I believed in.

On another occasion, years later, one morning when I was 18, I came out to find that someone had jimmied the vent window on the 1967 Dodge Polara my dad had given me a few months earlier, popped the door open, and stolen some tools, eight-track tapes, and my tape player. I was annoyed, but I knew it was part of living in Brooklyn.

I got the window fixed and bought a new eight-track player that was removable from under the dashboard and could be hidden. And that was that, until a few weeks later when I was out with Tom Kennedy. TK's dad had recently passed away and his mom wanted to reward him for graduating from Brooklyn Tech and receiving a free ride to a four-year college education. She used a portion of her husband's life-insurance money to buy him an incredible white Firebird Formula 400. It was the most beautiful ride I'd ever seen and whenever I was indoors and heard that deep rumble on the street, I'd think, "There goes TK."

One night, TK and I'd been out to Coney Island and he'd just dropped me back home at about 1 a.m. Minutes later, I heard that unmistakable growl of his Firebird, followed by the honking of his horn.

I ran outside to see what was going on. TK had driven up my narrow one-way street in the wrong direction to get to me quicker.

"Ronnie, I saw two guys trying to break into your car again! I stopped and told them to get lost—that we'd be coming back together and they'd better be gone."

I immediately took off on foot to where I'd parked my car. I rounded the corner and, unbelievably, the two of them were still there! One was keeping lookout while the other worked the vent window with my own screwdriver, the one stolen from me the last time around!

I charged the one with the screwdriver at full speed, grabbed the screwdriver, scooped him up, and kept running until the back of his head was stopped by the concrete wall of the corner furniture store. That stunned him for a moment and I noticed his accomplice approaching. I had one hand on the neck of the guy at the wall and my other outstretched to stop the second guy's advance.

Just then, TK's Formula 400 rumbled up. He emerged with a knife in hand and charged the accomplice, who ran up Warren Street with TK in hot pursuit. The stunned guy came to his senses and we started going at it; eventually, I got the better of him. So he got my tapes and player the first time around, but this time, I got my screwdriver back and some satisfaction to boot!

The second guy got away from TK, who quickly returned to check on me. Meanwhile, someone called the cops and a sergeant and patrol officer arrived. The thief we had in hand begged them to arrest him. "I'll plead guilty to anything, man! Just take me! Don't leave me here with these guys!"

The sergeant's response was something like, "Listen, you thieving bastard, you're getting just what you deserve."

The cops left and I'll leave the rest of the story to your imagination.

That entire incident reinforced my belief in sticking up for myself and fighting for what's right.

Another thing was clear to me as well. TK had not only been a good friend since kindergarten, more than 12 years prior, but this incident proved his mettle beyond belief. We'd be close buddies for the rest of our lives.

CHAPTER 4

Brooklyn Tech to USMC

I'm a strong believer in young people receiving a solid education. So after graduating from Brooklyn Tech in 1970, I tried a couple of semesters at Bernard M. Baruch College of the City University of New York, before realizing that college wasn't for me. It wasn't college itself; my grades were good and I loved to learn. However, the City of New York had recently implemented an open-enrollment program in its university system, aimed at promoting a quality education for all. In short, anyone who wanted to attend one of the university's many city colleges, including Baruch, was admitted, regardless of grades or level of preparedness. If you had a high school diploma and wanted to go to college, you were in. That sounds pretty good, right? In theory, it was. But the administrators didn't consider how these kids would ever survive their first year, let alone make it through graduation. The greater impact of this well-intentioned policy fell on students who had applied themselves in earlier years and were now forced to re-visit lessons of old for the sake of a few.

In an advanced calculus class, I discovered that what sounds good on paper often isn't so great in reality.

One day, a fellow student was having trouble understanding the material, so the instructor asked him some basic questions. The entire classroom quickly realized that the student didn't comprehend fundamentals that most of us had learned as far back as our freshman year in high school. Here he was in our class without any of the tools necessary to keep up. The instructor, trying to be politically correct, I suppose, changed his lesson plan and commenced an abbreviated course in basic math to bring this poor kid up to speed. Sitting through day after day of these reviews, I realized this path wasn't for me; I dropped the class more than midway through the term. That seemingly insignificant decision had unexpected ramifications that would lead to a pivotal point in my life.

At the time, the Vietnam War was still well underway and all eligible young men were being drafted.

I was originally exempt under a student deferment and I mistakenly believed that my deferment was secure, provided I carried a course load of at least 12 credits. I didn't know that I needed to stay enrolled in those classes through the entire term to keep the deferment in force. Incredibly, with all our government had on its hands at the time— all the oversights, mistakes, out-of-control budgets, overpayments for basic items, battles against corruption, misuses of power, and shady deals, not to mention an extremely unpopular war to run—the Selective Service System proved to be amazingly on the ball.

And so, in January 1972, mere weeks after dropping that fateful class, I got the dreaded "Greetings" letter from Uncle Sam. I was bored with school and going nowhere with a part-time job, so the thought of this new experience actually excited me.

I learned that there were few ways out of the draft (moving to Canada, attending divinity school, and the like), none of which was for me. But in serving, I could also give myself the best odds of survival. The Selective Service System could randomly assign draftees to one of the various military branches, but the vast majority of them were destined for service in or around the Vietnam conflict. Many guys from our neighborhood were returning without limbs, severely and permanently disabled, or in coffins. I felt strongly that not only my welfare, but my very life, shouldn't be determined by an arbitrary assignment from the local Draft Board. Instead, I considered all the branches of the military by meeting with their respective recruiters. What I encountered was eye opening.

Recruiters have enlistment goals they must attain as part of their mission assignment. As a direct consequence of that scenario, it wasn't surprising that they painted rosy pictures for me. The Marine Corps recruiter was the exception. He described a training program (boot camp) that would be the hardest thing I'd ever encountered. He guaranteed hard work, physical demands, and literal ass-kicking unlike anything I could even envision. But, if successful, I'd be a member of the best-trained fighting force the world has ever known.

Many recruits, I'm sure, heard of the boot camp experience and ran for the door. Instead, I saw it as a choice I could make that would significantly enhance the likelihood I'd not only survive the war in Vietnam, but return intact.

The Marine recruiters administered an aptitude test on which I scored fairly high, enabling me to choose whether I wanted to do my boot-camp training on South Carolina's Parris Island or at the Marine Corps Recruit Depot (MCRD) in San Diego, California. Until then, I'd never flown on an airplane. I'd also never been to sunny southern California. I enjoyed the Beach Boys song "California Girls," and the feel-good vibe it always gave me. So I thought I'd see what was going on out on the West Coast.

This all came together quickly and I made these decisions without discussing them with anyone. I was 19 years old at the time and living at home with my parents, my grandmother, my mother's sister Gloria, and my younger brother Artie. One night over dinner, I told everyone I'd be leaving home for a while, that I'd joined the Marines and would be heading for boot camp in two weeks. No one believed me. I convinced them by producing the documents. At that point out came the rosary beads, and my mom, aunt and grandmother began praying together for my safety like I'd never seen before.

Given how close my friends and I were and had always been, it was no surprise that when it was time for me to "go to war," they were there to support me. We drove in a caravan to Fort Hamilton in Brooklyn for my swearing-in ceremony, to say goodbye and be together until the very last minute. I later learned that my dad followed us that night. He wanted to be with me too, but did it his way, from a distance. I'll always regret not including him in that ride with the rest of us. But at 19, that wasn't how we thought. If I only knew then what I know now.

After a bus ride to JFK Airport, I stepped aboard a plane for my first-ever flight. The huge jet flew us nonstop to San Diego.

The flight was at night, so except for distant lights below, I saw little of the country. Landing at the airfield near the Marine Corps Recruit Depot was uneventful. While a stream of other planes touched down, bearing enlistees from all over the U.S., uniformed Marines shuffled us off to a secure area. My experience as a member of the world's toughest fighting force began.

Herded onto a truck covered in military-green canvas, we stood in the dark, holding on to overhead supports for dear life, as we rumbled and lurched into the night, finally coming to a halt. The driver cut the engine. Minutes went by and we heard nothing. It was eerie. Finally, a meaty hand flipped open the canvas flap that covered the back of the truck and the yelling began. "Everybody out! Now!"

We scrambled out of the truck bed onto black asphalt "decorated" with painted yellow footprints.

"Stand on those footprints at attention and be quiet!"

From there we marched into MCRD and my life as a Marine recruit began.

The Few, the Proud

Over the next few hours, our hair was cut to the scalp, our clothes and personal belongings were boxed for shipment back home, and we were issued all we'd need for three months in boot camp.

There were four 72-man platoons, each called a series. Everyone in the series went through boot camp together, including basic and advanced training. We traveled as a group though MCRD and Camp Pendleton, which is about 40 miles north of downtown San Diego. We met people of every ethnicity and background, some of whom might be destined to save our lives, or change them forever.

About two months into boot camp, I first noticed a new guy in another platoon. At six feet four inches tall, he was difficult to miss, and I heard the drill instructors calling him Private Hughes. Our paths didn't really cross, but that changed one fateful day while I was in line at the mess hall. Hughes was standing with several other guys in front of me when some jerk tried to cut in front of him. Hughes shoved him back out of the line. The guy cut right back in, and this time tall, lanky Private Hughes threw an elbow that knocked the intruder backward about 10 feet. I found the sight rather entertaining and noted that this Hughes guy had some power.

The jerk picked himself up off the deck and walked to the back of the line, where he grabbed one of the metal food trays. Hughes never saw the cheap shot coming. I wish I'd been closer to stop it. The guy whacked him with the edge of the tray on the back of his head, knocking him out cold. He immediately started bleeding pretty heavily from the gash. The jerk took off running and I don't know what, if anything, ever happened to him. I do know that after Hughes was hauled off on a stretcher, stitched up and bandaged, he was back at full duty the next day. I remember thinking, that's one tough guy.

I later learned Private Hughes had just joined that platoon, having been previously taken out of training and placed in the hospital for a couple of months. He'd started boot camp months before me, but during one of the many long daily runs, he complained about foot pain. His drill instructor told him to ignore the pain, so he kept running. When a doctor finally examined his feet, he discovered they were both riddled with stress fractures. One tough guy, indeed! They removed him from his original platoon, placed him in the hospital to heal, then reassigned him to our series—a development that proved to be very important in my life.

Hughes and I graduated boot camp at the same ceremony and were assigned together for advanced infantry training. We were no longer recruits. We were now Marines and afforded the opportunity to lead relatively normal lives, like being able to speak to one another. I learned his first name was Dan and that he was from a rough South Philadelphia neighborhood, not unlike mine in Brooklyn. He came from a large close family and seemed like a really good guy. We started hanging around together, playing pool and drinking beer at the Enlisted Men's Club, then were assigned together at Camp Pendleton. We got into a couple of scrapes with hotheads who'd had a few too many. Dan proved to be a tough and loyal friend and I soon knew we were going to be buddies for a long time.

Although we all assumed we were headed to Nam, just prior to our graduation, President Richard M. Nixon announced that "de-escalation" was commencing immediately. That meant that no one else would be shipped to the war. Suddenly, the Marine Corps had to find somewhere else to send us.

Off to Exotic Barstow and Project Transition

Dan and I ranked as the top two of our advanced training class of 90 students, earning us the right to choose the posted duty station where we wanted to serve. There were selections from all over the world—Japan, Spain, Hawaii, and various desirable spots around the States. We'd agreed to try to be stationed together and Dan said he'd always wanted to see Japan. To his shock, I told him I thought we should take the two available openings in Barstow, California—not exactly a garden spot in the Southwest.

Back then, Barstow was basically a wide spot in the road, a small high-desert town on the highway from Los Angeles to Las Vegas. It was miserably cold in winter and hot as hell in summer. The Marines stored weapons and vehicles there between conflicts, because the lack of humidity and potential rusting was favorable for the equipment. Additionally, a major rail line provided easy transport of tanks and other equipment to the U.S. Navy base in San Diego, whenever the need arose.

Dan and I discussed requesting Barstow at length. I urged him to wait to see Japan until we made some money and could do it in style. I pointed out that Barstow was just a two-hour drive to Las Vegas, where I had three sets of aunts and uncles who'd be more than happy to feed us and give us a place to bunk. Unless there was another war, we'd have Monday-to-Friday, nine-to-five jobs. We could spend every weekend in Vegas where my three cousins, who'd lived there for many years, could show us the ins and outs. Dan eventually agreed and we took those two billets for Barstow for the balance of our two-year enlistments, much to the amazement (and pleasure) of the other 88 guys in our class, who now had a shot at the plum stations we'd passed on.

With the war winding down, the country was faced with another dilemma. Servicemen by the thousands were returning with limited

civilian skills and hitting the unemployment rolls hard. The government's solution was a program called Project Transition. It enabled a
serviceman to get on-the-job training from a civilian employer for up
to six months prior to the end of his tour of active duty. The government
still paid the Marine, and the civilian employer received his services at
no cost for those six months, hopefully helping the serviceman start a
career and keeping him off the dole.

With my customary over-attention to detail, as we served our time
in Barstow, I studied the military rule books on Project Transition and
found that a soldier could ask his commanding officer to approve an
assignment in another city or state, provided the military could maintain "reasonable monitoring" over his performance, grooming, and
training.

Wow, I thought. How great would it be if Dan and I could get
approved for Project Transition in Las Vegas? My mind reeled with the
possibilities.

I researched the military guidelines line by line and began to build
our case. My immediate supervisor, Sergeant Alvarado, drove to Las
Vegas with his wife almost every weekend. He could monitor us. I spoke
to him and he was fine with it. Now all we needed was to find employers
willing to take us on and we could submit our requests to our COs.

Before enlisting in the Marines, Dan had worked as a silkscreen
printer in Philadelphia. In Vegas, the colored panels of slot machines,
known as "slot glass," were screen-printed. So were the reel strips
mounted inside the machines on revolving drums that displayed the
7s, bars, cherries, and other symbols players hoped to line up to win
jackpots. Dan found a printer willing to take him on under the government's guidelines and we were halfway there.

I had no particular skill before enlisting, but I was always good
with numbers, so I thought I'd try my hand at dealing blackjack. The

problem was, most new dealers came out of a dealing school, then made the rounds, looking for jobs in the casinos. To comply with the program's guidelines, I needed to find a place that would let me learn on the job.

After pounding the pavement and knocking on a lot of doors, I found a willing employer at a real hole-in-the-wall joint in downtown Las Vegas called the Carousel. The owner, Phil Gimmer, appreciated my service in the Marines and wanted to help.

In fall 1973, prior to our last six months of service, Dan and I turned in our Project Transition requests to our individual commanding officers. My captain's response was quick and unequivocal. "No fucking way!" he bellowed. "You can't go to Vegas while still on active duty and train to be a casino dealer. Go get a job in Barstow! Pump gas or something!"

I calmly pointed out that everything I'd requested was clearly spelled out in the manual. "Not only is my request within the written guidelines," I said, "it represents the true spirit of the program—for Marines to learn a trade to be used in civilian life and keep them employed. That's precisely what this job provides. It's a real career in Las Vegas, not just killing six months at a filling station. What would that train me for?"

"Not happening," came the gruff reply, as he motioned me toward the door.

One great thing about our military is that it provides an appeal process that goes right up the chain of command. "As high as the presidency," is how our drill instructors put it. So after my CO's emphatic denial, I appealed to the battalion commander. He, too, abruptly rejected my request, without even hearing my justifications or reviewing the supporting documents.

The base commanding general was next up the ladder. Here, I met an open-minded senior officer who actually took the time to hear me out. I worked my way through the inception of my plan, its rationale, and the history of the rebuffs I'd received and their lack of any reasonable justification.

"Sir, my blackjack training at the Carousel Casino is a fulfillment of all that was envisioned by the framers of the Project Transition program. I even have a written promise from the owner of the Carousel that at the end of my transition and eventual discharge from active duty, I'll have a full-time position waiting for me."

He listened intently and perused the accompanying documents before looking me in the eye. "My compliments on your presentation and for not quitting in the face of multiple denials. Tell your new boss at that casino that your request has been approved and to save your position before it goes away." But then he added, "The Marines need men like you. I'd like to keep you. How about re-enlisting for four years and with that commitment, I'll immediately promote you to sergeant?"

Thanks to two meritorious promotions I'd received, I was already an E-4 corporal by my 15th month of military service. His offer would make me an E-5 sergeant after just two years of active duty, an uncommon attainment of rank in such a short time. I thanked him, feeling quite honored, but respectfully declined, more dedicated to my commitment to Dan to do this together and excited about starting a new phase of life in Las Vegas.

I headed out the door, proud that I hadn't given up and pleased to prevail in what was just and fair. With my victory, Dan's application for Project Transition sailed through the approval process.

The Marines had taught me well. Failure was not an option.

CHAPTER 5

Vegas or Bust

Dan and I arrived to "conquer" Las Vegas as part of Project Transition in October 1973. A dynamic duo, we were excited about the unknowns ahead of us and prepared to face them side by side, as we'd done everything else for the 18 months we'd been friends.

When I got started at the Carousel Casino, Phil Gimmer introduced me to his casino manager, Greg Abdo, who in a small but significant way changed my life. Because Greg was Syrian and I was Lebanese, we instantly developed a common bond. Being a Marine didn't hurt my cause either. Greg appreciated my service and was happy to train me. He was a true patriot.

My first day on the job, Greg said to me, "Here's the deal, Ron. I understand that according to Project Transition rules, I can't pay you. But I'm going to cut you a check every week and put it in an envelope in the cashier's cage. After your discharge in six months, that envelope is yours." Then he added, with a twinkle in his eye, "I don't think it breaks any of the rules, does it?"

"That's more than generous of you, Mr. Abdo. I just want to learn a skill, but this is really appreciated. Thank you."

We shook hands and just like that, I was in the casino business. Well, just barely—my casino salary back then was minimum wage, a whole $14.40 a day. I also learned that tips averaged $3 to $5 per day, per dealer.

People unfamiliar with the inner workings of gaming are often surprised at the degree of technical knowledge and proficiency it takes to be a good dealer. In addition to being thoroughly conversant with the rules of each game, it's very important to be quick, smooth, and accurate. The more hands you deal, the more the casino makes and as we all know, the odds are stacked in favor of the house. Even today, if you go into a smaller joint in or around downtown Vegas and you see a dealer who's shaky and choppy, it's an indication that he or she is either a "break-in," the casino term for newcomer, or just not very good—nothing that a little more time and experience wouldn't improve. Conversely, when you walk into a higher-end property, you'll see the dealers handling the cards expertly, the sign of a well-trained and experienced professional.

My six-month apprenticeship at the Carousel could not have gone better and I had a great time, not only dealing the games, but also observing and learning about the casino business. I'd always made it a point to keep my eyes open, soak up everything I could, and prepare myself to take full advantage of the next opportunity when it presented itself.

Six months into dealer training on Project Transition, I received my honorable discharge from the Corps and once again, I was a civilian, free to chart my own destiny. As much as I appreciated Greg and all he'd done for me, I also knew it was time to start earning a better living. Perhaps I'd even be able to afford a car and get off that Honda motorcycle that brought me to town.

Moving Up in the Casino Business

Then, as now, if a casino was looking for dealers, the job application process was fairly simple. You introduced yourself to a boss and hoped he was hiring. If he was, he'd send you to a game and put you through a live audition on a table. During my time at the Carousel, I'd grown proficient in both blackjack and roulette.

One afternoon, I headed down the street to the Four Queens, where tips were running $20 to $25 a day, compared to the $3 to $5 I was seeing at the Carousel. The pit boss, Frank Riolo, and a dealer on shift, Mike Arnold, auditioned me on blackjack and roulette, and I walked away that day with a new job. Back at The Carousel I told Greg Abdo about the new job at the Four Queens and, as always, he was gracious and wished me well. He also handed me the envelope with six months' pay, just as he'd promised. It totaled just over $1,500, a healthy down payment on a new 1974 Pontiac Grand Prix.

My first Christmas working at the Four Queens, I was invited to a Christmas party back in Brooklyn that all my childhood friends would be attending. Mike Arnold and I were on a break from the tables and we'd become good friends, playing softball together and hanging out after work. I was rather depressed that I couldn't afford to fly back home for Christmas, and my sadness was probably apparent as I was speaking to him during our 20-minute break. He'd only known me under a year and we had become pretty friendly. Money wasn't flowing in for either of us from this downtown Las Vegas dealing job. To my surprise, Mike offered to lend me the money for the flight to New York. Though I declined, because I didn't have the room in my monthly budget to repay him in a reasonable time frame, I'll never forget his incredible offer of kindness and generosity. To this day, more than 40 years later, both Frank Riolo and Mike remain very good friends of mine.

My stint at the Four Queens almost ended abruptly. Early on, my floorman, a cordial older guy named Jack Collins, told me, "Don't let customers into the pit," which, of course, I already knew. So there I was, my first week on the job, when a casually dressed man came walking toward me, right between my roulette table and the adjacent blackjack game. I put out my hand and said, "Sir, you can't come this way."

He replied, "It's okay," and kept coming.

I wasn't moving and he was clearly startled as my outstretched arm abruptly halted his forward advance.

Jack Collins came running over frantically and said, "Oh my God, Mr. Garrett, I'm so sorry. Are you okay?"

Just my luck, it was Jimmy Garrett, vice president of the casino, though not in the typical boss's suit, dressed down that day with no name badge.

As Jack yelled at me, it seemed pointless to say that he was the one who told me not to let anyone past me, Jimmy looked like a customer, and I was just following orders.

Before I could say anything, Mr. Garrett said, "I like this new kid, Jack. He didn't know me and he was protecting the house!"

I got a pat on my shoulder with a "Good job, kid," as he passed by. I'd dodged a bullet.

Working at the Four Queens was definitely an upgrade in terms of compensation and soon I knew what it felt like to walk around Las Vegas with some extra money in my pocket. Even then, I had my eyes on bigger things. After a couple of months, I made it a point to start dropping by Strip hotels, where the major money and action were. Those jobs were golden and not easy to get. You needed "juice," the industry term for having connections or just knowing someone in a position to help you. The better the earning potential of the job, the stronger your juice needed to be.

I'd heard plenty of stories about guys who just walked into cold-call auditions at a Strip property and got hired, because the pit boss or casino manager had just let someone go—a rarity in practice, but a possibility for someone without juice. So after my noon-to-eight shift at the Four Queens, I hiked up and down the Strip in my black and whites, the dealer's standard white dress shirt and black slacks, for two hours, hoping I'd find myself in the right place at the right time. Unfortunately, I struck out everywhere for months, unlucky with my timing.

For the moment, I was stuck at the Four Queens with the opportunities to work on the Strip right in front of me, yet just out of reach. That didn't mean I wasn't still thinking about my next move. An uncle through marriage, Jimmy Dumont, knew Fred and Ed Doumani, brothers who'd recently purchased the real estate that the Tropicana Hotel-Casino, (a.k.a. The Trop) occupied. Jimmy set up a meeting between Fred and me in the Blue Room Lounge at the Trop.

After introducing ourselves and sitting at a table, Fred said, "Your Uncle Jim called me. What can I do for you?"

"Well, sir, I recently got out of the Marines. I've worked downtown for a year; I've put in my training time. I'm a good dealer and I'm just looking for a chance to make more money."

Fred nodded, then stood and told me to come with him. Using a casino house phone, he made a call upstairs to the administrative offices. A few minutes later, a well-dressed man emerged from the elevator, saw Fred, and greeted him warmly.

He glanced at me, then said, "What can I do for you, Mr. Doumani?"

Fred put his hand on my shoulder and said, "I want you to give this kid a job. He's a great dealer and comes highly recommended."

"You got it, Fred." He turned to me. "When would you like to start?"

I told him I wanted to do the right thing at the Four Queens and give them notice. They'd treated me very well and I'd become friends with many of my co-workers. This included pitching for our company softball team, where I'd led us to victory against the Golden Nugget team, whose pitcher was a guy named Steve Wynn.

I went back to the Four Queens, gave them two weeks' notice, and finished out my time, all the while waiting for the call from the Trop. Two weeks came and went, but the call never came and suddenly, I found myself out of a job. This went on for several weeks, with car payments and rent due and not much money in reserve. I was patient for as long I could be, but finally realized I had to do something.

I returned to the Trop, found Fred, and told him what had happened—or more accurately, what hadn't. "With all due respect, sir, I need work. I'll be a dishwasher, a busboy, anything, because I'm about to get evicted."

He gave me a funny look. "What the hell are you talking about?"

"Your guy never called me about the dealing job. I gave my two weeks' notice and finished up my time at the Four Queens. Here it is, a month later, and I haven't heard a thing."

Visibly upset, Fred once again called his manager. This time, when the man stepped off the elevator, there were no niceties. "I thought I told you to give my friend a job."

The dapper executive flushed with embarrassment. "I'm trying to work him in, but I—"

Fred stopped him with a raised palm. "Put him to work. On any shift he wants. Now!"

Flustered, the man turned to me. "What shift would you like?"

I knew the answer before he even asked the question. "Swing shift, seven p.m. to three a.m."

"And no audition," said Fred. "Just hire him."

Fortunately, I was good enough to prove myself on the job.

Dan Hughes, whom I'd convinced to come with me to Barstow and Las Vegas, was by now doing very well at the screen-printing company where he worked.

I finally had my foot in the door at the Tropicana, on the Las Vegas Strip, the promised land for dealers.

CHAPTER 6

Meeting Joan

My late wife of more than 34 years, Joan, was the absolute sweetest person I've ever known. She never once spoke a bad word about anyone and was generous, loving, and the greatest wife and mom anyone could want. I'll never forget the day in 1972 when we met.

I had a flight out of Las Vegas, nonstop to New York, for Christmas. My Brooklyn buddy Joe Aboushanab knew I wanted to visit home, but fresh out of boot camp, I couldn't afford to fly. He sent me the money so I could spend the holidays with friends and family.

I was driven to the airport by my Aunt Gloria, who was living in Las Vegas with her husband and gave Dan and me a bed and meals when we first arrived with barely two nickels between us. I was still on active duty, dressed in full uniform and waiting for the boarding announcement. Out of the blue, my aunt pointed out a cute young blonde gal seated in the gate area with a girlfriend who was apparently seeing her off. With a little chuckle, Aunt Gloria told me that as I'd passed by to approach the boarding agent, the girl had stood up, snapped to mock attention, and saluted with a big smile on her face, taking her seat again and giggling with her gal pal.

The plane was huge, but hardly anyone was on it. As I settled into my seat, the flight attendant told me that the pilot, a former Marine aviator, had instructed her to comp me anything I wanted. She offered me champagne. I thanked her and said, "Maybe later." As she left, I walked up to the cockpit, knocked on the open door, and loudly proclaimed, "Permission to enter, Sir!" (My fellow Marines will see the humor in that.) The pilot rose, turned, and shook my hand. We exchanged Marine talk, reveling in the camaraderie and indescribable bond among fellow Marines. It's hard to put into words, but it's a wonderfully warm feeling that the few, the proud, share to the core of who we are.

When I returned to my seat, I noticed that the girl who had earlier saluted me, was sitting directly behind me. Was it a signal? Should I initiate a conversation and risk being shot down only to fly for five hours beating myself up mentally? Or should I say nothing and be bored and regretful the whole way? Assess, analyze, decide, implement, and live with the results, right?

We took off and finally I thought, what the hell. I turned around, smiled, and said, "Hi." She smiled back and returned my greeting. Whew, a great start. I asked her if I could move back and join her over a glass of champagne. She said that would be nice. We introduced ourselves and I learned her name was Joan and she was one of seven kids, the daughter of a banker who relocated to Las Vegas from Oregon. Joan was working as a pharmacist's assistant while attending the University of Nevada, Las Vegas (UNLV). Friends had invited her to join them for Christmas and see New York for the first time.

I motioned to the flight attendant and politely asked for two glasses of champagne. She quickly returned with our drinks, announcing, once again, that they were complimentary, as the captain appreciated my service. Wow! A couple years earlier, I'd never even been on an airplane and now, a flight attendant was my literal and figurative wingman. Joan was impressed.

At the end of the flight, I asked if I could call her in a couple of weeks. To my great joy, she said yes.

We landed and deplaned. Joe Bush was at the gate, along with Joan's friends picking her up. We parted with a warm, long, hand-holding goodbye. As Joe and I walked to baggage claim, he asked who she was.

I said, "Joe, she's a great gal I just met and talked to for five hours. I think she may be the one!"

Back in Las Vegas and a couple of weeks later, I called Joan. We started dating regularly over my weekend visits to Vegas from the Marine base and fortunately, her family embraced me like one of their own. Joan visited me at the base in Barstow once (via a Greyhound bus) and was impressed by the rows and rows of tanks and amphibious assault vehicles stored there. We dated for a couple of years during the completion of my military service and thereafter. We grew closer and closer and toward the end of 1974, I purchased an engagement ring with a tiny diamond in a thin gold setting. It came in a small blue box, which I still have today, with a hinged top and a white-satin pillow base wherein the ring was mounted.

Tucked inside into the upper lid, I placed a small piece of paper. I wrote, "Will you marry me?" and drew two small square boxes below that could be checked either yes or no.

When she arrived, I handed her the jewelry box with a pen. She looked at me and asked what the pen was for. I said, "Open it and you'll know."

She opened it, read the note, looked at the ring, and said, "Yes, I love it! I will marry you, Ronald Thomas Coury!"

CHAPTER 7

Into the Bar Business

By 1975, I'd been dealing blackjack and roulette at the Tropicana for more than a year. I was making decent money, but as always, I was itching for my next opportunity and keeping my eyes open for the chance to make something happen. However, now I had a wedding to arrange.

One of the first people I told about my upcoming nuptials was Fred Doumani. Of course, I wanted to do the right thing and extend a wedding invitation to the benefactor of my great dealing job on the Strip.

"Congratulations!" he beamed. "I wouldn't miss it for the world. Where's the reception?"

I told him the Blue Room Hall, a little venue upstairs at the Tropicana.

He patted me on the arm. "Let me talk to food and beverage. I don't want to make any money on you. I'll make sure they just charge you at cost."

I certainly wasn't expecting this and thanked him once again for his incredible generosity. Our reception, with food and drinks for over 100 people? Fred had them charge me $800. A friend for life! Even now, more than four decades later, we try to have lunch together every few months.

We had the wedding in Joan's parish church, with her family, my parents, aunts, and uncles, and 100 other guests, mostly casino co-workers, in attendance. It was a wonderful day.

After a whirlwind honeymoon over an extended weekend, enjoying the ocean breezes in La Jolla, California, we settled into a 1,200-square-foot duplex home with a common wall and a one-car garage in the Spring Valley area. I bought half the duplex, Dan bought the other half—each of us with VA loans for zero down and a house payment of $300 a month. Dan and I would no longer be roommates, but living side by side was the next best thing.

Joan had been driving a Volkswagen Beetle with no air conditioning, which was intolerable in the often-oppressive Vegas heat. So I bought her a new Chevrolet Monte Carlo with air conditioning. Now, between her Monte Carlo and my Grand Prix, plus a partnership in a small boat and a mortgage, my budget was maxed out. I was making a decent living, but I was also spending it all. As a dealer, whenever I was on a dead game and had to just stand there, I thought about what I could do to make more money.

My first consideration was that I knew Joan wanted to have a family—and I wanted Joan to be a stay-at-home mom. I'd get a second job if I had to. I felt strongly that I didn't want our children to be home without their mother there.

Another factor that weighed heavily on me was that my dad had lost his three brothers and a sister to cancer. He'd survived colon cancer himself in the 1960s. With my family history, I felt it wasn't a matter of if I'd get it, but when, which created an added sense of urgency. With only a month or two of expense money saved, what would I do if I got sick for six months? I needed a way to earn income whether I could physically show up to work or not. The question was, doing what? Owning my own business would fit the bill, but what did I bring to the table? I didn't have an attorney's shingle or a doctor's license or even a college degree.

Then it hit me. I could work as a part-time Realtor, showing homes on a schedule I could dictate and doing office work on my own time, while still dealing in the evenings. I could earn extra money to buy or start my own business when I could afford it. Excited, I attended real-estate school, passed the state licensing exam, and set out to find a broker who'd hire me.

I started dropping in on different brokerages to get a feel for how they operated and whether or not I thought any of them would be a place I'd like to work. One day, I stopped by a Jack Matthews and Co. office, not far from my home, and introduced myself to a broker named Steve Schneider. Apparently, my timing was perfect and after an interview, Steve offered me a position that I gladly accepted.

When I got home, Joan asked me how the job search had gone. When I told her about Steve, she said, "If it's the Steve Schneider I'm thinking of, he was my tenth-grade English teacher!"

A quick review of photos in her Bishop Gorman High School yearbook confirmed it. Talk about a small world. I went to work for him part-time; we got along great, and to this day he's a close friend.

Since I was fairly well-known at the Tropicana, it made perfect sense to make it my "farm," the community or business a Realtor focuses on to generate listings and sales. I told people what I was up to, distributed my business cards all over the property, and before long, anyone at the Trop looking to buy or sell a home usually came to me.

At that time, most of the roulette dealers were Cuban. If you walked into a Vegas casino, you'd see 20 blackjack tables and one or two roulette tables at the end of the row. In Cuba before Castro took over, it was just the opposite, with many more roulette wheels than blackjack tables. After the revolution, Castro closed the casinos, so suddenly a lot of Cuban roulette dealers were out of work. Many of those who could get out of Cuba came straight to Las Vegas looking for jobs. I didn't speak Spanish, but I got along very well with them, including José Martinez, who asked me to list his duplex. Pretty soon it was sold.

Hearing of my success with José and other people around the property, my pit boss, John Napoli, approached me one night as I was coming off my game. "Hey Ron, my daughter's a bartender and I was thinking I'd like to buy a little bar for her as an investment," he said. "I figure she can run it and I'll own it and earn some extra income. Think you can find me something?"

On my way home after my shifts, I'd started stopping by a nice little place in the same shopping center as my real estate office, the Suburban Lounge West. It didn't have a kitchen, but neighborhood people came in to socialize and have a drink. Video poker had yet to be invented, so unlike the bars of today, it had only two or three old-school slots with pull handles. One day I made it a point to walk into the Suburban during regular business hours, when I knew the owner, Ted Walsh, would be in.

After introducing myself and exchanging pleasantries, I got straight to the point. "I'm a Realtor. I work nights at the Tropicana and my twenty-one boss asked me to find him a bar to buy."

"No kidding." Ted smiled. "I used to deal too. The thing is, Ron, I get approached all the time."

"I'm not fishing for a listing here, Ted," I replied. "I really have a guy who's ready to buy."

Ted looked me over, assessing me. Finally he said, "Okay. I'm not going to list the place, but if you bring me an offer that I like and the deal goes through, I'll pay you a commission."

"Fair enough," I said. "What kind of price are you thinking?"

Apparently, he'd been thinking about it for a while, because he shot his answer right back at me. "A hundred thirty-five thousand. With thirty-five down, I'll carry the paper." He also gave me some preliminary numbers on what kind of business he was doing to take back to my pit boss.

I told John Napoli about the Suburban and, to my surprise, he waved me off. "That's way out in the boondocks," he said. "Hell, they still ride horses out there. I want to be in the middle of town, preferably around Paradise Road."

"Okay," I said. "I'll keep looking."

The Bar I Had to Have

But this deal had gotten my attention. The more I thought about it, the more I liked it.

By 1979, TK and Tommy Bear had relocated from Brooklyn to Las Vegas, following me out here to seek their own fortunes. Dan, the Bear, and TK had joined me at this bar for drinks many times and we all liked the place. The Bear, incidentally, became a casino dealer, learning how to deal from me on an old blackjack table I'd purchased from the Tropicana after their remodel. Since it was an actual table I'd worked on, nostalgia played a role in my keeping it. Tommy Bear rose through the ranks, eventually becoming a pit boss at the Wynn Hotel-Casino.

Though in 1979 I was only 27 and a little green, I was a common-sense thinker, a problem solver, in great shape, and had a decent education. I was good with numbers and a fast learner. I could ensure that the bar would stay friendly and peaceful and I'd keep the place clean and make it inviting and safe-feeling. I didn't have bartending skills, but I could hire people who did. This was before the television show "Cheers," but I knew I wanted to run a local bar where everyone knew everyone else's name.

I planned on getting to know all our customers, as failing to remember them each time they walked in could become embarrassing. It would be easy enough to implement a "tickler" file system with index cards to help remember people and the details about their lives that they revealed to me. Maybe they had a bald head or a big red nose, whatever trait I noticed first would lead me to their card, which would contain everything I learned while getting to know them. Their wife's and kids' names, their son's baseball team record or daughter's ballet or singing hobby, the kind of car they bragged about driving—anything and everything that would make them feel good to think that I remembered them so vividly. I would ask them about such things time and again when they came in.

Sure enough, it turned out that this made them feel so important and they were so proud of being recognized and engaged by the owner of the place, they invariably brought friends with them to witness the celebrity-like treatment they always received from the owner and employees of the Suburban. It proved to be great for business.

Best of all, Dan was interested in partnering and would help me at the bar as his work schedule allowed. I was confident it would all work out fine if only I could make this place mine!

At the time, however, the Suburban West was beginning to develop a reputation as a rough place where the customers were running the show. Ted Walsh was a pretty tough guy himself, but his other bar, the Suburban Lounge East, was across town and very close to his home. Out of convenience, he spent most of his time there and not at the West location, where the mostly petite female bartenders were unable to maintain control. The presence of an owner was sorely needed.

In my view, this was a perfect opportunity for me. I'd run things with a fair but firm hand and the word would go out that this was a friendly, safe, peaceful place with an owner on-site to deal with any problems. Ladies could come in unescorted and be respected. And if the girls came in, I knew the guys would follow. I was confident that my concept would work.

It's important as a businessman to know what you don't know. I knew I wasn't a bartender and didn't want to be a full-time manager. I'd need someone I could trust to work the bar on prime shifts, handle the money, and manage the bartenders. That would leave me free to do the accounting, banking, advertising, ordering, schmoozing, and anything else that fit between my casino-dealing night hours and my Realtor duties. I didn't have to look far.

My lifelong buddy, Tom Kennedy, had now lived in Las Vegas for more than four years. TK had attended college in New York and, while a student, had driven a cab in some of the city's worst neighborhoods. During our frequent phone calls, I told him about the good life out west and urged him to come out and give it a try. Upon graduating, he did exactly that, staying with Joan and me until he got on his feet. In fact, at the time I was trying to buy the Suburban Lounge, TK was a bartender on the Strip, at the original MGM Grand (now Bally's). Dan liked the idea of offering TK the manager's spot and when asked, he accepted. He'd work four or five swing shifts and manage the place with me.

It was all coming together nicely. Only one thing was stopping me. Actually, 35,000 things—dollars!

Right around this time, José's duplex sale closed and one of the services I provided to clients was to personally deliver their closing documents and proceeds check, hoping it would give them another reason to use or recommend me as a Realtor. Fortuitously, José's closing check was for almost exactly $35,000. The writing was on the wall.

As was my custom, I talked my idea over with Dan. "Even if I can convince José to invest his money with us, we'll still need operating capital."

We thought about it and realized we could go to the bank, refinance our cars, and pull a little money out. We would beg and borrow wherever we could to scrape together the extra couple of grand we'd need.

The next day, I went to see José and deliver his closing package.

"What are you going to do with the proceeds?" I asked.

"I don't know, Ron," he said, eyeing his check. "I think I'm just going to put it in the bank."

I had my pitch rehearsed and ready to go. "Look, José, a bank is going to pay you maybe five or six percent. I'll pay you twelve."

"Why?"

"I want to buy this business and I need thirty-five thousand for the down payment."

José couldn't have considered it for more than 30 seconds before he pulled that check from its paper clip, signed it over, and slid it across the table to me.

After thanking him, I said, "José, I don't have this kind of equity in my home to protect you with, but I really want to do this the right way. I'm going to document this loan, secured by my own house."

"Do whatever you want," he said. "I've been watching you for a while now. When other dealers go on break, they run down to the break room and play gin rummy or tonk for money. Not you. You're always reading. You took the real estate exam. You're going to do something big in life and I believe in you and trust you."

I hurried over to Ted Walsh and told him I was ready to make the deal. However, there was another bend in the road I hadn't anticipated.

"You're a day late, Ron," he said. "Another regular of mine, Wade— you know him—also wants to buy the place."

I knew Wade and his wife well. "Wow, Ted, I don't know what to say. I borrowed the money; I'm ready to go."

"Yeah, well, so is Wade."

My mind began to race; I hadn't come this far to be denied at the finish line. "Wade and I are at the same price?"

Ted nodded.

"Tell you what. If you'll add the difference to the note, I'll give you fifteen thousand more—a hundred fifty thousand total sale price with the same down payment and I'll waive any commission." My philosophy thus far in life was based less on the actual cost of something and more on how much a month it would cost me. My new offer only increased my monthly note by $160. Whether this venture succeeded or failed, it surely wouldn't ride on $160 per month, so why not try?

Still, it was a gamble. I didn't know if his friendship with Wade would override his business sense, or worse, if Ted would use my offer as leverage to get Wade to up the ante. By the terms of my offer, I'd owe Ted about $1,750 a month. I'd never run a bar before and I wasn't planning to quit my job at the Trop, covering myself in case the venture was a total flop. But I didn't need to let Ted know all that.

After a minute that felt more like an hour, Ted stuck out his hand. "You've got a deal."

We shook and just like that, I was in the bar business.

Now the only question was, could I pull it off?

CHAPTER 8

Suburban West to Suburban Graphics

My first child, Joe, was born in 1978, which gave me a sense of urgency about making the Suburban West a success. Dan and I owned the place for six long hard months before we started to see growth in popularity and profit. More people started showing up and staying longer. They felt welcome and safe and the place was much cleaner than it was when we took over. Still, I had to be vigilant about smoothing out rough edges from time to time.

One example was a customer who chewed tobacco. One night I watched as he spit his tobacco juice onto the carpet. I couldn't believe my eyes. "What the hell are you doing?"

"I always spit here," he said blithely.

"Do you spit on your carpet at home?"

"Well, no."

"Well, I'm the new owner here. This is my home, and you don't spit on the carpet here either."

He looked at me like I was nothing more than an annoying gnat and said, "You ever hear the expression, 'The customer's always right'? Why don't you get me another beer and leave me be?"

Before he knew it, he was on his ass in the parking lot. In the early days, this joker wasn't the only guy to leave the hard way.

An interesting side note about Marine training. The endless running and exercises introduced a key factor that explains how a smaller, less muscular guy can win a fight against a larger, seemingly stronger opponent. *Stamina!* All the workouts over 90 days of boot camp instilled in us a level of stamina that would keep us in the battle when others might find themselves exhausted. Aside from the hand-to-hand tactics we were taught, that level of endurance turns the tide no matter whom we might find ourselves up against. Stamina, combined with fighting skills and a never-quit mentality, would serve me well for the rest of my life.

Even though we'd managed to turn the ship around at the Suburban, our profit margins were minuscule. We were operating on a wing and a prayer, and the wing was tattered.

As we were trying to make a go of it, living week to week, worrying about payroll, bills, vendors etc., I was called out from my office one afternoon by my day-shift bartender. "Ron, a guy out here wants to see you."

I went out and introduced myself.

"I'm Izador Auerbach from the Service Industry Local," he said, offering me his card. "You can call me Izzie. We want to unionize your bar."

That was the last thing I needed at the time. But I leveled with the guy. "I'm a small operation; I didn't even know you came after bars this size."

"We're doing a recruitment campaign," he said, with a slimy leer.

"Look, I'm barely making payroll as it is. I can't pay the kind of union wages you guys make the hotels cough up. This is a survival thing."

Dusting some imaginary lint from his jacket, he said, "Well, there's surviving and then there's surviving."

I was lost. "What the hell does that mean?"

"What it means is, you can either go union or maybe we can work something out, where you pay me directly every month—so you *won't* have to be in the union."

"I have a partner," I said, eyeing his first and last names and middle initial on the business card. "He's just around the corner. Wait here a few minutes while I go see what he thinks." He didn't need to know that Dan worked a good half-hour away or that I could be at the back door of Jack Matthews Realty in seconds. I hustled out, thinking I just might be able to find something on him in the assessor's parcel records we kept on microfiche in my realty office.

Luckily, he had an unusual name and I got a home address that had to be his. I wrote it down on a piece of paper, pulled out my snub-nose Smith & Wesson .38 revolver from its ankle holster, emptied all the chambers, and crumpled the paper around it. Then I rushed back to the Suburban, where he sat waiting for me.

"So, did you talk to your partner?"

"Yeah, as a matter of fact I did," I said, sliding the paper and gun across the table, "and here's your answer."

He looked at the revolver, uncrumpled the paper, and turned white as he saw his home address.

I said, "Buddy, I know one thing for sure. You're threatening to screw with my livelihood and my family's future . . . and if you do, I'm going to engage with yours." I paused to let it sink in. "I know that when you go back and tell your bosses what happened here today, I could end up with pickets and God knows what else. So here's my deal: If I never see you or one of your people ever again, I promise you'll *never* see me again. And this," I pointed at the gun, "or that," I motioned toward the paper, "won't matter to you."

My eyes were filled with rage and my voice had all the determination and deliberate slow-talking emphasis I could muster. I knew in my gut that this was potentially serious, depending on his frame of mind and what he told his bosses. Would he go back to the union and tell them they had no shot with me? Or that I'd threatened him? Would he urge more harassment for the bar? Were they in on his little bribery scam or was he acting alone?

All I knew was I wanted to scare the shit out of this guy so he went away and never came back. Disappearing for 10 minutes, then reappearing with his home address, was unusual, to say the least. There was no computer screen to go to. There was no Internet, where you can look anyone up in 60 seconds. He had to wonder, how the hell did I get it so quickly? The gun itself may or might not scare the guy, but passing it to him indicated that I wasn't the least bit afraid of him.

It worked. He left the note and without another word walked out. I never saw him again.

With that out of the way, I got back to work.

Dealing Days Are Done

In 1980, one year after we purchased the Suburban West, I realized we lacked a critical factor in achieving greater success there. While we enjoyed terrific traffic, many customers left when they got hungry. Our frozen pizzas heated in a toaster oven and the fresh popcorn we offered weren't cutting it. Although many intended to return after eating, understandably, most didn't. We needed to serve real food. To do that, we needed a kitchen. To build a kitchen, we had to come up with $10,000. Even then, it would be a bare-bones lean-and-mean operation with a charbroiler, two deep fryers, and a refrigerated salad table. We'd offer a basic menu with typical tavern mainstays like burgers, steak sandwiches, chicken wings, French fries, and salads.

As for the money, Dan and I lacked that kind of liquidity. My parents didn't have it either. Eventually, I borrowed from an aunt in Pennsylvania. We opened the kitchen, paid her a fair interest rate over the next three years, and business improved significantly, as we could hold on to those customers who would have left otherwise.

When you're in business for yourself, no one brings you a map with problems and fixes outlined. Your eyes, ears, brain, and gut are all you have. You need to take a step back and observe, assess the problem, then develop and implement solutions—all on your own.

Even after you've cured what ails the business, you continue to keep an eye on the matter; the problem will surely resurface if you aren't diligent in its management in the long term.

Though we were operating profitably, the crazy money that came along when video poker arrived on the scene was still in the future, so I wasn't exactly getting rich. Dan, still working at the print shop, had developed such a strong reputation that he was promoted to print and art department manager at Bally's Distributing, a subsidiary of Bally Manufacturing, which was the leading manufacturer of slot machines in Las Vegas, if not the entire world, at the time. Dan was in charge of a busy crew that silk-screened glass fronts and reel strips for Bally's newest slot machines, as well as for casinos that occasionally changed their existing machines or wanted to customize new machine purchases. Our arrangement was that I ran the bar, while Dan kept his job, but he helped me as he could. On Sundays, for example, we went in and deep-cleaned the restrooms. Revenues were so sparse, we couldn't hire a janitorial service. In fact, I couldn't hire a bouncer or a payroll clerk—I did it all.

Working three jobs—Realtor, dealer, and bar operator—I was running myself ragged. So, after a couple of months, with faith that the Suburban West would continue to grow, it was time to give my notice at the Tropicana.

Usually in the gaming business, if you tell them you're leaving, you're done that day. The bosses don't want to risk lame-duck stealing or performance at a reduced level of customer service. Fortunately, I'd demonstrated a level of integrity that my bosses respected.

One example of this was our system for distributing tips, or tokes as they were called. Each shift's designated toke manager compiled a list of who worked that day, then wrote each name on an envelope, leaving the envelopes in the tip containers. Then the swing-shift dealers on the tip committee divvied up all the tips we received over the previous 24-hour period and deposited equal amounts into the designated employee envelopes. This occurred each day at 3 a.m. in the empty casino showroom.

Over time, we began to suspect that the graveyard toke manager was putting in too many envelopes and collecting for people who hadn't actually worked, stuffing more money in his own pocket. This type of activity was more than frowned on; if a dealer was found to be taking money from his fellow employees, things often turned violent.

I was on the tip committee and we knew we needed to find out if a fellow employee was stealing from us, and specifically, who it was. I wasn't afraid of getting involved and taking action, so I volunteered to transfer to graveyard shift and keep my own list of who was and wasn't working each shift, so we could compare it to the envelopes that the suspected toke manager was submitting. Sure enough, after a couple of weeks of undercover recon, we identified him and proved his guilt.

We took the body of evidence to management and the dirty dog found himself out on the street, jobless. As far as I was concerned, he got off easy.

Suffice to say, my reputation as a straight-shooter served me well when it came time to say goodbye to the Tropicana. Confident that I wouldn't do the wrong thing, my bosses let me serve out my last two weeks and leave with dignity. I've always appreciated that show of faith.

On my last day, a few of my fellow dealers came to a tie-and-apron-burning ceremony I held at the Suburban West and just like that, I was down to two jobs, running the bar and selling real estate. Those dealers were so supportive of the shot I was taking to get out of the daily grind that the Suburban West soon became a popular stop for them after their shifts.

The Niche Finder

Even before becoming a bar owner, I was well aware that Vegas was a transient town, but now, the high turnover rate meant I had to constantly build a new customer base. In the bar business, like most businesses, if you're not growing, you're dying. There's an inherent loss of customers due to divorce, relocation, termination of employment, old age, drinking problems, and a host of other factors we can't control. I realized early on that due to attrition, I needed to constantly seek new clientele.

Fortunately, I developed a knack for generating good publicity and eye-catching ideas for the bar. But back then with no websites, blogs, or social media to spread the word, we relied a great deal on word of mouth. Luckily, my real estate office had a state-of-the-art copy machine. I asked my broker, Steve Schneider, if I could use it from time to time to run off flyers when I had an event going on in the bar. He said "Sure," so for a long time when I had something to promote, I hand-drew a flyer, made a bunch of copies, grabbed a staple gun, and went from hotel to hotel posting my flyers in the dealers' break rooms. I offered a special or discount of some kind to each hotel's employees, so I could track results, night by night and property by property. Usually, no one stopped me, but if I was on a property I wasn't that familiar with, I just wore the traditional black pants and white shirt, so I looked like I belonged. Then I followed the dealers as they went on break and slapped up a few of my flyers before security discovered me. This would be impossible to do today, as most casinos have customized dealer shirts, but a white shirt and black pants were the standard dealer uniform in the 1970s and '80s. Sure enough, business continued to grow, along with our profit margins. Hotels that turned out stronger and spent better were more frequent recipients of my flyer runs.

If I had to give myself a title or occupation description after four decades of business activity in Las Vegas, I'd call myself an observational entrepreneur, a "niche finder." With nearly every venture I've undertaken, Dan and I identified a niche in which we could do things better than they were currently being done. This mindset was easy to execute in a young, growing town like Las Vegas.

In the 1970s and '80s, visionaries willing to go for it found Las Vegas to be a prime setting for fulfilling their entrepreneurial aspirations. I was the niche finder who pulled together the concept, funding, and implementation, while Dan was the best partner possible for any project, sharing ideas and duties and riding the wildest and most fun-filled roller coaster of life anyone could ever imagine.

When you can demonstrate a need in any area of industry, your job is to find a cure, believe you can implement it, raise the money to do so, form the team, and make it happen: a new business is born.

Generally, I took up to a year establishing a new venture, running it hands-on, day-to-day, and setting the standards for excellence, before preparing to move on. Moving on means freeing up your time to find the next challenge, which can only happen if you select the right management team to fill your shoes when you aren't there. If the company could generate the revenues and profits set under my direct management, the right manager would take over the operation, doing no worse and hopefully better with the foundation I'd established.

Hard work, good decision-making, and some luck usually lead to success, financial rewards, and a sense of accomplishment that recharges your batteries and leaves you looking for the next niche to fill. It was always true, in my case.

The Next Big Thing

Knowing myself and the goals I was setting, it was no surprise that even as the bar revenues began to rise, I grew restless, looking for the next opportunity. As I was thinking about it, I said to Dan, "You're so good at what you do, why don't we open a silk-screen print shop?"

Dan's first response was, "Bally's makes the machines; Bally's prints the glass; I work at Bally's. Who would we print for?"

I had to admit that my buddy had a point. "It just seems a shame not to use your talent. We really should figure something out. The question is, what?"

A regular at the Suburban, an old cowboy named Jimmy, hailed from Texas and, like a lot of the regulars, considered the Suburban his home away from home. If I ever had a beef and was outnumbered, Jimmy always had my back. He was also a hell of an artist. He could grab a cocktail napkin and in a few seconds sketch out a little masterpiece—really amazing stuff.

At the exact same time that Dan and I were trying to figure out our next move, the coffee shop next door to the Suburban went belly up. Thinking about the suddenly available space, I remembered what I'd gone through as a new business owner trying to raise awareness and attract customers. Any new enterprise needs signage above the door, in the windows and throughout the store. I found a publication that listed the names of all the companies that had recently applied for a business license and suddenly, all I could see were dollar signs.

I said to Dan, "Let's rent the space and open the Suburban Sign Company. Jimmy can do the hand painting and if we get a big job, we can call in your company to do the screen-printing. Then you can bill us and we'll mark it up and deliver."

Soon the Suburban Sign Company was up and running—and, once again, I had three jobs.

Every day, I stocked the bar in the morning and if I didn't have a lot of real estate appointments scheduled, I put on my Suburban Signs sales hat and started calling on all the newly opened businesses I'd researched. I showed them Polaroids of our work (remember, this was the Dark Ages of the early 1980s) and damned if I didn't start selling $25,000 or more in signs each month. Things went great for a while, but our new operation had one significant Achilles' heel.

Jimmy just couldn't stay out of the bar and away from the beer. I didn't care if he drank while he painted. I just needed him to keep pace with all the sales I was generating. Long before digital printers, individual signs were painted by hand. Many times, I came back from beating the streets and found Jimmy at the bar, rather than working in the shop.

"Jimmy, I'll have the girls bring you beer, but you've got to go next door and paint."

Unfortunately, as anyone who's gone round and round with a problem drinker knows, it's a non-stop struggle and, over time, I realized I didn't want to keep arguing with him. I told Dan, "We've got to pull the plug on this—let's just expand the bar into that space." I figured my foray into the printing business was at an end.

Except for one huge development.

Bally's Distributing employed a man named Si Redd, who sold slot machines, but liked to tinker with new ideas and developed a little game called video poker. He immediately took it to his bosses at Bally's, who essentially laughed him out of the office. "Slot players don't want to interact with the game. They want to pull handles and pray for sevens," said one senior manager. "Besides, the real gaming is at the tables!"

At that time, he was right. In that era, 70 to 80 percent of the casino floor consisted of blackjack, craps, and roulette. Slot machines were relegated to the periphery of the casino, a place for a cigar-chomping crap-shooter to park his wife while he did the "serious" gambling. What nobody, including Si, realized was that his invention was about to revolutionize the gaming industry. Today, when you walk into a casino, you'll see the floor is more like 80 percent machines and 20 percent tables — a complete reversal.

To Si's credit, he didn't fold. "I'd like to build these machines whether you want in or not," he told the "brains" at Bally's.

"Suit yourself," they replied. "We just need a non-compete agreement that you won't build slots for ten years and we won't build any interactive poker games."

Si went off and started Fortune Coin, which later became IGT (International Game Technology), a company that in 2017 had amassed total assets of $15 billion. As IGT grew and grew, it became a serious competitor for Bally's Manufacturing. Game inventors, designers and packagers around the world began thinking, "Hey, why did we let Bally's own this market for so long? Look at what this one guy did!" And just like that, gaming entrepreneurs everywhere started building and distributing various types of gambling devices.

In the wake of all this, one day Dan wanted to talk. "Remember a while back how you were thinking that we ought to open a graphics shop?"

"Hell yes," I said.

"The time might be right," he said, "now that there's a worldwide market in slot manufacturing. These guys who build games don't want their own print shops, so they'll have to use an independent shop that protects their confidentiality and proprietary work. This could be big!"

Based on the opportunity and my faith in Dan's abilities, I was prepared to go all in with him. Sticking with the good luck we had with the Suburban name, we called the new business Suburban Graphics. It started with me, Dan, two other employees and an SBA loan of about $100,000. We took over a 5,000-square-foot leasehold space with a small office in the front and we were in business.

When IGT built their operation in Reno, they had their own print shop. Luckily, their sales outperformed their production capability and we got some of the overflow. Within a few years, we were booking up to $200,000 a month in sales from IGT and Bally's alone. Our shop would one day grow into 48,000 square feet of production space on three-plus acres with 120 employees and more than $12 million in annual sales. But until then there were still several years and many unexpected dramatic twists in the road ahead.

CHAPTER 9

Suburban East

In 1983, soon after I turned 31, I started hearing that Ted Walsh, whom I'd bought the Suburban Lounge West from, was having difficulties operating his Suburban Lounge East location. Actually, it boiled down to one difficulty: A series of poor life choices were distracting him and sucking up all his time and money, driving his business into the ground. I learned from a bartender there, who was married to a former dealer I knew from the Tropicana, that the beer and liquor distributors had cut off his deliveries, which forced his bartenders to run to the adjacent supermarket to buy beer and liquor—one or two six-packs and bottles at a time—to sell over the bar. They couldn't even get a delivery COD, because there was never enough cash on site to pay the driver. On the infrequent occasions that Ted walked through the door, it was just to empty the register, desperate to satisfy other obligations he felt were more important.

I felt for the guy, but I also saw an opportunity for Dan and me to purchase the Suburban Lounge East, which had a reputation as a great bar in an outstanding location in a busy shopping center. Owning both Suburbans was a natural for us—if we could catch it before Ted let it slide further or someone else picked it up.

I dropped in one day and was lucky enough to find Ted there. I knew it would only cause bad feelings if I didn't broach the subject in exactly the right way. I eased into the conversation. "I'm really loving running the Suburban West," I said, casually looking around his place. "If you ever want to sell this bar, I hope I'll be your first call."

"Funny you should mention that," he said, nearly as casual. "I actually have been thinking about getting rid of it and moving on to something else."

I tried to keep playing it cool. "Really? How much would you want for it?"

"Well," he leaned closer, "I'm not showing anybody my books."

No surprise to me, as he was selling single beers out of six-packs.

"It's a good store with a solid customer base," he continued. "I'd let it go for two hundred fifty thousand."

That was obviously a ridiculously high price in its current condition, but I kept playing my cards close to the vest. Given his rumored difficulties, I knew he'd want some cash right away. And I could make that work in my favor. "Interesting," I said, "but I don't have that kind of cash on hand. Would you do a deal with terms like we did with the West? You know from our past experience that your monthly checks will come like clockwork."

"I could do that," he replied eagerly, immediately snapping at the prospect of having a regular flow of money and no counter-offer on his inflated asking price. I could almost hear him thinking, let's sign this guy before he wises up.

"What will you take as a down payment?"

Ted didn't need to think about it very long. "Sixty thousand against the two fifty purchase price."

"Sounds reasonable," I said. "I'll be back in a bit with the deal in writing."

I calculated an interest rate and monthly payments and stipulated that the first installment would start six months after we closed escrow.

I needed time to get the place performing before being tied to a large monthly nut.

Ted was all for it, except for the six months. As I suspected, he needed to open a cash pipeline as soon as possible.

"Ted, the thing is, after I hand over the sixty grand, I still need to buy your inventory and stock up on what I'll need to make a go of this place. There's only so much water in the well. So I'll need to start churning revenue to pay you back. My monthly payments to you will have to begin after a short ramp-up period. I'm coming in at your asking price and we both know that anybody else will grind you."

Another thing we both knew was that he wanted his hands on that $60K down payment and he wanted it now. "Okay," he said, "but while the title company is doing all the paperwork, will you release the down payment to me?"

"Of course, as long as the deal is all signed with no back doors that could kill our agreement." This was a bit of a risk, as I knew it would take a couple of months to get approved by the county and state liquor and gaming boards in order for escrow to close. But I had an ace up my sleeve.

When I told Dan that I hadn't countered the full asking price and agreed to release the down payment before escrow closed, he looked at me like I was nuts. But then I told him the rest of the tale.

After the down payment of $60,000, the balance due was $190,000 paid over 15 years with monthly payments due the first of each month. Ted's payment would amount to $2,280 per month, just $500 more than his checks from Suburban West. I could cover that even if my ultimate plan didn't work out. At 12 percent interest, he'd receive payments totaling $410,000 over 180 months.

"Big bucks, right?" I said to Dan. "But these optimistic numbers keep him focused on meeting me at Nevada Title, tonight, to get all the documents executed and have him legally bound. Then no one can come in at the eleventh hour and get this deal away from us, and Ted can't change his mind and back out."

"Okay, but what do you think will really happen?"

"I'm not sure, but I do know that with a guy like this, everything will be subject to change over time—and probably not too much time. Offering these terms will keep Ted from shopping the deal and that's the priority at this early stage."

I'd opened escrow at Nevada Title with Mona, whom I knew socially from the Suburban West. She and her husband, George, were regulars there and we'd become good friends. Luckily, we had a great relationship and I called and told her I needed her to stay as late as necessary to get this signed by all parties before another day passed and anything could change or go wrong.

Once fully executed and put in motion, the only remaining problem was that all our cash was tied up in our other ventures and we didn't have the $60K down. My plan was to approach Bobby Boris, who sat on the Tavern Owners Association's Board of Directors with me. He'd owned a couple of successful neighborhood bars for many years. Knowing that Bobby was well-heeled financially, I went to him and said, "I'm looking to borrow a hundred grand to do a deal for Suburban East. Are you interested?"

"I was going to take a run at that place myself," he said, "but it sounds like you beat me to it. I like how you operate, so rather than a loan, I want a piece of the place."

"Bobby, with all due respect, I've already got a partner. I just need a loan. You know me. You know your money is safe with me and my word to repay is good as gold."

He thought for a moment. "Okay, a hundred grand. Twenty percent interest, all due in one year."

"Son of a bitch," I said with a smile. "You're hoping I can't make the payments and you become a partner that way. You don't want to own it outright—you want me in there running it."

This time it was Bobby's turn to smile. "Make the payments and it's a non-issue."

We shook on it. He funded the loan within days. It was another gamble, but I figured I had the edge, and even if worst came to worst, it wasn't like I stood to lose my house. I was betting on my belief that another card would be turning soon with Ted.

I put the deposit in escrow and Ted got his $60K immediately. That left us $40K for operating expenses and the deal was done.

Waltzing off with the Suburban East

As the new owner of the Suburban East, I took a hard look at my immediate situation. The beer and wine coolers were completely bare, the power bills were months in arrears, and the place was just weeks away from getting shut down completely. That worked to my advantage though. There wasn't much inventory to buy from Ted at close of escrow, which preserved most of my remaining $40,000. Based on the solid credit I'd established at the Suburban West with my suppliers, I could load up on product at opening, sell it quickly, and pay for it the following month. The payments would be made from sales, not from the remaining start-up cash.

And Ted thought that by getting his full asking price, he'd made the deal of his lifetime. Except for one little problem—he burned through the initial $60K in a shockingly short time. Even I was surprised at how quickly he started calling and asking for an advance on what I owed him.

"Sure," I told him. "Will five thousand work for you?"

"Absolutely, Ron. That'll be great, thank you."

"Thing is, Ted, when I give you the five, you're going to sign a receipt for ten."

There was a pause on the other end of the line. "Why would I do that?"

"Because I didn't get into this deal to lend you money. Consider it interest. The five thousand I'm advancing you is cash I need to advertise, buy product, remodel and operate. If I'm going to start paying you early, I need to make some major changes in my financial planning."

"Screw you, you bastard." And the line went dead.

Again, I didn't have to wait for long. The very next day, my phone rang again. "If I take your deal, can I get the five today?"

"Sure," I said. "I'll have the check waiting."

I was truly sympathetic to Ted. Rumors abounded about his financial desperation and the causes contributing to it. I've known people who needed cash fast and would do nearly anything for it with no thought for tomorrow. However, Ted had made his own bed. Nobody put a gun to his head to accept my terms.

He rushed over and signed the receipt for $10,000. I made a point of explaining the terms of the new note, which clearly stated that the advance would be applied to the first couple of payments, rather than the balance owed on the principal. That little detail was critical for my idea to work. He thanked me for being so flexible and understanding.

He called again a few days later.

"Hey, any way I can get another five?"

"Sure," I replied. "Same terms as before."

He came, signed for $10K, and walked away with five.

After the third $5,000, I made my play.

"Hey buddy, I could use another five," Ted told me over the phone. "When's a good time for me to come by?"

"Sorry, I can't do it."

Stunned silence. "What do you mean?"

"Ted, I've already fronted you fifteen thousand. How much cash do you think I have lying around? Paying you five thousand a week isn't terms on the sale. It's more like a cash deal. I haven't been licensed here yet. Hell, escrow hasn't closed, so I don't even officially own the bar. I've got some major risk here. Can't you get the money somewhere else?"

I swore I could sense him sweating over the phone line.

It was time to play the card I'd anticipated. "Tell you what I'll do. I have a Treasury bond for fifteen thousand I can liquidate. I'll pay the penalties that cashing it out will cause. But only if it wipes out the rest of the loan and I don't owe you another cent." The $60,000 deposit and $30,000 in cash would give Dan and me the place for a mere $90,000—and we'd own it outright.

I had no such Treasury bond. But he had to think I was doing all I could to raise money and hand it to him. Once again, the only answer I received was a dial tone. And who could blame him? After subtracting the money I'd advanced, he still had over $400,000 coming his way with payments over time if he could just hold out. But I was pretty sure he couldn't. Immediate cash always trumps good judgment, when financial demons are running the show.

Late the next afternoon my phone rang, almost as if we had an appointment. "Can I get the fifteen thousand today if I accept the deal?"

"To tell you the truth, Ted, I don't know."

"What do you mean, you don't know?!"

"It's already four o'clock. We've got to sign paperwork at the title company. I'm not sure we're going to make that all happen before closing time."

"You gotta make it work, man. You gotta help me out. Please."

I sighed. "I'll see what I can do. I'll call you right back."

I couldn't dial Mona's number quickly enough. "I just made the deal of the century and I need this thing inked before Ted changes his mind, gets an idea for finding money elsewhere, or even just goes to sleep."

"Ron, are you kidding me?" she asked. "He's really going to sign the bar over to you for just fifteen thousand more?"

"All I can tell you, Mona, is we need to sign this deal fast."

I immediately called Ted. "I got Mona at title to agree to stay open until we're done. She's drawing up the documents as we speak. If you really want your cash, meet me there at six."

Damned if he wasn't there at 5:59, ready to sign. A few strokes of the pen later, he had his 15 grand and Dan and I owned the Suburban East, free and clear from Ted! That was the good news.

The bad news was I'd used up a lot of the loan from Bobby and I still had a bar to remodel and get running, and pay Bobby back.

And I did exactly that. My managers and I laid the new carpeting ourselves, I worked around the clock to make sure every little detail was addressed, and we somehow managed to get the doors open as soon as we were licensed. I spent 18 hours a day, seven days a week, at the East location, meeting and greeting, running out riffraff, advertising, all the same things that made Suburban West a hit. Before long, the place was packed and our gaming and bar sales were going through the roof.

At the end of each month, I looked at what I could comfortably pull out of the business to send to Bobby Boris. Lo and behold, we paid him back in six months, half a year ahead of schedule.

The day I handed over the final check, Bobby said, "Kid, if I knew anything like this was possible, I would have put in a pre-payment penalty. I never imagined for a second that you'd pull this off. I was sure you'd come back begging for more. But good job. I'm happy for you."

A fellow former Marine, James Fusco, came to work for Dan and me as the manager of the Suburban Lounge East. He was out of town that fateful night at Winners or he would likely have been there with Bob, Artie, Arthur, and me as we dealt with the Nielson theft matter. All for the best, as we had one less attorney to hire and James was spared the agony and uncertainty that the rest of us faced.

As for Ted, well, we never saw each other again. I'm sorry to say that things continued to go downhill for him. I heard from a friend who owned a bar that he popped in from time to time, looking rough and hustling pool for a few bucks.

My duty was to the partnership Dan and I had. The acquisition of the Suburban East was a coup for us and helped to continue building the little empire we dreamed was someday ahead of us as we walked guard duty together in the Marines back in 1972.

CHAPTER 10

Keeping Order

At this time, I was 32 years old, owned two bars and a screen-printing business, all with Dan, and sold real estate on the side. I spent most of my time shuttling between the two bars, working hard and playing hard.

Many people believe that running a bar or restaurant is the same as patronizing one. You hang out with friends and enjoy good food and drink—kind of like being on a perpetual vacation. Don't get me wrong, owning this type of business can be fun and rewarding, but it's not all glitz and glamor. In addition to the grueling work and long hours, you also have to be willing to step up and show people who's in charge. In an establishment where alcohol is served, things can get out of control and if you allow that to happen, it can ruin your livelihood. Even though I'm a generally friendly person, I'm more than willing to do what's necessary to protect my interests, staff, and customers, as occurred on more than one occasion.

In front of the Suburban West was a little freestanding kiosk called the Fotomat. I became acquainted with the girl who worked there and always made it a point to wave and say hi when she was on duty. She dated a tattoo-covered, Harley-riding biker named Rick, who also was a semi-regular at the bar.

One night, I parked my Cadillac near the back door to leave a space out front for customers. I came in to find the place jumping, but the look on my bartender's face told me something wasn't right.

She motioned toward Rick and said, "He's had too much to drink; he's acting like a real jerk. It's a problem."

I told her I'd handle it and made my way over to Rick.

"Hey Rick," I said politely, but firmly. "It's time to go."

Rick glared at me through red, drunken, and drugged eyes, and started to give me crap. Rather than debate the matter, I put my hand on his shoulder and leaned in more closely.

"Here's the deal," I said. "If you just get up and leave, you can come back tomorrow. If you make me throw you out, I'll have to eighty-six you for thirty days. It's up to you."

"Eighty-six" refers to when a business ejects someone for bad behavior and doesn't want him or her back. But the term has an historical basis. It was slang for many mob and business or neighborhood dispute resolutions, not uncommon in this tough western town of years past. To be 86'd originally referred to that dreaded one-way ride to the desert. Short for eighty miles out and six feet under, it's an appropriate term for someone being led to a car, against his will, for his last ride.

But this was no time to give Rick a history lesson. He stood up, started to throw a punch, and that was that. He went out the hard way. I locked the rear door behind him and went back to the front door, where I sat with some buddies, enjoyed drinks and checked the IDs of incoming patrons.

About an hour later, my partner Dan arrived, clearly upset. "I just parked out back," he said. "What the hell happened to your car?"

Curious, I went outside and saw my tires slashed, the vinyl roof cut, windows broken, and headlights smashed. It didn't take Sherlock Holmes to figure out who was responsible. "That asshole Rick," I muttered under my breath.

I asked around the bar and found out Rick's complete name and address. The next day, I huddled with my general manager, Bobby, and my brother, Artie, and told them what I was going to do. "You know the fish market across Jones Boulevard? I want you two to run over there and buy the biggest fish they have. Then head over to the Hallmark store and pick out a gift box and some wrapping paper. See Shelly there; she'll wrap up the fish for you."

Then, in a scene straight out of *The Godfather*, I had them take the gift-wrapped dead fish to Rick's door, ring the bell, and take off before Rick saw them.

The next day, a cop buddy of mine, Tony Manzi, who worked the day shift around the Suburban West, stopped in. "Hey Ron," he said. "Any chance you're having a problem with some guy named Rick?"

"You bet I am. I just had my car towed to Cashman Cadillac for a couple grand worth of repairs because that son of a bitch vandalized it. Why?"

Tony gave a slight smile. "I was cruising the neighborhood and he waved me down. Ron, he's shitting a brick. He thinks he screwed with the wrong guy. He said, 'I was drunk, I messed up Ron's car because he threw me out of his bar, and when I woke up, there was a rotting fish at my door. I think I'm a dead man walking. The guys at that bar are from New York and have a reputation that scares the shit out of me.'"

Tony looked at me intensely. "I'm not going to ask if you're responsible, but Rick wants to know if he can meet with you and if I'll sit with the two of you to ensure his safety."

I said, "I'm happy to talk to him."

But just in case the meeting didn't go well, this was an opportunity for me to gather more intel and keep Rick wondering. I went to Bobby. "When Rick pulls up, I want to note the make, model, and plate number of whatever he's driving. Make sure he sees you writing it down."

Sure enough, Rick saw Bobby in the parking lot and when he

walked in to find Tony and me waiting for him, he already looked like a beaten man.

"You called the meeting, Rick. What's up?"

So nervous he could barely sit still, he replied, "I want to know if whatever damage your car suffered last night gets paid for by me, is there peace for me or am I a dead man either way?"

I looked at him calmly, not betraying any emotion. "It's going to cost a lot to fix the damage and I've had to rent a car. If I'm reimbursed and made whole, the slate is clean. You have my word."

He looked like the governor had just called at the last minute, ordering a stay of execution. "Let me know how much and I'll bring you the cash."

"Are we done here?" Tony asked, standing to leave.

"W-w-well," Rick stammered. "When I pulled into this lot just now, somebody wrote down my license plate. If it's over, is it really over?"

Tony looked to me.

"Just doing recon in case things don't get settled, Tony."

"Fine," Tony said. "Rick, I know Ron. If he says the slate is clean, the slate is clean."

Within a few days, the three of us got together again. I stated the amount due and Rick laid out thousands of dollars in cash. We shook hands and that was that.

Big Bad Chris

As I say, running a bar can be a wild experience. A couple of months later, one of my customers came running in, quite agitated. "You know Billy who rides that green Honda motorcycle?"

"Sure."

"Well, he was so drunk he didn't want to ride it home, so he fell asleep underneath this old pickup truck outside. The driver got into the truck and started to pull out without knowing Billy was under it. He needs help!"

I ran outside with Bobby and Artie to find the truck resting on a high curb between the paved side street and the dirt lot. It was high-centered and couldn't move now. Billy was trapped, screaming from underneath it! Thank God, the truck hadn't crushed him to death, but he was pinned and we had to get him out. The three of us tried to lift the truck high enough for Billy to slide out, but we couldn't manage it. It was one of those vintage trucks that looked like it was built of cast iron. Then I remembered Chris Hancock, a six-foot-eight monster of a man who was inside having a beer.

"Go get Chris!" I shouted to Bobby.

In a matter of seconds, Chris emerged from the bar.

"Chris," I said, "can you go to the front of this pickup and lift it up?"

Honest to God, just like the title character in Jimmy Dean's old song "Big Bad John," Chris gave a mighty groan and damned if he didn't lift that truck enough for us to pull Billy free. Miraculously, he was still alive and an ambulance sped him to the hospital.

"Come on, big guy," I said after all the dust had settled. "Tonight, your drinks are on me."

Not everyone knew that despite Chris's immense size and strength, he was a sweet guy at heart, a real teddy bear who'd give you the shirt off his back.

But a few months later, I was working in my office when the bartender contacted me on the intercom. "Ron, you gotta get out here. Chris is out of control."

Chris had a booming voice and he'd had more than a few drinks.

He wasn't hurting anyone, but he looked and sounded so intimidating that people were leaving.

I approached him cautiously. "Chris, you have to quiet down. I'm losing customers."

"Fuck you," he growled at me.

Okay, so the puppy dog does have some bite, I thought. But I wasn't about to back down. "You and I both know I can't bounce you out of here. Don't make me shoot you where you stand. You've got to go and you're out for thirty days. You're costing me business. The people you scared might never come back."

Just like that, Chris's belligerence turned to penitence. "I'm sorry, Ron." And he peacefully stood up and lumbered out.

We always saw Chris on check-cashing Fridays, when many of the neighborhood construction workers made us their hangout of choice. The following Friday, the bartender stuck her head in my office. "Ron, you're not going to believe this."

She led me to the back door and opened it. There was Chris, sitting in the bed of his pickup with a six-pack parked on our side lot. He called me over and handed me a $100 bill. "I know I'm not allowed inside for thirty days, but I want to buy everybody a round of drinks."

For many of our regular clientele, all roads led to the Suburban. Chris was no different and that was how he dealt with his suspension.

Like I said, it can be a crazy game.

CHAPTER 11

Sign of the Times

Back when I was first trying to promote the Suburban Lounge West and before we opened the Suburban Sign Company, I noticed how many cars were driving right past us on Spring Mountain Road. So I ordered a sign, which we installed on a four-by-eight sheet of plywood supported by two anchored posts out in the frontage-area flower bed. Talk about grassroots marketing!

Designed to advertise the Suburban name and whatever specials we were offering at the time, it worked great until a county code-enforcement officer named Rod Johnson came along and told us we had to take it down. Apparently, it violated some sort of regulation. Knowing how effective that sign was, I didn't want to turn my back on the idea, so after taking down the sign, I bought a used Ryder moving truck. We put "Suburban Lounge" on the sides and the rear and added our comical motto, "Best Burgers in Town. You Can't Beat Our Meat!"

On the lower level of each side panel, I installed tracks where I could slide in pre-printed, 12-inch-high plastic letters, much like an old-style movie marquee. We also mounted a hinged clear-plastic cover that could be locked for protection from vandalism or foul weather. I parked the truck on the adjacent gravel parking area that I'd helped create. Here's how the extra parking spaces came to be.

When I first acquired the Suburban West, a cinderblock wall separated a nice strip of potential parking area from the main shopping center lot. The space belonged, technically, to the community via the Las Vegas Valley Water District. But no one ever used it for anything. The only reason it was never paved was because beneath it were pipes to an adjacent reservoir and if the District needed to do a repair or upgrade, they didn't want to have to jackhammer through concrete or asphalt. For months, I never saw a single person from the Water District, or anywhere else for that matter, use or enter the area.

One night at about 2 a.m., I was talking across the bar with three local construction workers and patrons of the Suburban. Freddy was a welder, Adam was a heavy-equipment operator, and Alan drove a huge dump truck, which he happened to have with him.

"Man, I'd love to see that block wall come down out there," I mentioned casually. "I'd have another thirty parking spaces right next to this bar. If the Water District ever had to get to the pipes, we could just ask everybody to move their cars. Except for Suburban customers, no one else in this shopping center would park there." The closer people could park to our entrance, the more apt they were to stop in.

To my surprise, Alan said, "I can knock that mother down in a half-hour with my truck."

Freddy chimed in, "My welding truck's outside. I can cut the rebar."

Adam added, "I work for an asphalt contractor up the street. I can go get a back loader, load all the blocks in Alan's truck, and drop them all in our dump."

I laughed, thinking they were joking.

"We're serious," they said. "It'll be fun and we'd be done real quick."

"Well," I said, "it's going to be loud and it's the middle of the night. If we don't get shut down trying, there's a case of beer in it for each of you if you can pull it off."

That was the deal closer.

It took an hour to get everything organized and outside it was very quiet. Alan maneuvered his truck in place, revved it up, backed full speed into the wall, and BOOM! About a third of it went down. This was going to work! Alan kept at the wall, Freddy broke out his welding equipment, and Adam got to work with the backhoe. In less than two hours, that wall was gone. Our customers could now drive in and park just steps away from the door. It turned out to be great for the business.

On the rare occasion that people came by from the Water District to enter the reservoir area, they didn't even realize a wall had been there in the first place. It was all good. I had that extra parking lot the entire time we owned the Suburban.

Anyway, I parked the old Ryder truck, the Suburban Lounge's 40-foot billboard on wheels, in that lot, adjacent to the busy street and facing all that daily traffic. Sometimes I lent it to employees or good customers who needed to move heavy furniture, etc. No problem—it was a rolling ad for our bar.

But then came the day that the county-code agent, Rod Johnson, paid me a second visit. He motioned toward my truck. "It's gotta go. You know you can't have signage like that."

"Rod, it's not a sign," I protested. "It's a truck. If it's a sign, why am I paying the DMV to put license plates on it? It's a vehicle, according to the state of Nevada, and it's not stored permanently. It moves! You want a ride?"

He couldn't argue with that logic, so he took another approach. "Well, you've got to move it anyway; the code says you can't park vehicles on unimproved property."

I didn't know why, but Rod seemed to have it in for me. However, I wasn't about to give up without a fight. I went to see Manny Cortez, our county commissioner at the time. I knew he lived right up the street from the Suburban and drove by every day. I told him there was a problem with the truck and the county.

"I love the Suburban," he said, "You've got a great reputation in the neighborhood. We have no beef with you."

"Maybe you don't, but a guy in code enforcement named Rod Johnson sure does," I replied. "I don't know why he's breaking my balls, but first he comes in and tells me a small four-by-eight sign in my planter bed is a violation, so I get rid of it. Now he says my truck's a sign when, according to the state of Nevada, it's a vehicle."

"I know the truck very well," he said. "It's clean, it's got a nice paint job, and it runs." Manny picked up his phone and a couple of minutes later, Rod Johnson appeared at his door. "Rod, I presume you know my constituent, Ron Coury, from the Suburban Lounge?"

Rod glared at me. "Yeah, sure."

"I understand you've got a problem with his truck."

"Yes, sir. It's a vehicle and it's parked on an unimproved lot, which is against code."

Manny thought for a moment. "Have you ever had a problem with Ron?"

"No, not really. He had an illegal wooden sign, but when I told him about it, he removed it."

"What problem are you trying fix now? Have you received any complaints?"

"No."

"Do you really think this is the best use of your time?"

Rod just shrugged.

"Listen, Rod, the truck isn't parked on unimproved property. Unimproved property is raw land with rocks and bushes growing and tumbleweed blowing around. This land has been graded and there's gravel spread on the dirt for dust control. In my view, it's improved enough for parking a car or a truck or whatever. So how about you leave Ron alone?"

"You're the boss."

I never heard from Rod again and the truck sat there until Dan and I built another bar, re-painted the Ryder, and moved it there to promote the new place.

This is another important lesson for entrepreneurs, whose livelihoods can be buffeted about by politics, personalities, and the whims of code enforcers and union organizers. Manny Cortez knew the code well enough to interpret it in a way that was advantageous for me. It gave our business a huge boost.

Remember, if you're going to play the game, always read the rule book. And if a call doesn't go your way, don't just sit and take it. Put up a fight. You never know. Things might just break in your favor.

CHAPTER 12

Protect and Serve

Most of the younger generation has no idea of who John Wayne was. When I was growing up, he was a hero of mine—a patriot, a loyal friend to his pals, and by all accounts a real good guy both on and off the screen. Some scenes of his that have always stuck with me came from the last of his movies, *The Shootist* and *True Grit*.

In one scene in *True Grit*, he's escorting a bunch of bad guys he caught, single-handedly, back to stand trial. Suddenly, he's confronted by a band of thugs intent on setting their cohorts free. As the gang encircles them, John Wayne rests his hand on his gun and asks them a simple question. "I'm willing to die trying to get these guys back to face justice. My question is, are you willing to die trying to take them from me?"

In one of his films, *Big Jake*, he famously said to Richard Boone, "Now you understand. Anything goes wrong, anything at all—your fault, my fault, nobody's fault—it don't matter. I'm gonna blow your head off. It's as simple as that."

And finally, a line the screenwriters and industry-rag reporters all agreed was vintage John Wayne in real life. It was written for "the Duke" to recite in his final movie. "I won't be wronged, I won't be insulted, and I won't be laid a hand on. I don't do these things to other people and I require the same from them."

I believe those few lines represent a window into the soul of a man who was a true friend to his compadres, a fierce enemy to those who might harm him or his loved ones, and an American who set standards that we could all admire and strive to emulate if we had the collective heart, mind, and body to back up those motivational, yet simple, sentiments.

This goes along with the principles that drill instructors instill in all recruits in Marine boot camp: "We train you to always avoid a fight. However, we also train you to handle yourselves in the event that a conflict is unavoidable. Whether you win or lose, make sure the other son of a bitch knows he just tussled with someone he never wants to fight again. The tenacity and discipline you recruits will learn here will become a part of your core, coupled with the stamina and skills you develop in your months of training. You'll possess all the tools to be a force for right. A force to be reckoned with. A force to stand up to adversaries here in the States or anywhere in the world our beloved Corps may send you."

Having My Back

In running our bar, I became good friends with many of our customers, including Norm Ziola, a Las Vegas Metro homicide detective. Norm was a big supporter of another good guy named John McCarthy, elected Clark County Sheriff in 1979. After taking office, McCarthy appointed Norm the Sheriff's Adjutant.

Back when slot machines accepted Eisenhower silver dollars or legal minted tokens, one of the most tried-and-true methods of slot thievery was known as "slugging." The perpetrators replicated the size and shape of silver dollars with lead slugs, fed them into the machines, and collected the payouts in real dollars. When their slugs started to come out as winnings, indicating the hopper was drained of real money, they knew it was time to move on to the next machine or bar. Sluggers could get away with this for several days, because most bar operators didn't own their machines or have keys to them—only the slot company did. And the slot company performed a count once a week.

One day on our weekly "drop day," the route guy came by, opened the machines for the count, and gave me the bad news. Over the course of the past week, some slugger had been hitting us hard. I didn't know who it was, but I did know I had to catch him in the act. I told my bartenders, "If anyone who doesn't buy any Eisenhower dollars from you plays the dollar machine for an extended period of time, call me."

A few nights later, the bartender on duty buzzed the intercom line to my office. "This guy out here's been playing the dollar machine for a good long while and he hasn't bought in for a single buck."

I stepped into the bar from my office and started surreptitiously eyeballing the suspect in question. Slugs are heavy and hard to conceal and sure enough, this clown had a leather satchel between his feet. He was playing away—dropping three "coins," pulling the handle, dropping another three, pulling the handle. I knew a bunch of slugs make a different sound than a sack of Eisenhowers, a kind of dead thud. I edged closer and up behind him. Then I quickly kicked the satchel and heard the thud. "You're my slugger!"

The words were barely out of my mouth when he took off on the run. I went after him, and everyone at the Suburban knew that if I was running after someone, something was up. I chased the guy out the door and into the parking lot. Unbeknownst to me, several of my customers were following. The guy was high-tailing it down Spring Mountain Road. Even though I was a pretty fast runner, I couldn't catch up with him. He barreled across Jones Boulevard and continued sprinting toward the Strip.

I wasn't gaining any ground, but I wasn't about to let him get away, so I pulled my pistol and yelled, "Stop or I'll shoot!" I fired a shot into the dirt of a vacant lot, just to scare him and hopefully stop him. The shot only succeeded in making him flee faster. If I couldn't catch him before, I sure as hell wasn't going to catch him now.

Next, I heard footsteps charging up behind me and turned to see my buddy Norm, the sheriff's right-hand man. The first words out of his mouth? "Where is he?" I laughed a bit and said his crime didn't warrant the death penalty. I told Norm I just shot into the dirt. It would either prompt him to stop or ensure he wouldn't return to my place with his lead slugs. We had a good laugh and went back to the bar to have a drink.

A short time later, a bartender from a nearby establishment showed up and said, "Damn, we just had a customer come in white as a ghost and said somebody over here was shooting at him!"

I never caught the guy, but I also never saw him again. And I never forgot the way Norm was right behind me in case I needed him, which only deepened my loyalty to my friends, our cops, and my commitment to helping them out whenever I could. It wasn't much longer until I had my chance.

No Questions Asked

One night I had to park at the far end of the Suburban's parking lot. Since all the adjacent businesses were closed, it meant my bar was having a good night. I walked toward the bar, came around the corner, and noticed a parked police cruiser. As I got closer, I saw that a cop I knew, Walter Davis, was in trouble, trying to break up an altercation between a known punk named Joe and his girlfriend Debbie, one of my waitresses. Debbie regularly called in sick while she recovered from beatings from this asshole, a six-foot-plus drug abuser. He had Walter pinned, banging his head against a brick pillar. Walter was barely conscious and bleeding badly; I could easily see his head couldn't take much more.

Walter needed help—nothing to ask, nothing to say. I raced toward them.

Before Walter could choke out a word, I punched Joe in the face, spun him around, and let loose with a roundhouse kick to his midsection, which buckled him over.

Walter immediately struggled to gain his senses and called for backup on his lapel mike. Then, between the two of us, we wrestled Joe to the ground, but whatever he was on was giving him incredible strength. Walter and I each had an arm and couldn't get them behind him to be handcuffed.

The call "Officer needs assistance! Fight! Fight!!" sends shivers down fellow officers' spines. If they can, they drop whatever they're doing and rush to assist.

I knew that for me, that call was a double-edged sword. I wanted to continue to help Walter, but I didn't want to be in the middle of a brawl with a cop as other officers arrived, not knowing whose side I was on. I could get hurt by one of them thinking I was in a two-on-one against Walter. My instincts and training kicked in and my attack became even more brutal. I wasn't limited by any police policy guidelines.

One technique we learned in the Corps was that in a true fight for life, there are ultimate fight-ending moves. We're trained to tear out the Adam's apple and throat area or remove an eyeball. Joe will never know how close he came to one of those final life-altering maneuvers, as I heard Walter's backup approaching. Just as the other units came screaming up, Walter and I managed to get the handcuffs on him. I quickly backed away with my hands up.

Cops jumped out with guns drawn. The well-trained officers

immediately assessed me as no threat. They came to Walter's aid and helped him up, head bloodied and out of breath, but otherwise in generally good condition. Walter told them what had transpired, identified me, and shared what I'd done for him. They all shook my hand or high-fived me, expressing gratitude for jumping into action and helping one of their own.

Honorary Deputy Sheriff

Not too long after that, in my role as a Realtor, I was showing a pit boss named Jack and his wife Marilyn a home they were considering purchasing. I had them both in my car. As we drove across the Strip, an elderly white-haired woman was making her way along the sidewalk when suddenly, a shirtless kid appeared behind her, hit her hard over the head with something in his hand, grabbed her purse, and began running in the same direction I was driving! I saw the kid run into the Tropicana Hotel's parking lot, with which I was very familiar.

"Hang on!" I yelled, swerving into the lot, trying to pursue the kid as he zigzagged through the parked cars. At this point, I didn't yet have a concealed-weapon permit, but I did keep a pistol in my glove box for protection. Knowing I'd never catch him while I was driving, I slammed on my brakes, grabbed my gun, and jumped out to give chase.

Seeing me, the thief began racing toward a fence along the back of the Trop's courtyard rooms, a three-story motel-like building directly behind the main hotel tower. Because I'd parked in this area as an employee, I knew something the kid didn't. He was heading toward a dead end. What I didn't know was what he'd used to strike the old woman. Crowbar? Pipe? Maybe even the butt of a gun? I was well aware of the dangers of over-reacting and taking an unwarranted shot; however, I also knew that I wanted to be prepared for whatever might happen.

As he reached the fence and realized his predicament, he broke to his left. Anticipating this reaction, I'd made up ground and gotten behind him. As he turned, I swung my pistol, caught him in the back of the head, and he went down like a sack of potatoes. He hit the asphalt, which on this day was hot enough to fry eggs.

I kicked his weapon, a length of metal pipe, out of his hand. "Stay down!" I ordered, pressing on his chest with my foot.

"The pavement!" he cried. "It's burning me!"

"Yeah? And how do you think the old lady you just cold-cocked feels?"

At that moment, Tropicana security rolled up and leaped out of their cars, guns drawn. Casino security guards were armed back then, something few casinos allow today due to liability and litigation concerns.

I immediately put my hands up. "This guy just knocked an old woman down right there up the street, stole her purse, and I caught up to him here."

"That's great, but right now I need you to put your weapon down."

I complied as Jack came running over, followed by Marilyn. They verified my story and I gave the guard my business card with my pager number on it (Remember those? Before cell phones!) in the event they or the police needed to reach me.

As we walked back to the car, Jack started laughing. "That was something else, Ron. Not only did you jump out of the car while it was still running, you left it in gear! I had to slide over behind the wheel to keep it from smacking into a row of parked cars."

When I got home that night, Joan told me that a Metro cop had stopped by. After explaining what had happened, he asked, "Does your husband have a carry permit for that gun he carries?"

She had no idea and told him so. My gun was registered, but I couldn't legally carry it in a concealed manner.

"Okay, well, tell him if he doesn't have a permit, he ought to apply and get one."

Shortly after, the *Las Vegas Sun*, the afternoon daily newspaper at the time, wrote a nice story about the entire incident. People noticed!

At this point in the development of Las Vegas, it had never occurred to me to get a concealed-carry permit. As I said before, it was still the Wild West in many ways. A lot of people carried guns and I doubt many of them had permits. However, I wanted to play by the rules and soon got my license to carry.

A couple of nights after the Tropicana incident, Officer Walter Davis came into the Suburban Lounge with a big smile on his face. "Between helping me out and catching that purse snatcher, Sheriff McCarthy wants you to know you're on his radar. You've got something coming."

I had no idea what he was talking about until I found out I'd be receiving an award for my actions. A few days later, Sheriff McCarthy came to the Suburban with a badge naming me an Honorary Deputy Sheriff in the Las Vegas Metropolitan Police Department. The badge bore my name and it replicated the exact badge worn by the Department—a seven-pointed gold star. It was inside a black, foldable wallet. Clearly visible in front, through a transparent plastic cover, was an ID card to go with the badge, which came with an official Certificate of Appointment signed by the Sheriff, identifying me as the recipient of the appointment. A true honor!

When the Sheriff handed it to me, he said, "I saw the article in the paper, where you caught that purse snatcher. Later, I read the internal report by Officer Davis about you helping him out of a jam. If you're going to act like a cop, you should carry a badge. Here you go, Ron. Thanks for helping my guys."

To this day, the newspaper article and Certificate of Appointment awarded by Sheriff McCarthy are two of my most prized possessions.

CHAPTER 13

Limo Wars

As I mentioned earlier, I've always been a niche finder. Sometimes it seems like niches find me as often as I discover them. As drinking and driving laws became more strictly enforced in the 1980s, whenever I traveled out of state and knew I'd be having a few cocktails, I hired a limousine. Invariably, the driver was dressed in a clean black suit and tie, half the time looking better than the people he was driving. In Vegas back in the 1970s and '80s, by comparison, most drivers employed by our local limousine companies dressed casually. Many wore satin baseball jackets with their company logo, and casual baseball caps. The condition of the cars was also less than stellar.

Whenever I hired a limo with friends or a group in town, usually a stretch limo, I thought, "This is Vegas, the Entertainment Capital of the World. Shouldn't we have cream-of-the-crop limousines with drivers who represent the epitome of elegance and luxury?"

Looking into it, I found out that one company dominated the transportation market in town. Sin City Charters owned private planes and helicopters for hire, 50 full-sized buses, 750 cabs, and more than 300 limousines. But they had only two stretch limos. There was an obvious need for a quality limousine service in Vegas featuring stretch limos and it felt like a niche I could fill.

In 1984, I started researching what it took to open a limousine company. The industry was regulated by the Nevada Public Service Commission, commonly known as the PSC. The first thing I heard was that a new limo license hadn't been issued in Vegas in decades. The laws were written in the 1940s by a lawyer who had worked for one of the existing companies. This lawyer later became a judge, a state legislator, then a justice of the Nevada Supreme Court. The rules were so restrictive that, in effect, they'd created a monopoly that was nearly impossible for anyone new to penetrate.

At the Marine base in Barstow, when I was told that training as a dealer didn't fit within Project Transition guidelines, I read the rules and discovered that, indeed, it did. So I applied the principle of "reading the rulebook" once again. I learned that the state law making it so hard to get licensed was designed to protect the existing certificate holders from any competition. I couldn't believe my eyes. Aren't competition and survival of the fittest what capitalism is based on?

I further learned that an applicant must show a need in the community for the service applied for and provide proof that the new license wouldn't create an adverse economic impact on the existing companies. Apparently, the law was completely successful in preventing newcomers from entering the business. In the last two decades, not one applicant had successfully cleared those two hurdles. When others applied, they faced an army of "interveners," including the major limo companies, a local charter-bus company, and several taxi operators, all pleading little to no profitability. There it was: Simply show that your company hardly turned a profit and any new license issued could hurt your business with an "adverse impact" and the state wouldn't license the newcomer. They knew they had a good thing going and weren't about to let anyone else grab even the smallest piece of their pie.

Despite this daunting information, I still believed an opportunity existed. I talked to several hotel doormen who were customers at the

Suburban and they all echoed the same sentiment. "Oh man, it would be great to have a quality limo company in this town!" said Bob, a Caesars Palace doorman. "Do you know how many big winners stroll out of the hotel, money spilling out of their pockets, and ask me to get them a nice limo? I'm ashamed at what shows up! And it hurts my tips."

When others told me the same thing, I asked them, "If I apply to the PSC and have a hearing, would you be willing to testify that there's a need for a top-flight limo company in Vegas?"

Most were afraid to alienate the existing limo companies, but one or two said they'd appear on my behalf, so I started building my case.

Part of the application required me to show that I was fit, willing, and able to operate a limo company. I felt strongly then, and still do now, that in most cases, if you apply good judgment and reasonable business principles and practices, you can succeed in nearly any business. However, with a state regulatory agency like the Public Service Commission and the odds stacked against me, it wouldn't hurt for an experienced operator to testify that he was a contracted consultant to a newbie like me. In my interactions with Presidential Limousines in San Diego, I'd gotten to know Gerry, one of the managers, who'd recently opened his own limo company. Gerry agreed to be my consultant and soon became another friend for life.

Several of my Suburban customers were employees at local limo companies and when I asked them how business was, they told me they were often so busy, they had to turn customers away. That was exactly what I needed to hear. If the existing companies had more business than they could handle, how would picking up their leftovers create an adverse economic impact? To further strengthen my case, I tried to rent some of their limos and 90 percent of the time, the dispatcher told me, "I'm sorry, sir, but no cars are available." And when one did show up, I took photos of the torn seats, ripped carpets, and drivers who looked like big-city hacks. Everything pointed to the fact that not only wouldn't I hurt the existing companies, I'd also be filling a serious need for luxury stretch limos.

After preparing with my attorney, Justin Young, I went before the PSC, brought in the witnesses I'd gathered, and did a thorough and compelling job of making my case. The existing companies were so used to winning, they didn't take me seriously. After two days of hearings, the commission issued me a license limited to stretch limos. To further ensure I wouldn't hurt the competition, they also stipulated that I couldn't solicit business at the airport; I could only pick up there if a customer had a pre-arranged reservation—a restriction the other companies didn't face. Despite the uneven playing field, I was ready to run a quality service and fill the niche I'd discovered.

With everything in order, I went out and bought two beautiful stretch limos, a Cadillac and Lincoln Town Car. Presidential Limousine Service was in business.

The PSC required limos for hire to be identifiable, but the regulation was vague and I found an easy way to comply. My contention was that when people hired a limo, they wanted to feel like they owned it, so I didn't put any signage or logos on my cars, only personalized license plates: "Pres 1," "Pres 2," and so on. By comparison, the competition plastered their names and phone numbers on the doors just like cabs— the only thing missing was a roof rack featuring advertising for local strip joints.

Vegas stretch limos had a traditional bar and TV, but nothing else, not even a bottle of water. Presidential cars provided a bucket of ice and free bottled water. And through my liquor supplier, I could buy a decent bottle of champagne for about $2.20. I didn't sell passengers alcohol, but in addition to the ice and water, I stocked the cars with complimentary champagne and mixers. If a passenger requested something special to drink, the driver picked it up. To comply with liquor laws, the drivers were reimbursed directly by the customer. We also gave a single-stem red rose to every lady in the party. It was truly going to be a high-quality service.

The Big Boys Take Off the Gloves

The ink was barely dry on my Operating Certificate when two of my competitors filed an injunction request in District Court, claiming that the PSC had exceeded its authority in issuing my certificate to operate stretch limousines when the Nevada legislature had never clearly defined a stretch limo; therefore, my license should be rescinded. The District Court issued the injunction. We were closed, for now!

I immediately mounted an appeal, which in Nevada means going directly to the State Supreme Court—the same court where the former attorney for one of my competitors now was a sitting judge. As always, the wheels of justice turned slowly and I still had the expenses of the business, with no revenue to cover them.

Finally, we had our day in the Supreme Court and it seemed as if common sense and the law would go in my favor. One compelling point Attorney Young made in my defense was that if I'd been limited to operating only black-colored limousines, while the Nevada Legislature had never defined the color black, PSC officers would certainly know if we were compliant. Similarly, without any legislative assistance, these state officers, fully trained in transportation matters, were well able to identify a stretch from a standard limousine and my limitation could be fully enforced. After hearing both sides' arguments, the Chief Justice said, "I'm no expert, but if I'm sitting on my porch and two limousines go by, I'm pretty sure I could tell the standard from the stretch without having to place a call to the state legislature." Hearing that, we felt pretty good.

Weeks later, the Court issued their findings.

The ruling was unanimous.

Against us.

So much for common sense, fairness, and the law.

I reapplied to the PSC and made my second presentation. By now, I'd learned a lot and made it bigger and better than ever. This round of hearings took 13 days, not only grueling, but expensive, as certain costs, such as the court reporter, were on my dime.

This time, the existing companies were locked and loaded for battle, looking for a way to mow down my proposed business once and for all.

During one round of questioning, an intervener's attorney asked me, "What are you doing with the cars that you aren't licensed to operate?"

It seemed like an innocent enough question, which I answered truthfully by testifying about where they were parked. That night, one of the cars was extensively vandalized and I came home to find Joan in tears.

"They've been calling all day," she said, trembling. "Threatening to hurt or even kill you!"

"Who?" I asked, my blood boiling.

"They don't say. They just make their threats and hang up. You can hear them on the answering machine."

I played back the messages. The threats were random and varied, ranging from bullets coming my way and a car bomb, to going to a deep watery grave wearing concrete boots in Lake Mead. These cowards had Joan frazzled beyond belief and naturally, I took a fight-back posture as I considered all the possible variables.

I immediately took the recordings to one of my cop friends. He listened to them, but just shook his head, gravely. "I'd like to get these bastards for you, Ron, but legally there's nothing I can do. You need more."

"Like what?" I angrily replied. "You guys telling my wife I'm dead?"

"I'm sorry. As soon as they make any kind of move, we'll nail them, I promise."

The next few weeks were torture. Each day, I checked under my car with a mirror, searching for suspicious-looking devices, before starting the engine. They say that in a car blast, it's the compression that kills you. So I started mine with the door open and one leg out, hoping any blast would throw me clear with only minor injuries. I carried a concealed pistol and always tried to assess my surroundings and people's movements around me. In restaurants, sitting with my back to the wall, facing the door, and ready for the unexpected—from whatever direction—was the new norm for me.

The threats on my life kept coming and I was under tremendous pressure from Joan to pull the plug on the whole plan. The problem was, I'd spent a ton of money on the cars and making my presentations. Plus, I'd be caving in to injustice and bullying and I just couldn't bring myself to do it, even as Joan was begging me to walk away. I tried to reassure her that they were bluffing, but she finally asked me to move out for her peace of mind and the safety of our kids, leading us to separate and even divorce until we reconciled and remarried several years later.

Uncle Louie Makes Me an Offer I Had To Refuse

I didn't know who was behind the intimidation, but Bill Bunton, a former driver who'd been promoted to shift manager for one competitor, was, I thought, a gangster wannabe and to this day, I suspect it was him. One of their drivers was in my bar one night and I asked him about Bunton. The driver described him as a former gentlemen's club bouncer who lost his job for being too aggressive with customers. He went to work for the cab company as a mechanic and later a limousine driver. He was rumored to have dated the office manager for a short time; she promoted him to lead driver and eventually the company's day-shift manager.

The owners of Sin City Charters were three sisters who inherited the business from their father when he died back in the 1960s. Bunton had them fooled into thinking he was their knight in shining armor who would do anything for them and the business. So when I came along as a threat to their near monopoly, it was the perfect opportunity to show them he was serious—by trying to scare me off.

The thing is, I knew real gangsters. Back in Brooklyn, my dad walked the straight and narrow, but some friends he grew up with were connected. A close neighbor I called "Uncle Louie" was a high-ranking made guy with one of New York's Five Families. At one point, when I was a kid, he went to prison. But before he left Brooklyn, my dad told Louie not to worry—he'd watch out for his wife and kids while he was gone. Whenever anything went wrong, Louie's wife Isabel called my dad, who was very handy and could fix anything. When Louie got out, he told my dad that if he ever needed anything, all he had to do was ask. My dad took care of his own business and never accepted Louie's offer.

One night in the midst of this limousine fiasco, I was working late at Suburban West when Uncle Louie showed up, unannounced, with a bodyguard who seemed like he was eight feet tall. After a hug and hello, I asked him what brought him all the way out to Vegas.

Louie had been shot seven times in a highly publicized single incident and one nearly fatal bullet to the throat had left his voice extremely gravelly—a perfect voice for his persona. Apparently, news of my David and Goliath battle with the limo companies had made its way back to the old neighborhood. "I heard about the trouble you've been having," Louie rasped. "Your mom is worried. You know she walks by my social club at night on her way home from church and I always have one of my guys walk with her."

"I didn't know that, Uncle Louie, but I'm grateful for it."

He leaned forward. "I owe your father and he'd never let me do anything for him. Let me take care of this for you, Ronnie. I can make sure these guys will be out of your life, forever."

I'd be lying if I said I wasn't tempted. But . . . "Uncle Louie," I said, "I'm building something here. I've got a gaming license and a real estate license. If something happens to these limo jerks, it's all coming back on me. Even if they aren't just bluffing and hit me when I'm not looking, I'll go down with a smile, knowing that all hell will break loose when you show up again and make things right. Until then, and I say this with love and respect, please let me try to fix it my way."

Louie gave me a tight nod, stood, kissed me on both cheeks, and headed back out into the night. As I watched him go, I was reminded that sometimes, the only way to fight fire is with fire. Bad guys don't play by the rules; to beat them, you should be prepared to color outside the lines yourself.

This lesson was still fresh in my mind as I arrived for the next hearing day at the PSC. As luck would have it, when I stepped into the elevator, the wannabe gangster, Bill Bunton, was standing there. The doors closed and it was just the two of us. A quick glance around the ceiling perimeter revealed what I'd hoped. This old building's elevator lacked surveillance cameras. I pressed the emergency-stop button.

"What the hell are you doing?" he asked, full of his usual bluff and bluster. I pinned him to the rear of the elevator wall, my fingers pressed against each side of his Adam's apple. The throat hold, taught to me by my chief drill instructor in boot camp, was amazingly effective. When properly used, it ensured immediate attention and total compliance by its recipient.

"Listen, you piece of shit. You have no idea what you're in for. The death threats to my family and the destruction of my cars stops now or you'll be fucked more ways than you can imagine. I know you're at the heart of these tactics. From this day forward, whatever happens to you and yours is on you. You're messing with the wrong guy." With each word I squeezed harder and harder on his throat, my fingers moving closer and closer to touching behind his Adam's apple. It's a crippling maneuver and he felt it. My tone and eyes were filled with rage and he stood there, stone cold, with his eyes wide open, in shock as my warning to him went uninterrupted.

I released my hold on him, then restarted the elevator, and we arrived on our floor. Bunton never said a word, but the death threats and vandalism immediately stopped. I guess I was right about him being the source of the anonymous threats and damages I'd encountered.

Round Two of the Limo Wars

Once again, I made my case to the Commission that my company would fill a need without having any adverse impact on the existing limo businesses. During one exchange, a competitor's attorney claimed that I'd violated the regulation stipulating that the name of the company be displayed on the vehicle. He pulled out a picture showing that "Presidential Limousine" was not displayed on the sides of my cars, comparing it to a photo of one of their cars. "When you were previously in operation, you provided no such identification and who knows what other codes you've failed to follow," the attorney said, like he'd just delivered the knockout punch.

I just smiled back. "I didn't break any law. I completely followed the code."

He affected his best look of disbelief and confusion.

"A limousine has four sides. While the other companies seeking to keep me from operating display their names on the left and right sides, I've identified mine on the front and rear. My license plates have my company's name on them. If a plate is good enough for the DMV to identify the ownership of a vehicle, it should be good enough to identify the company operating the vehicle."

Now his look of disbelief and confusion was for real. He thought he had me, but had absolutely nothing to counter my assertion.

We took a short recess and in the men's room, I found myself standing next to the Chairman of the PSC, Chris Johnson. I didn't think it was appropriate to speak to him, as he was presiding over the hearings, but to my surprise, he asked, "Where'd you do boot?"

"You served, sir?"

"Damn right. Parris Island!"

I felt that my chances at getting a fair hearing had just improved dramatically, but the good old boys wouldn't just roll over. If one of the existing companies could successfully assert that it was barely profitable, any business Presidential booked would significantly impact its bottom line, forcing the PSC's denial.

As an applicant, I had access to the financial records that the existing companies filed each year—banker's boxes full of them. I pored over the reports and discovered that, despite their fleets of cars and years in business, all claimed they were barely breaking even and, in some years, even losing money. Using an old accounting trick, they pumped up expenses so there was no visible profit.

One of the largest expenditures was for gasoline. Through further research, I found that one company owned its own gasoline tanks for fueling their taxis and limos. I took the total miles driven from one segment of the report and the total fuel expense from another and determined that the limos' miles per gallon were ridiculously low. By throwing all the fuel expenses for cabs and limos onto the limo side of the ledger, they artificially lowered the limousine company profits to eliminate potential competitors like me. If the fuel costs were properly allocated, their limo business was extremely profitable.

I also looked at the salaries of the company's employees and officers and saw there was no breakdown.

With Bill Bunton on the stand, I whispered to my attorney, "Ask him what he makes a year."

As soon as Justin asked the question, Bunton turned his head to look at his company's general manager, Rod Stone, who held him in a death stare. Stone was the face of the three gals who owned Sin City Charters. They maintained a very low public profile and let Stone run the day-to-day business.

"I'm not going to answer that," Bunton fumed.

"You're under oath. You have to answer it."

Bunton shook his head. "The owners of our company don't want me to disclose privileged information."

Justin's counter came swiftly. "Wouldn't you acknowledge that salaries are one of the larger operating expenses? We need to verify that salaries, as well as all other expenses, are reasonable and customary for the industry."

"I have no knowledge of those figures," Bunton stammered. "You'll have talk to the financial people."

Chairman Johnson picked up the thread. "Mr. Bunton, your company has presented you as the spokesperson and representative of the business. Either answer the question or don't come here and assert that your company is barely profitable."

With a second look at his boss, Bunton stuck to his guns. "I'm sorry sir, I can't answer that."

Johnson replied, "Well then, for the record, we're going to assume that these companies are financially quite healthy and there will be no adverse economic impact by issuing a license to a company to operate a few additional limos."

Sure enough, the Commission issued me another certificate. My two cars were back on the streets earning and I bought two more to help me out of the financial hole dug by all the delays and legal acrobatics.

But just when my business began seeing terrific daily rentals, along came another petition for judicial review, this time questioning the adequacy of the public notice issued by the state prior to my hearings. This was a technicality that any reasonable court would recognize as a weak tactic, but it was well established that I wouldn't get a straight hearing in any courtroom in the state, not with my opponents' political and judicial influence.

When I knew how I wanted to proceed, I met again with my attorney. "I'm not even going to try to beat them on this bullshit technicality in an obviously skewed court system. Instead, I'll just file a new application every couple of months. I'll get a certificate as Limousine Company A while I'm applying for Limousine Company B, with a pending application for Limousine Company C. Because it takes so long for my competitors to file for judicial relief and get a hearing, every time I get shot down by the court, I'll have another certificate approved by the PSC and keep the limos running under whatever company is active." Justin, a great guy and extremely practical, understood completely and concurred with my plan, offering to help in any way he could if I later required it.

I filed the paperwork under many different names—Monarch, Galaxy, Luxury, whatever I could think of—burying the system with applications. In the meantime, I worked night and day to keep my limo operation in the black.

As insignificant as it might initially seem, the cost of car washes was cutting deeply into my profits. Each car was washed and detailed after every run, and local car washes charged exorbitant markups for limos. To solve this, for a short time, Dan and I ran our own automated car wash. Our limos could roll through anytime they wanted, saving us at least $240 a day; multiplied by 30 days of operation in a 24/7 town, that was a ton of money—not to mention the profits we generated on the car wash.

With the bars, the limo company, and the car wash, I needed a little more help in handling all the businesses. My Brooklyn buddy, Tommy Bear, was living in Vegas and came on board as manager of the Spring Valley Car Wash. I also asked my dad to move out from New York and work for us. He and my mom would be closer to both their sons and grandkids, which they'd love, and we'd get another 100% trustworthy employee. They made the move and our family was all together again.

I continued to flood the PSC with applications and plan for hearings. One day, my phone rang and it was Rod Stone himself, the general manager of Las Vegas's preeminent limo service and one of my fiercest opponents. He wanted to meet at a restaurant to talk. He selected a Denny's. I preferred to have a home-court advantage. A popular place for locals run by a super gal named Amy Liles, Amy's Café, was a regular morning stop for me, a good place for a great breakfast and a chance to plan my day, which was usually full and sometimes hectic, running multiple businesses simultaneously. While I could eat at any of the restaurants Dan and I owned, I'd be visited by customers wanting to shoot the breeze and by employees with issues.

Amy was a hardworking single mom, raising a daughter, Emily, who worked the counter. Amy's girlfriends waited tables. Danette and Charlene were friendly and caring, taking the time to know their regulars and all the events that filled their daily lives. Amy, Emily, Danette, and Charlene all knew a lot about me; they listened when I needed to vent or left me be when I needed to focus. Either way, Amy's served to settle me into a good frame of mind to attend to business. It was the ideal place for my meeting with Rod Stone, home turf where I could control the setting.

Cloak and Dagger

By all accounts, Stone was a decent sort, just a businessman, and I doubted he was directly involved in the threats and intimidation tactics I'd experienced. I was fairly sure his underlings were playing these tough-guy games, and probably without his knowledge, but I had to be smart and safe about it. I didn't trust any of my competitors. I agreed to meet Stone, but I wasn't about to arrive unprepared. My cousin, Arthur Charles, was a big powerful guy who got a job done, whatever it took. And I had Bobby and my brother Artie, also good with their hands, plus a couple of friends who were legally armed and ready to back us up.

I called them together and laid everything out. "I doubt this is a setup and there's a shallow grave waiting for me out in the desert, but I'm not taking any chances. I'm meeting him at noon, at a place I picked, and I want you guys there at eleven fifteen, seated at different tables around the restaurant. I'll also have two guys waiting in the parking lot, in case I have a problem getting to and from my car." Was I paranoid? Maybe. But in the Las Vegas of that era, you couldn't be too careful. While I didn't share my concerns about this meeting with Amy's team, they would surely inform me if anything seemed out of whack with customers or their behavior. I'd planned things as well as I could for my own safety.

I arrived early and when Rod came in and joined me in my preselected booth in an open area along the windows, he had no idea that my guys surrounded him. When he joined me, Amy herself was standing at my booth, exchanging pleasantries. For Rod to feel the location was less than neutral couldn't hurt my position. Just chatting casually with Amy at my booth accomplished that goal.

Amy excused herself as soon as Rod arrived. "I have to tell you, Rod, I was pretty surprised to get your call," I said. "I'll admit my interest is piqued. What do you want?"

He sighed. "I'm getting copies of applications from all these start-up limo companies and you're the proprietor of every one. What are you doing?"

"Hey," I said, "even though we both know my company has every right to be in business and is no threat to you, I don't think I can beat you in court. Even if I could, I don't have the deep pockets to finance repeated legal battles. I can't afford to be shut down again, and being right but out of operation does me no good when I've got car payments to make, a family to feed, and businesses to run. So every time you succeed in voiding a certificate of mine, I'll have a new one ready to operate. When I show up at hearings representing myself, you're paying lawyers and investigators and I'm going to drain *you*. You're not going to drain *me*.

"However, I'll make a deal with you. I just want a little piece of this pie. Get off my back, let me run my business in peace, and I'll sign a contract promising not to operate more than fifteen stretch limos. You now have more than three hundred limos and very few are stretches. I can't hurt your core business."

He looked down at the table for a moment. "The thing is, Ron, if I let one competitor in, others will think they can do the same. The market's only so big and I have my marching orders. How about if we just buy you out?"

That, I never saw coming!

I pointed out to Stone that Vegas was getting somewhere in the neighborhood of 15 million visitors a year and that in the blink of an eye, we'd be seeing more like 40 million. "The market is limitless," I said.

"You may be right, but we're not willing to take that risk." And then he handed me an envelope. Inside was a check for $100,000, a lot of money in the 1980s.

I handed it back to him and said, "That's not going to work for me."

"What would?"

"Well, I need to go through my check register and calculate everything I've spent so far, including legal fees and debt balances. I'll also throw in extra for time and aggravation. When I give you that number, you can buy me out or not. I really don't care. There won't be any negotiation."

I walked out and my guys peeled off one at a time, Stone still unaware I'd been covered on all sides. A big wave to Amy and her gals concluded the tension-filled morning and left everyone in a relaxed state of mind.

I went back through my records, came up with a figure, and called Rod.

"Okay," he said, with no debate and no counter. "Come down to my office tomorrow at eleven and we'll wrap this up."

I arrived to find Bunton and the CFO waiting along with Stone. His flunkies weren't ready to give up without a fight. "Mr. Stone, sir," said the CFO, "we can beat this guy. You don't need to buy him out."

Stone gave him a look that said the discussion was over. "I don't want to spend money fighting Ron. This is just a business deal."

In that moment, my suspicion that he'd had nothing to do with all the violence, harassment, and bullying I'd been subjected to seemed to be confirmed. In fact, over time we grew to become friends.

Stone then handed me another document. "I know we didn't discuss this, but what would you say to a non-compete for five years? Otherwise, I could buy you out and you could turn around and open another company or advise someone else how to get licensed. My employers would like some assurances."

"Be happy to, Rod, for another twenty-five thousand."

Before his CFO or Bunton could open their mouths, Stone turned to them. "Write the damn check."

The Las Vegas limo-licensing scene changed when the regulatory environment shifted and a number of new companies found their way into the industry, adding hundreds of charter vehicles to the Las Vegas streets. Casinos also began buying their own limos. All the competitors I faced in 1984 continued to grow as well.

But that all developed years later. In the 1980s, with the mid–six figures in buy-out money we received, Presidential Limousine proved to be a highly profitable niche we filled for a relatively short time. We demonstrated that the little guy can win, but the true test of this principle was just ahead.

CHAPTER 14

Dust to Dreams

With my dad helping me in Vegas, I could once again focus on looking for new opportunities. Dan and I divested ourselves of the car wash, so I had more time to generate new ideas on how to grow our little empire.

Due to county and city codes and gaming regulations, most bars in the Las Vegas area couldn't operate more than 15 machines—a rule for which the big casinos had lobbied in an effort to severely limit competition from smaller operators. However, a bar owner could apply for a non-restricted gaming license to operate more than 15 machines, provided he had a location in a jurisdiction that was suitable under their local code. More machines, live table games, and a sports book were all possible with the right location and licensing. I really wanted to get a piece of this pie and began to envision a neighborhood place that served great, reasonably priced food and drinks, adding value to the community, while generating the kind of revenue expanded gaming could produce.

When I shared my vision with Dan, he agreed. Knowing that what we wanted wasn't possible in Las Vegas, we found the perfect spot in the Ashby Heights neighborhood of the City of Opportunity, a growth area with little tavern or gaming competition in 1988. The city name was also quite appropriate, as we looked for a place to expand our earning potential: The zoning codes Opportunity provided fit right into our hopes to grow in gaming operations.

I located a half-acre property that, built out, would have nearly 300 parking spaces thanks to the adjoining shopping center. Every other business in this soon-to-be-developed center would close at around 5 p.m., meaning ample parking spaces for our patrons during prime evening hours. Best of all, it had C-1 zoning issued by Opportunity, which qualified it for casino use. It was everything we'd been looking for and we bought the property for $270,000, a premium price for a half-acre at the time.

As anyone who has operated a business or built one from the ground up will tell you, having the vision and the land is only part of the challenge; permits and approvals from various local and state entities are another part. Both restricted and nonrestricted gaming licenses are issued via the Nevada Gaming Control Board, the investigative and enforcement arm of the Nevada Gaming Commission. The Control Board investigates applicants thoroughly and makes a recommendation to the Commission based on their findings. Getting approved for a restricted license (15 or fewer slot machines) is a relatively simple process. Obtaining a nonrestricted gaming license is an entirely different matter. The application is a small book in which you divulge every aspect of your life, good and bad. Furthermore, the process is set up so that the applicant has to foot the bill for the entire investigation, which in those days could run anywhere from $25,000 to $60,000—money the state kept whether you were approved or not!

The board was, and is, very thorough. It's not unusual for them to send investigators to wherever you lived decades ago—in any city, state, or country in the world—and talk to neighbors, teachers, and friends. And, of course, there's the usual criminal background check. Felonies? Forget it. Gross misdemeanor? If fairly recent, denied. Bad checks? Screwed vendors? General unsavoriness? You're in for trouble. The code says, in effect, that it's the licensee's responsibility to uphold the moral integrity of the gaming industry in word, thought, and deed. You might be tempted to roll your eyes at this, given the sordid history of gaming in Las Vegas, but in this day and age, the government takes it all very seriously. I knew of a restricted gaming licensee whose license was pulled after one too many arrests for driving under the influence.

All that said, Dan and I weren't even at the point of applying for our nonrestricted license just yet. We still needed to get a use permit for the casino from the City of Opportunity. We assumed that we'd move smoothly through the process and began excitedly thinking about the new establishment. Brimming with optimism, we met with an architect to start giving our vision some physical shape.

Leaving No Stone Unturned

An early thought was to have very high ceilings—18 feet and higher. We'd learned that tobacco smoke stops rising about five feet below ceiling level. With 10-foot ceilings, the smoke settles at about eye level, so why not let it gather where people won't have to breathe it in? We also planned to install air purifiers and buy top-of-the-line barstools to make our new establishment a comfortable place to hang out. If customers' backs aren't hurting from the poor support of a cheap bar stool and eyes aren't stinging from cigarette smoke, they'll likely play video poker for two hours instead of 30 minutes. Or if they just came in to drink and eat, they might stay longer and spend more money.

Gaming is prevalent throughout Nevada and while Ashby Heights was a small and relatively new area, Opportunity had already given preliminary approval to a couple of places in the immediate area, and both were larger than what we were proposing. So the community had already shown they didn't have an issue with gaming and alcohol in their part of town.

Boards and councils generally look for a gradual imposition of heavy commercial use on their residential communities. A casino is considered heavy use with regard to traffic, parking, numbers of customers, etc., so a buffer between that casino and the residential area is considered ideal. In our case, our property fronted on Main Street, a major thoroughfare and a huge advantage for us. Surrounding us on four sides were planned shopping centers, undeveloped commercial lots, and a large industrial complex backed by an expressway. Beyond these commercial and industrial buffers were multi-family apartments and condo neighborhoods. Most important, the needed zoning was already in place. Surely, no one could rightfully object!

Dan and I also conducted a survey of nearby residents. We wanted the poll for planning purposes and, if the results were what we expected, for presenting to the city council as support for our application. Nearly every response reflected a desire for high-quality dining at a reasonable cost. The nearby residential area was starved for anything other than fast food, and reasonable prices were a priority. Of course, a good way to subsidize the cost of high-quality affordable food was with gaming revenue.

Buoyed by the results, we closed escrow and obtained a tavern use permit and a restricted gaming license. At the very least, we could build, open our doors and start earning.

We also applied for the nonrestricted gaming permit, completely in line with the zoning already in place. The city's zoning criteria spelled out precisely how many square feet you could construct on a certain-sized lot, and we designed our structure to be two stories and 9,500 total square feet—completely within those standards. All told, we did everything right in providing the Opportunity Planning Commission with what they needed to give us a speedy approval.

My cousin Arthur had cooked at the famed Tower of Pizza on the

Las Vegas strip and another Vegas locals' favorite, the Venetian Italian Restaurant on W. Sahara Avenue. His proven skills provided us the ability to offer an extensive fine-dining menu, as well as typical coffee-shop fare—literally, something for everyone. Since this was long before cell phones, we also installed courtesy phones, offering free local calls in every booth in the dining room. Receiving a page (remember digital pagers?), our customers could use the courtesy phone in their booth, access their messages, return calls, and continue socializing with little inconvenience.

We included a large horseshoe-shaped bar and TVs everywhere to showcase sporting and entertainment events. To further set us apart from most bars, we planned to stock 120 of the finest beers from around the world. We worked out an innovative numbering system, enabling the bartenders to quickly locate whatever beer a customer ordered, no matter how obscure the brand. We tinted the doors to the walk-in cooler, so they weren't brightly lit, but easily accessible. We wanted a dark, elegant, classy bar—a really cool place that anyone in the area could consider their home away from home.

We bent over backwards to create a place we were proud of, where people would come and stay for a while.

In the second-floor office, we installed interior windows, from where we could see the bar and restaurant floors, in order to supervise and maintain the highest degree of customer service. Artie and I realized that standing and overlooking the public areas felt like we were on the bridge of the starship USS Enterprise of *Star Trek* fame. My brother had always been a huge *Star Trek* fan, so we had a sign painter put NCC-1701 (the starship's ID number) on the office exterior, facing the front door. Some people got the joke and others had no idea what it meant, but we got a kick out of it.

We needed a name for our new place. Dan and I went to the local library and looked through the Yellow Pages of other cities seeking a unique and catchy tavern name. After hours side by side, as Dan and I so often worked, we both sparked to the same name of a place in Colorado, WINNERS!

Everything seemed to be falling into place. Right? Wrong!

CHAPTER 15

Questionable Ethics

Hundreds of people showed up at our 1988 Planning Commission hearing. I made my opening remarks and provided a detailed explanation of our plans, all of which had been enthusiastically embraced by the majority of the surrounding community, according to our survey results.

The problem? Happy residents rarely attend hearings like this. The vocal minority beat the drums of dissension and appear in droves, while the majority remain silent at home. True but sad—regulatory bodies are often misled into believing this vocal minority is expressing the wishes of their entire constituency. I hoped my description and our drawings would alleviate everyone's concerns, and we succeeded to a large degree. But in the eyes of many, we couldn't be trusted.

Their mistaken belief that we would one day become a large hotel-casino type of gaming project was fueled by a persistent, negative, behind-the-scenes, and untruthful rumor mill spawned by a local activist and, in my view, hypocrite, Stanley Gunster.

In all of my life's travels and experiences, it's hard to think of anyone more unlikable than Gunster. Not because he opposed my project—anyone in public service deserves to have an opinion and vote on it. However, what Stan did to Dan and me was unforgivable. More about that later.

"You can't fight City Hall," right? We've all heard that saying. But taking a screwing like Gunster orchestrated wasn't in my DNA. And it wasn't just financial. He played some role, in my opinion, in an effort to put me in prison for up to 50 years. I would not allow that to happen without some form of retribution. Always make the other SOB know he was in a fight and he will never mess with you again!

Gunster later managed to become an Opportunity city councilman; he wasn't one yet, but he was active on city committees. He and his errand boy, a local gadfly, had stirred several attendees of our Council meeting into a fury and there was simply no getting through to them. The planners voted, recommending denial to the City Council.

Stunned, Dan and I huddled to review our options. We didn't want to begin a new relationship with the City of Opportunity by going forward with our application, getting denied by the Council, and having no choice but to sue for judicial review to get a court to grant what we were rightfully entitled to. Who, in their right minds as businessmen, would want to start off in a new city with a lawsuit against its regulators? But we'd already begun construction and the place couldn't be the profit center we envisioned long-term with just 15 machines. Dan and I strategized at length, refusing to be beaten and trying to determine the smartest play.

We learned of Mark Milano, an influential lobbyist in a large Nevada lobbying firm. He was born and raised in Opportunity and knew nearly everyone in this small town's government. He had a proven track record of consistently winning Council approvals for his clients. We met with him and described both our plight and our detailed plan. He agreed with our strategy, accepted our retainer, and began working on what we hoped would be a new application and smooth-sailing approvals within the next 18 months, after we'd developed a track record at Winners. Little did we know that we'd disclosed our entire plan to someone I now feel was a mole within our midst and who would prove to be in bed with Gunster! At the time, we weren't aware of a friendship amongst Opportunity power brokers that dated all the way back to their childhoods and were now in major positions of authority in government. In fact, these nefariously incestuous relationships were known to few persons outside the Opportunity golden circle.

In the meantime, we completed construction and got ready to open the tavern and restaurant with 15 slot machines. We were convinced that once the community got to know us, enjoyed our menu, and saw what a quality facility we operated, most of our detractors would disappear and we could obtain approvals to increase the gaming within our walls. Certainly, with Milano's lobbying, the Council would be converted to our cause and do the right thing. The opponents would also get to see how relatively small our operation was and that it truly wouldn't intrude on their lifestyles, but complement the existing commercial community. I knew we'd never get 100 percent support— no one does. But once we were up and running, I was confident we'd convert the majority of naysayers.

Problem was, we had an adversary, seeking every opportunity to ruin us.

In August 1989, Winners' doors opened. For now, we were Winners Lounge and Restaurant; hopefully, one day we'd become Winners Casino. Several newspapers and television stations came to cover the big event and we were met with tremendous community interest and support. Our food and beverage areas were soon enjoying brisk business around the clock and the slot drop was far better than projected. Due to the higher overhead of running a facility of this size, we wouldn't realize great profits, but it looked like we'd cover the debt service, be marginally in the black and after some time cure the shortfall of machines and gaming tables.

Better times were sure to follow!

However, we were also well aware that we needed a year or two of operations to give Milano the ammo he'd need to win us approval from the City Council for more gaming. We gave him ammo, all right.

The times that followed turned out to be the worst!

CHAPTER 16

Pete Nielson

Winners opened with a good crew. As an owner, I operated as I always had, getting to know all the employees and learning a little about them and their lives.

One of them, Pete Nielson, stood out, because he was always asking questions about the operations and me. I thought he was a bright, curious, and ambitious 20-year-old who would make a good long-term employee. When he turned 21 and could legally serve alcohol, I promoted him to server. He was part of the Winners family and I treated him as such.

One night, I was sitting in our dining room, talking things over with my managers, when the conversation turned to the Thursday Night Pistol Team we ran out of the Suburban Lounge West. Nielson was within earshot when my brother, Artie, asked about my concealed-carry permit and how I liked my preferred concealment method: a snub-nosed .38 in an ankle holster. He was contemplating his own method of concealment. It wasn't a secret; we were legally licensed to carry.

Typically, when I called it a day, which could easily be the middle of the night, I went home, took off my ankle holster, and safely put my pistol away for the night. On one such night in November, just four months after our grand opening, Artie, who was the general manager at Winners, gave me a call to tell me we had a problem with one of the employees.

"Who is it?"

"Pete Nielson."

This was more than a surprise; it was a disappointment. I wanted to see what Artie found in person. I splashed some water on my face, got dressed, and decided there was no reason to bring my gun.

Most gaming bars in the Vegas area have office areas that also serve as their slot count rooms. In our office upstairs at Winners, we counted the coins and tokens from the machines, placed them in money bags, then zip-tied them, so they'd be openable and available for sale again as needed. If, during the course of any shift, 24 hours a day, seven days a week, a bartender was running low on nickels, quarters, or dollars, a manager came up to the office, snipped a zip tie with wire cutters, grabbed the necessary coins or tokens and put them in a can or rack to take back downstairs. Because of this, there were always discarded bags and clipped zip ties lying around—small piles on the floor you'd see in the office of any small gaming establishment. It was all cleaned up at least once a week, usually before one of our scheduled full-site inspections.

When you're ringing up restaurant and bar sales, the cash register creates two records of each transaction. One is an individual receipt for the customer and the other is a contiguous roll of paper called a detail tape, for business records. The detail tapes track every transaction on each register. They're either pulled and saved by the owner or sent to the accountants for bookkeeping.

I walked into the office that night to find Artie waiting for me with detail tapes for the most recent shift, spread out in long strips on the floor, while Bobby, standing next to him, looked like he just heard that someone ran over the family dog.

"Nielson's stealing from us," Artie said. "And you're looking at the proof."

As anyone who runs a cash business can tell you, you've always got to be on your guard for members of your staff skimming from you. In the case of a restaurant or bar, here's one of the ways it works.

A party of four comes in and sits at table number seven, served by a waiter like Pete Nielson. They order a round of drinks while they peruse the menu. The register opens a check for table seven, which for the moment only has four drinks on it. After a while, table seven orders food, and Pete goes back to the register and inputs the items. A short time later, someone orders another drink and fries and dessert and over the course of the evening, the check gets built up until it's time to close it out for, let's say, $149.

Pete brings the customers the check; they pay the $149 and leave a $30 tip on top of it. He comes back to the register and voids out $80 on the bill, so now it looks like the total due for table seven is just $69—and the difference of $80, plus the $30 tip, goes right into his pocket.

Now, a server isn't supposed to be able to void a check without a manager's key, which is how an owner prevents such abuses. Unfortunately, our register system was improperly programmed when we opened, just months earlier, and my people didn't catch the error, allowing an unscrupulous employee like Pete to void out checks at will.

How could I be so sure this wasn't just a run of bad luck for a waiter whose timing was off? Well, if it was, the bad luck happened eight times during one four-hour period, all clearly traceable in the detail tape. Nobody's that unlucky. There was no doubt: Pete had a scam going.

How did we learn of it? Foolish Pete, so proud of his thieving acumen, confided in our waiter, Patrick. "Let me show you how to make some extra money," he said to Patrick one evening.

Unbeknownst to Pete, Patrick had worked for my cousin and head chef Arthur in a prior restaurant setting, something no one but top management knew. After learning of Pete's scam, Patrick relayed the information to Arthur, who in turn told Artie. Artie pulled the detail tapes, tracked each of Pete's transactions by his employee number and I got the call.

Angry and betrayed, I turned to Bobby. "Go down, ask Pete to come up, and we'll confront him. Unless he's got a hell of an explanation, we'll fire his ass and turn him in to the cops. Then we can move on and be glad we caught him sooner than later."

Artie and I each took a seat, and by this time Arthur had joined us. A minute later, Bobby returned with Pete. As soon as I saw Pete's face, I knew he was guilty.

Trying to cover, Pete put on his best "innocent" smile. "Hey, what's all this?"

"Well, Pete, we've got a problem." I motioned to the rows of register tapes covering 15 lineal feet of office floor. "We know what you've been doing."

Any doubts I might have still harbored about his guilt instantly dissolved as he lurched for the door. My guys were faster. They tackled him. On the way down, Pete's face caught the edge of the open office door, scratching him. They picked him up and deposited him in a chair directly across from me. "Artie," I said, "get the Opportunity Police on the line."

Pete began to shake his head. "No, please don't call the cops. Let me pay you back. I'll sign a confession and you can fire me. Just don't call the cops! I'll go right to jail, because I'm wanted in California!"

Hearing we'd hired a known criminal knocked me back another step. "How could you get a work card from gaming and the liquor board if you're wanted somewhere?"

"I don't know," he stammered. "When I moved to Vegas, I just applied for it and got it." Visibly upset, he said he was getting sick. I motioned to the adjoining restroom and he went in, knelt down and vomited. He splashed water on his face and head, and returned to his seat. His face and hair were dripping wet, but that was of little interest to me at the time.

The Cops Get Involved

I weighed the pros and cons of calling the cops, and my lenient nature and initial affection for Pete won out. Asked how much his thefts totaled, Pete indicated he never kept track. After doing some quick calculations based on how long Pete admitted to his manipulations, I said, "I'd say you owe us somewhere in the neighborhood of well over two grand. Pay it back, we'll call it even, and you can be on your way."

But first, I wanted to learn all I could, such as who else he'd told, who else might be doing the same thing, and how big the total collective theft might be? He briefly mentioned his girlfriend Barbara, who worked graveyard shift, but spent most of the time talking about having a drug and gambling problem that compelled him to steal more than he was earning.

During our discussion, things were calm and quiet. They were so cordial that the office door wasn't even closed after he entered, as evidenced by his cheek striking its edge during his escape attempt. As it was a busy Friday night, Artie went downstairs to check on things and when he returned, he had a small container of oil from one of our deep fryers.

"Look at this, Arthur!" he said. "It's so dark you can't see through it. We're packed with customers, the oil looks dirty and our food is coming out under specs. You should have changed it last night."

I just stared at Arthur. He knew my disappointment, as I always insisted on quality, which meant not going into a weekend with marginal oil consistency. He should have changed the oil in both fryers on Thursday night. He knew he'd screwed up, but now wasn't the time for a reprimand. Artie set it down at the end of the desk and continued listening to my talk with the amazingly observant Nielson, who heard it all.

I handed Pete a legal pad to write out his confession. I also had blank forms of promissory notes we used for loans I sometimes advanced for bad-check settlements and we worked out a monthly payment Nielson said he could live with. When he was done, I read it and told Bob to escort him off the property.

"Thank you so much, Mr. Coury," Nielson said. Suddenly I was "Mister" Coury. "I'll pay you back in full."

Bob returned to say that when Pete walked out the front door, two police cars in the driveway had their engines running. "Pete saw the cop cars and ran into the desert behind the building."

I guessed he mistakenly assumed we double-crossed him and called the cops anyway. It didn't matter much to me at that moment.

We waited hours for graveyard shift to begin and the chance to confront Pete's girlfriend Barbara. She'd be terminated as well. Big shock! She was a no-show. Pete surely tipped her off.

After talking things over until 2 a.m. or so, we walked downstairs and as I approached the front door to leave, in came a force of police. It was like a raid. A sergeant I knew named Mike came over and said they had one of my people at headquarters, with his dad, and the kid was telling an amazing story. Mike asked if we could go up to my office. I said sure, as I always cooperated with the cops in Vegas and Opportunity without reservation.

We went upstairs and he started asking me questions about Nielson, what had transpired that night, and what condition the kid was in when he left. After examining the condition of the office, Mike even commented that the story Pete was telling was unlikely to have occurred there. I wasn't sure what he meant and as I was about to ask, another visitor arrived. Detective Ted Banich, a dry, impersonal, Neanderthal-looking guy with light hair and a decent build walked into the office. Mike told me Banich would be taking "the case" from here.

I thought, case? What the hell?

I wondered again if Nielson believed the cops' presence as he exited earlier was a double-cross, so he came up with a story of his own to detract from the severity of his theft. Time would tell.

Detective Banich asked me what happened that night with Nielson. I described it in full, totally open about everything that occurred.

Banich said, "I don't believe you. Mr. Nielson stated he was beaten for nearly two hours. He claimed you zip-tied his hands together and forced them into hot grease, tried to drown him in the toilet, put a gun to his head to force a confession, and had your guys hold him down as you dropped heavy five-hundred-dollar bags of tokens on his hands and relentlessly beat and kicked him on your office floor. I see money bags over there, a bathroom right here, a cup of grease on the table— all consistent with Mr. Nielson's story."

At that point, Mike re-entered and announced the arrival of the crime-scene unit.

Crime-scene unit?

Detective Banich instructed them to gather the broken zip ties in the corner of the room, fingerprint the toilet, take the cup of grease, and search for a gun. He asked me if I was carrying and I said no. Clearly, Pete assumed I was carrying and that would feed into his tale quite nicely. They searched me and found no gun.

Processing all this, I started running down our defense, chapter and verse. Nipping it in the bud would put an early end to this fiasco before lawyers were needed and criminal charges got unfairly filed.

"Did Pete Nielson go to the hospital or need medical attention?"

Banich said, "No."

"Good. Now take a look at my three managers and me." Arthur Charles was a 280-pound beast, Artie weighed in at about 225, Bobby was a former Metro Corrections Officer and Marine in excellent physical shape, and at 185 pounds, I worked out every day and was at peak fitness. "Do you really believe we could beat up anyone for two hours and he wouldn't need a doctor or have a broken bone or significant marks on him?"

I went on to explain everything as it had actually happened. "Pete begged me not to call the cops and got sick in the bathroom. And you'd find zip ties on the floor of every bar in town with dollar machines and coins in money bags."

"Why is there a cup of grease at the end of the table?"

I explained why and asked if Nielson's hands were burned. Such injuries didn't exist when he left. But did he inflict them on himself to support his fabricated version of events? Did his dad help concoct a scenario to support Pete's tale? Was he that clever?

"What did Nielson's hands look like?" I asked.

None of these relevant factors seemed to matter to Banich. This Dick Tracy wannabe curtly responded, "You answer my questions; I don't answer yours."

That was when I knew for sure. He had an agenda and it wasn't to gather facts. He was there to gather evidence in support of the conclusions he'd already reached. Or were they conclusions he'd been told to reach? Photos were taken of the office before anything was removed or changed.

Getting more concerned that Pete and his dad faked some injuries to support their narrative, I pointed to the rows of register tapes on the floor and said, "If we had him down there, beating and kicking him, why aren't the rows of thin register tape ripped and destroyed? Surely, he would've squirmed and fought and resisted this supposed two-hour beating. Also, if his hair was dripping wet from the alleged forced drowning and we pulled him out of the bathroom and threw him down, as he claims, why aren't these register tapes wet as well? Put a drop of water on them and they turn blue, due to the type of register paper we use!"

Banich just didn't care. He had a crime, maybe the biggest case he'd ever been assigned, and seemed determined to make the facts fit his scenario, rather than let them disprove the allegations. And it didn't take long to prove me right about this cop. As I watched his unit check for fingerprints on the toilet, I asked them to check the top of the bowl, not just the bottom. Anyone getting sick who has hugged the porcelain goddess knows where their hands end up. If he was pushing his way up and we were pushing him down, wouldn't his hands be at the top of the bowl?

"Not necessary," Banich said with a smirk and a shrug.

I asked if they'd test the edge of the door for skin or blood from when Nielson scratched his cheek and was again told: "Unnecessary." And off Banich went.

I wondered if he might be doing the bidding of a city that knew we'd be coming after them for the gaming-use permit we were entitled to. What else could explain his seemingly agenda-driven mentality? Time would tell, and my worst fears proved to be supported.

As I drove home in the wee hours after my first encounter with Detective Banich, I sensed this would be a battle and ultimately, a war for which my entire life had (hopefully) prepared me.

Fighting Back—Hard

The next day at work, I told Dan about the previous night. He listened intently. When I was done, he instantly concluded, "We need to take this seriously. We need a criminal attorney to advise us."

I noted the subtlety and steadfast camaraderie in his response. None of what he said included the terms "you" or "me." It was "we" and "us" on all things relating to this Nielson mess—on that day and every day till it was over. If a battle was coming, it would be fought head-on by us as a team. We lacked the financial resources of the city, but took a disciplined approach to creative strategizing, problem solving, a refusal to quit, and legally taking on those who'd come after us, whoever they might be.

My next surprise came early Thanksgiving morning, 1989, just six days after Pete was caught stealing. I was awakened by a phone call from Tommy Bear. He'd worked until 4 a.m. and read the daily morning newspaper, which had just come off the presses. He filled me in on the page-one story about how criminal charges had been filed with the DA's office for prosecution against a casino owner named Ron Coury and three of his managers. That was Banich's next classless move to embarrass and inform us as to how they were proceeding.

I'd remained naively hopeful that the DA would review and reject the case. I thought it might go civil, as many cases with questionable supporting facts did. For Banich to release his report to the press, with details only he could have devised, reinforced my belief that the city had its own agenda regarding me. And these false accusations gave them a vehicle to dispose of our eventual civil disputes with them.

Artie and I were hopeful all week that it would go nowhere and hadn't told our parents about any of it. It would only cause them undue stress. But now, the page-one newspaper account, in excruciating detail and entirely devoid of our side of the story, would shock them.

I immediately called Artie and woke him up, just as Tom had awoken me. I suggested we go to our parents' house, grab the newspaper from their driveway, and tell them, in our own words, what actually happened, as opposed to what they'd see in the paper. Our mom had a bad heart and this page-one story could kill her. We could provide our side of the story and soften the impact of learning that both of their sons could face years in prison.

As if I wasn't already motivated to mount a huge defense, this move by Banich so infuriated me that nothing would stop me from proactively battling on our behalf. Hoping for the best with a jury wouldn't be near enough to respond appropriately. Not in this situation. With the number of felony charges filed, might a jury, assuming they could believe the OPD for the most part, think where there's smoke, there's fire? Even if we disproved most of Nielson's lies, might they slap us with a minor guilty verdict on something? Even one sign of guilt by a jury would be devastating, civilly and for my licensing with gaming. This was not a risk I could take; leaving our destiny up to a jury was untenable.

Proving Pete Nielson to be the liar that he was, to say nothing of his thievery, rendered me a fanatic on a mission to prevail in these false criminal charges and against the City of Opportunity with our use permit hopes.

I knew I was being set up—I sensed it within every cell in my body. My name was well enough known in Opportunity, from the Planning Commission meeting, the media coverage of the opening of Winners, and no doubt having been bandied about by Gunster behind closed doors, so that when Pete Nielson showed up at the police station that night, telling his wild tale about Ron Coury and his people, phones started ringing. In the many hours between when Nielson ran away from the cop cars at our entrance until Banich showed up at Winners, there'd been plenty of time for these conspirators to sic their attack dog on us.

Any remaining doubt I might have entertained was erased when my lawyers obtained Banich's written report. He lied blatantly when he asserted that I lied to him when asked about a gun. Of course, as a dishonest cop with an agenda, portraying me as a liar during his investigation served the ultimate purpose of his behind-the-scenes masters in city government. Banich was a tool, an errand boy, doing the city's bidding against someone they knew would be coming forward for expanded gaming and likely to sue the city if denied. Mark Milano, Banich, City Attorney Brenda Beals, and Stan Gunster, all longtime friends, knew what we had planned and, I assume and must believe, this was their scheme for trying to dispose of me.

We were going to war!

CHAPTER 17

Further into Political Adversity

When the story about Nielson hit the newspapers, I found myself the talk of the town. Trust me, this is something you never want to be.

Few people ever experience the debasement and embarrassment caused by having one's reputation trashed via such media tactics. Everyone I encountered for the days and weeks following that newspaper headline was supportive, but I couldn't walk away without wondering, did they believe it? What do they think of me now? Will my reputation ever be restored?

At the same time, I was touched by the people who knew, beyond a shadow of a doubt, that I'd never commit the alleged crimes. One of those friends was Las Vegas Metro Undersheriff Eric Cooper. A fellow former Marine, I admired and respected Eric immensely. As friends, we had years of wonderful and memorable experiences together. He and his wife Linda were regular patrons of the Suburban Lounge West and we were on one of my sponsored pistol-shooting teams together. Eric and I shot together in an organized outdoor competition using three weapons, including a machine gun, a pistol, and a shotgun. I'd been honored to be asked by Linda and Eric to emcee a ceremony held by the local Boy Scouts organization to recognize Eric for his years of support; this was a grand formal event, with nearly 1,000 people in the room, dinner, and a number of speakers paying tribute to an extremely popular undersheriff and all he'd done to support scouting. I was deeply touched to be asked by them to perform the master-of-ceremonies duties. I also accepted Eric's invitation to join him on the board of directors for the Marine Corps Support Counsel of Southern Nevada. Eric and I grew to be close friends, loyal to each other over decades of great times together. As soon as he saw the news, he called me. "What is this crap?"

"It's a long story. Of course, it's bogus, but I still have to deal with it."

"Well, I'm going to help you," he replied.

Eric called the Opportunity Police Department and the DA at the time, Matt Moore, and tried to set them straight, vouching for me. He later told me that DA Moore just sighed and said, "I know this case sucks, but for some reason OPD has pushed for Ron to be prosecuted." The chief of OPD informed Eric that he believed much of this was political, but he was being told I was a bad guy. Clearly, Gunster and his minions had gotten to him and Banich.

"I tried to make it right," Eric told me, angrily. "But these guys are really after you."

Along with the possibility of a long prison sentence, I also had to think about what would happen if a jury found me guilty of even one of the counts. I'd be liable for damages in a subsequent civil suit, Nielson's true end game and side benefit to dodging the ramifications of his theft. I'd surely lose my gaming license and probably have to liquidate nearly everything I owned to pay lawyers and whatever damages might be awarded to Nielson. To say I was motivated to prove my innocence and come out on top is the understatement of the century.

And then it got worse.

Booked!

A month or so later, the four of us had to go through the booking process with the Opportunity Police. By then, we'd hired our defense dream team and to avoid the scene of cops rousting us at home, the lawyers arranged for us to appear voluntarily at the Department for the formal booking process.

As soon as we presented ourselves at the counter, the desk sergeant foreshadowed what was to come with a kind of evil glee in his grin. Four officers marched out and promptly handcuffed each of us behind our backs, then walked us to a row of jail cells and placed us each in one.

Even not knowing how the process would unfold, I understood that OPD was getting a perverted pleasure from dragging it out and putting us through all those unnecessary dramatics. It was a typical Banich move to stage a display of authority and chest pounding.

Still, the emotional shock of being handcuffed and sitting in a jail cell, both for the first time in my life, is impossible to overstate. I waited there, behind bars, thinking that this could be a preview of the next 50 years of my life if the Opportunity authorities and Pete Nielson had their way. These were my most serious and introspective moments ever. I not only felt acutely the loss of my own liberty, but I couldn't help thinking about the countless innocent people who'd been railroaded into prison by an abuse of power. It motivated me to believe—beyond any and all possibilities—that this effort to put us away would not succeed.

One by one we were led from the jail cells to a booking area where we were photographed, fingerprinted and processed. At the completion of the booking process, we remained in the cells for what felt like hours for no reason, other perhaps than for the cops to go out for coffee and donuts, giving us time to stew and stir, while our attorneys waited for us out front. At least they left off the handcuffs as we sat.

Finally, in the most ridiculous pretense of all, they put the cuffs back on as we were led from the cells back to the desk sergeant's area and our lawyers, as if we'd cause trouble just before we were released!

An experience few people will ever encounter, it's set in stone in my mind. But while the powers of Opportunity played their little games and tried to scare us, it only cemented my resolve to pull out all the stops and fight with all the tenacity I could muster to ensure that none of us ever spent another minute behind bars.

The Defense Gears Spin

When the news hit the papers, I went to work forming a team of defense attorneys. I told my lead attorney, Chuck Thompson, that the situation was urgent. "This is serious," I said. "We need a solid battle plan and we need it now."

We put together the defense team, then hired a private investigator. When Mike Wysocki showed up the next day at Chuck's office, I recognized him immediately as an occasional Suburban West customer. He was a tough, shrewd and honest retired cop who'd opened his own private investigator business. I filled him in on what had happened and could see his investigative mind working. I leaned forward in my chair. "I want to get this resolved as quickly as possible and I can't rely on a jury to clear me."

He leaned back and said, "The first thing we need to do is learn everything we can about Pete Nielson and why he said he was wanted in California."

I handed Mike a copy of Pete's employment application that had his Sacramento, California, address on it, so he could follow that lead.

"I've also dug up quite a bit," I replied. "Since all this came down,

I've interviewed all my employees and discovered that Pete's not the nice young kid I took under my wing. He's been selling drugs and has burned some of my people in different ways. And he's been hitting relentlessly on Julie, one of my bartenders, who's like family to me."

Mike nodded with the steady demeanor of a guy who's seen it all and then some. "I'll get right to work. Let's see what I can find in his last hometown."

"This can't go to trial, Mike. It's too risky with Pete having the OPD in his corner," I said. "I have an idea that could put an end to this well before any trial. I want you to befriend Pete. As you develop the relationship, I'd like to think at some point he may actually tell you how he set me up and created this whole bullshit story."

Mike considered for a moment. "I gotta tell you, undercover operations like that are very hard to pull off. They're expensive and I can't promise you he'll tell me . . ."

I stopped him. "I have some thoughts about how to make that come together." I knew from employees at Winners that Nielson had landed a job at the Peppermill Resort in Mesquite, Nevada, selling time-shares on the property. Of course, I was also aware that Pete was a money-hungry opportunist, which we could take advantage of. Finally, Pete had it bad for Julie.

The next day, I got Mike and Julie together and told them my idea. Julie had already come to me and said that she'd do whatever she could to help clear this up.

"The two of you are going to drive up to Mesquite, and Mike, we're putting you on a hundred-dollar-minimum blackjack table with a big stack of chips. Julie, you'll be very affectionate toward Pete. As Mike's playing, he'll throw Pete a handful of chips, turn on the charm, and invite him to join in and play. We'll use Pete's greed and opportunism to reel him in."

Mike used a lot of different identities in his investigative work. One of them was Mike Richardson, treasure hunter. He could really sell this; he'd previously worked for people where he actually did dive for treasure. He had some terrific still photographs to support this persona.

"Mike, your image to Pete will be that of the guy who does very cool things and, hell, if Pete ever wanted to join you on an exciting trip out of the country, no problem."

Armed with this plan, Mike, Julie, and a couple of Mike's investigators, Hank Yang and Jeremy Ausmus, drove up to the Peppermill—only to discover that Pete had been fired the day before. Disappointed and before driving back to Vegas, they were having drinks at a bar immediately adjacent to the entrance when Julie looked up to see Pete Nielson walking toward the front door, on his way out of the casino. We later learned that he'd come in to retrieve his final paycheck.

Mike said, "Damn, there's no time to set up. We're screwed!"

Thinking fast, Julie told Mike, "No, we aren't. Get to a table and buy some chips."

Then she jumped to her feet, ducked out a side exit, and ran full speed around the building to the entrance. As Pete stepped out into the parking lot, there came Julie, looking like she was just walking in. Pete thought it was his lucky day!

Julie immediately began to lay it on thick, paying Pete more attention than she ever had before. "Pete, how are you?" she gushed. "I can't believe what those pricks at Winners did to you."

Whatever skepticism Pete might have harbored at this convenient encounter had to be dispelled by the thought that he was finally going to get somewhere with the object of his dreams.

"I'm up here with a couple of friends," she said, continuing to spin her web. She threw her arm around him and purred, "Come back in and have a drink with us."

At this point, Pete would've been willing to follow her through a minefield. He had no idea he was a mere 10 feet from Hank's watchful eye as he tracked Julie's every move for her protection. They made their way back inside and Julie spotted Mike at the $100-minimum blackjack table. As she steered Pete over, he was completely unaware that two other guys were watching their every move. Jeremy was seated at the next table, able to hear every word should Pete blurt something out that would help our cause. Hank was situated across the pit, at a table facing Mike, appearing to be a happy South Korean visitor enjoying drinks and some blackjack. Julie sauntered up to Mike, wrapped her arm around him, and introduced him to Pete.

Pete leaned into Julie and asked, "So is this your boyfriend?"

Julie gave him a killer smile and whispered, "We're cool. We swap and swing all the time."

Mike flashed Pete a big smile, tossed some $100 chips his way, and said, "Be my guest and play these."

Playing with someone else's money and Julie rubbing his shoulders, Pete Nielson had to think he'd died and gone to heaven. And just like that, the hook was set. Over the coming weeks, Mike carefully groomed the relationship. And as I expected, Pete loved hanging around with Mike. The noose was about to get tighter around Nielson's neck.

Some time later, Mike called to say he wanted to meet at Chuck's office.

I walked in to find Mike waiting for me like the proverbial cat that ate the canary. "We got him."

I pulled up a chair, all ears.

"Our undercover operation is going great. Pete's starting to open up to me a little, but I just got back from California, where this kid screwed up big time. Apparently, he tried to boost a car he didn't know belonged to an off-duty policeman. When the cop came after him, punches were thrown and in a getaway attempt, Pete tried to run him down with a car! Pete was captured and arrested.

"Pete appeared at his preliminary hearing," Mike continued. "It was set to go to trial, but guess who made bail and skipped town?" Mike grinned as he pulled a sheet of paper out of his coat pocket and slapped it on the desk. "I give you a certified warrant for one Peter Nielson."

My own happiness was exceeded only by that of Chuck Thompson's.

"This is going away quickly, Ron. We'll get this to the Opportunity police. They'll follow protocol, arrest and extradite him—and there goes the only witness to this so-called crime."

Mike, appearing as an investigator retained by our legal team, delivered the certified warrant to Detective Banich. But the snakes weren't about to slither back under their rocks that easily. Banich had a mission assignment and friends he was watching out for! This warrant, in no way, would fit into his plan for me.

That night, Pete Nielson got together with his new buddy Mike and proceeded to tell him a story that revealed just how deep the vendetta I suspected in Opportunity ran. According to Pete, Banich called him and told him to come in. Mike assumed it was so Banich could tell Pete that he was going to be arrested and extradited to California. But that wouldn't explain Pete's joyful tone on the phone or his shit-eating grin when they met.

"Well, Pete," Banich told him, "Coury's people just delivered a warrant for you in California. There's no way you're going to be a credible witness against him with this hanging over your head."

Pete told Mike he'd assumed he was screwed six ways to Sunday.

"Not so fast," Banich had continued. "I just got off the phone with the Sacramento Police Department. I explained to them that we need your cooperation to go after a very dangerous big fish and convinced them to drop all the charges against you. All you have to do is get your ass out to Sacramento, go in, pay a fine, and walk right back out."

Pete smiled across the table at Mike. "Can you believe that shit? Am I one lucky son of a bitch or what?"

I was floored. The Opportunity Police Department at least, along with the city administration at most, was prepared to break policy and even the law in order to railroad me. Could this kind of abuse and corruption really be taking place in the country I so loved?

Chuck's jaw set. "That's it. We're not sharing anything else we learn with the Opportunity Police."

"I'm afraid we have another problem," Mike continued.

I shook my head. "The last thing I need is another problem, Mike."

"Pete's begun selling me marijuana, a crime he could be busted for. The thing is . . ."

"You're not a cop anymore," Chuck jumped in, finishing his thought. "You can't legally buy from him to catch him in the act." Chuck looked at me. "Even if we did present the evidence to the Opportunity cops, there's no reason to think they'd do anything about it. They'd rather rehabilitate him as a witness against you than do their jobs!"

"I might be able to make it stick," I said forcefully. "Let me take Mike into Las Vegas Metro Police and tell them everything he knows."

Chuck shook his head. "Ron, I used to be a DA. I know how it works. Cops are cops; they stick together. They talk to each other about everything. You, as a civilian, stand no chance when it's cop to cop, even with two different police departments. No one in law enforcement is going to hang out Banich."

"Chuck, I respect you and will always listen to your opinion, but my life is on the line here. We have to do something. We can't stop now when we have this much on Pete. I have a friend at Vegas Metro Police, who I totally trust. If you're right and I'm wrong, it's my future on the line. But I have to go with my gut on this decision and we need help from a trustworthy law-enforcement agency right now."

Chuck took a long deep breath and slowly exhaled, thoroughly unconvinced. "So how do you plan to play it?"

My hope could be distilled down to one name: Eric Cooper. I set up an appointment to meet with him in his office at Metro, right next door to the sheriff's office.

I told Eric about how the Opportunity PD dealt with the warrant against Nielson, then said, "Pete has started selling Mike drugs. Since Mike's no longer a cop, we need to develop this lead legally and we can't tell OPD about it. They've already proven their bias when it comes to me."

Without hesitation, Eric picked up his phone and moments later, the captain of the narcotics division had joined us. Of course, he knew Mike from way back, as Mike worked there as a cop years earlier. After explaining the situation, Eric told him, "I want you to have Mike work with one of your detectives. Mike will introduce the detective to this Nielson kid, then gracefully back out of the situation. Once Nielson trusts your guy, I'm damn sure we'll get hand-to-hand buys directly from Nielson without anybody else involved. He sold Mike marijuana, but word is he's pushing cocaine too. Make sure your people know not to toss this kid for a bigger player. No trading up. We want him and him alone. Ron is *my* friend and this prick is setting him up for a fall."

The captain turned to Mike. "You know Stu Marshak?"

"A little," smiled Mike. "He was my partner back in the day."

"Great. Introduce him to this Nielson character, then bow out of the situation when you can and let Stu work the case."

When the time was right, Mike introduced Stu to Nielson and it wasn't long before Pete started selling Stu marijuana directly. Smelling blood in the water, Stu pressed his bet. "Any chance you can score me some coke? I've got a big client group coming in and I'll need a lot." Stu, of course, knew that once the quantity of drugs sold exceeded a certain weight, it escalated in severity and became a trafficking charge.

Pete didn't stop to consider the possible ramifications. "No sweat. I can hook you up with all you need." He then confided in Stu that his dad had an arsenal stashed in the house they shared and was connected with some very big and bad people, which kept Pete in product and protected.

The Hearing

As things were playing out in our defense strategy, roughly seven and a half months after being officially charged, I found myself with Artie, Bobby and Arthur at that preliminary hearing in Judge Stabinski's court for second-degree kidnapping, false imprisonment, coercion, extortion with the use of a deadly weapon, extortion to collect a debt with the use of a deadly weapon, and coercion with the use of a deadly weapon—five felonies and a gross misdemeanor! It didn't matter how many slot machines Winners ultimately had if I found myself locked away in a penitentiary for decades.

At Deputy District Attorney Baird's request, the judge had all potential witnesses, including Pete's family and girlfriend, excluded from the courtroom. They'd be called in to testify as she determined. She put Pete Nielson on the stand to tell his story and he continued to alter the facts at will to support his prevarications. When he was done, the district attorney passed the witness. Now it was my guy's turn.

Chuck inquired, "When you and Mr. Coury were talking, didn't you ask him not to call the police, because you were wanted for a crime you'd committed in California? That you wanted to try to work things out between the two of you?"

Without much thought, Pete replied, "Yeah."

I didn't realize the significance of his curt and cocky response, but the other three criminal attorneys instantly did and jumped to their feet.

"Your Honor, we move to dismiss the kidnapping charge! Mr. Nielson asked Mr. Coury if he could stay in the room. How could he have possibly been kidnapped when Mr. Coury was about to call the police and Mr. Nielson begged him not to?"

Judge Stabinski agreed and just like that, he threw out the kidnapping charge. One felony down, four to go. Of course, even though Pete's case had taken a major hit, I was far from out of the woods.

Chuck had Pete draw an image of the office and bathroom on the courtroom blackboard. He then explained his false version of the event, perjuring himself repeatedly.

"Are you a drug dealer, Mr. Nielson?"

"No sir."

Good for another perjury charge later. We continued to get him on the record with everything our guys could think of.

"So, Mr. Nielson. As you've testified, during this intense interrogation, various managers are trying to push your hands into hot oil and you're understandably fearful that it will permanently maim you if they succeed."

"Yeah, it was scary."

"You also testified that, apparently, you broke the zip ties they bound you with in your struggle with them at the toilet, and to the best of your memory, one was hanging off your wrist."

I could see Pete getting nervous; he didn't know where Chuck was headed with this. But he was in too far to start recanting his sworn testimony now.

"Yeah, that's right."

"I'm confused. How, in the midst of this violent struggle to keep your hands from being immersed in hot oil, did the broken zip tie stay on your wrist?"

"It didn't."

"I see. So where did it go?"

"It fell in the oil," Nielson laughed, as if the answer were obvious.

"What happened to it?"

"What do you think? It melted instantly."

Now, I'd never tried to cook a zip tie, but I began to wonder that if his imaginary zip tie fell into the oil, would it be hot enough to melt it?

Judge Stabinski called a lunch recess, but before adjourning for the break, he admonished everyone, "Do not speak to anyone about what's going on in here. I don't want to taint any future testimony from a witness."

With court out of session, I turned to my co-defendants. "Come on, guys, we're going to Winners."

They looked at me like I was out of my mind. "Why?"

I smiled. "Because we're going to cook a zip tie."

The lawyers heard my plan and wanted to come along.

Back at Winners, we dropped a zip tie into sizzling hot oil and cooked it for 10 minutes. We fished it out to find it completely intact and fully functional, no melting whatsoever.

Our defense team conferred for a moment before one of them said to me, "Look. You're not getting out of this case during the prelim. Opportunity has a hard-on for you, so you're all eventually going to trial in Clark County District Court. We'll learn what we can during this preliminary hearing and keep it in the vault. At the trial, we'll pull it all out. Hell, we might just roll in a deep fryer and cook a zip tie, but for now we're not saying anything to anybody. We'll let Nielson keep talking, because every word out of his mouth only digs him in deeper."

Back for the afternoon session, we heard some interesting news. As soon as Pete Nielson went out the double doors of the courtroom for the lunch break, he huddled up with Barbara, Winners' graveyard waitress who was a no-show the night of the theft, along with his dad and other people he'd gotten to corroborate portions of his story. Once outside he gave them chapter and verse on what had gone on in the courtroom outside of their earshot. Paula, my brother Artie's girlfriend who sat in on the preliminary hearing, was outside and overheard every word.

When we resumed, Chuck told Judge Stabinski that he wanted to call Paula to the stand to share what she had heard. When she finished testifying, the judge turned a fierce eye on Nielson. "Mr. Nielson, what this young lady is saying—is it true? Don't lie to me."

Pete nervously cast his eyes to the ground, then muttered, "I was just telling my friends what was going on."

"Very well. At the end of our proceeding today, you'll spend the night in my jail for contempt of court."

At this point, Steve Stein leaned over and whispered, "Ron, I've been a federal prosecutor. I've been a defense attorney. I've been in the practice of law for decades. But I have *never* seen the supposed victim in the case thrown in jail. This is a first."

Pete's testimony continued. On a schematic on the blackboard, we had him draw where he was in the office. This would be relevant later, when compared to the photos the Keystone Kops took. Pete's supposed position on the floor, where he was thrown and beaten, his hair wet from the toilet, was directly on top of the neat rows of dry, undisturbed register tapes in the photos the crime-scene unit took that night. On either side of the tapes were desks. His story and stick figure of a body could only be atop those tapes, if his tale were true. There wasn't a crumpled register strip in the rows and rows of tapes. Not a tear! Not a wet mark! But all that we knew and were developing would wait for my actual trial.

Next up on the stand was Detective Banich. I'd worked at length with Chuck in preparing questions for Banich. We wanted him under oath and on the record. We'd gather his lies, but not point out anything contradictory. At trial, we'd expose and embarrass him in front of the jury for the liar and lackey that he was. I fantasized that it might even result in him, himself, ultimately being charged with some crimes!

Chuck asked Banich to expand on the statement in his report. Banich stood by his story about my carrying versus owning a gun, an assertion Chuck assured me no jury or judge would believe, given all the registered firearms I legally owned. There was no way any honest person would believe that I'd state I didn't own a gun with the virtual arsenal in my gun safe. He pressed Banich about whether he'd checked if the zip ties were cut or broken, the position and condition of the tapes on the floor, and his refusal to take prints off the entire toilet and tank. Our forensic analysts later would testify that all the zip ties had been purposefully cut and none were broken, as Pete testified. Under a microscope, broken zip ties have jagged edges, while cut ones have clean straight ends. Jurors would find scientific proof evidencing Pete's lie quite compelling. The tapes on the floor photographed by OPD wouldn't support the description Pete gave about the supposed battle that occurred directly on top of them. Fingerprints taken off the base would surely appear as Pete grabbed it to vomit. My request they print the sides and lid of the tank to prove he never was forced into it and never pushed up on it to save himself would be riveting testimony to a jury.

"Now, Detective Banich, didn't there come a time when you were presented with a certified warrant for Mr. Nielson's arrest?"

"Yes."

"Did you arrest Mr. Nielson and contact the issuing authority to arrange extradition?"

"No."

"What did you do?"

"Nothing."

"Did you speak to Mr. Nielson about it and, if so, what did you say?"

"No, I don't think so."

Banich didn't know that we had Mike learning everything that happened, directly from Pete, each and every day.

"Why not?"

"I didn't have time."

"Detective, please? You've testified that you've been a police officer for twelve years and a detective for five years. What does your police procedural manual instruct you to do when you learn you're in the presence of a wanted fugitive and have a certified warrant in your hands?"

His answer came cocky as could be. "I don't have the manual with me."

This would all make for very dramatic revelations to a jury in my eventual trial. I wondered about possible felony charges against Banich himself. Surely, his actions were serious criminal acts. And what about his co-conspirators? Did these people think the law didn't apply to them? Could they possibly believe they'd get away with this gross abuse of authority? My lawyers advised me to fight one battle at a time, so for now, Banich got a pass.

Our preliminary hearing ended and the case was referred to trial in the Clark County District Court, Criminal Division—a long way to go. Still, we got some satisfaction from Pete having to spend that night in jail as Judge Stabinski's guest. Mike, still under cover, heard the whole story the next day. Pete described how Banich told him to stay calm and keep his mouth shut about whatever "business" he helped him with. Pete described his comfy night in jail, where Banich spent hours with him in the open-door cell he arranged, assuring him the night would pass quickly and they'd get back to nailing me. Nielson could never wait to tell Mike, his new best friend, everything.

Our Own Little Trick

Despite the progress we were making, I was still far from seeing this whole mess rectified. Also, because of the undercover narcotics operation, Chuck and his team were constantly asking the District Court for extensions in my trial commencement date, managing to eat up months, while Stu Marshak continued to build evidence that would discredit Pete and ensure that it was him, not me, who wound up behind bars. Finally, the assigned criminal-court judge, the Honorable Tom Trupia, said to all four attorneys, "None of you can claim another conflict. Not another delay. We are not extending this trial again. It's going on the next date I assign. Am I clear?"

I'd still been having drinks every Thursday night at the Suburban West with Eric and Linda Cooper after our weekly indoor pistol-shooting competition. One night, we were discussing my Opportunity case and he asked where we were at. I said to him, "Eric, I don't know what we're going to do. The judge isn't giving us any more extensions and neither Mike nor Stu is done building the case against Nielson."

Eric thought hard and then asked, "Who's your DA now?"

"Ed Klee, why?"

Eric nodded, his wheels turning. "Linda and I know Ed. He's been wanting to get together with us for months now. Let me invite him up here next Thursday night for drinks."

When Ed Klee entered the Suburban that following Thursday

night, he gave Eric a big smile and handshake as he joined us in the corner booth. Eric was a very popular undersheriff who ran a fine police department, and it wasn't at all unusual for an assistant DA to want to hang out with him. We started eating, drinking, talking and having a fine time. At one point, Ed looked around and said, "I don't live far from here, but I've never been in this place. It's great. I'll have to start coming by more often."

To which Eric added, "Well, if you like it here, you should visit Ron's other places. He's got the Suburban Lounge East at Flamingo and Sandhill and a place over in Opportunity, on Main Street, called Winners."

Boom!

The words were no sooner out of Eric's mouth than Ed's face turned a unique shade of gray. "You're *that* Ron? Ronald T. Coury from Winners bar?"

"That's me."

"Oh my God!" He stood up, rushed to a courtesy phone, and immediately dialed his chief DA. After a few minutes, he returned to the table. "Ron, I'm your prosecutor!"

"Really?" I said, feigning surprise. "I heard my matter was given to a new Deputy DA, but I didn't know who my case was reassigned to."

He shook his head in disbelief. "I can't prosecute you. I've met you, I like you and now we've socialized together." Then with a sigh, he said, "I'll need to get a continuance. We'll have to assign this to a new prosecutor, who'll need to ramp up and learn the case."

And just like that, Eric had bought me the precious time I needed.

You can imagine Judge Trupia's frustration at hearing about this next delay. But he couldn't deny it, not when it was coming from the District Attorney's office. The trial extension was granted and we got the couple of added months we needed to continue the undercover operation on Nielson.

Pete Goes Down

Then came the break we'd been waiting for, in the form of a phone call from Mike Wysocki. "Hey Ron, can you get the attorneys together? I've got big news."

Chuck Thompson, Rick Wright, Steve Stein, and Don Green, my entire dream team, all gladly came to the bar. We'd spent years together in the trenches, working at a strategy that would protect me and Winners' entire management. No one wanted to miss this status update from our investigator, who'd worked undercover for well over a year. We were all very excited as we awaited Mike's arrival at Winners.

Mike came in beaming ear to ear and announced, "Gentlemen, as we speak, Metro is raiding Pete Nielson's house."

Steve Stein grabbed my arm and, with great foresight, said, "Hey Ron, someday this whole story could make for one hell of a book!"

Stu finally had enough to move on Pete and he moved hard. Not only had he gone after Pete for trafficking, but Pete's bragging about his dad's illegal high-capacity rifles stashed around the house, hidden in walls and floors, hadn't gotten past the undercover detective. The police had two issues. First, Pete's representations concerning his mistreatment at Winners were so inflammatory that if his comments were truthful, great care had to be taken when the case status necessitated a formal visit. And second, Pete's bluster warranted a raid with substantial firepower, so as to ensure the safety of Metro officers. The Metro narcotics team, SWAT, and Forfeiture Squad were there tearing the house apart, searching for contraband, weapons, etc. From what I later learned from Mike, the house was left a mess. No weapons of any consequence were uncovered, just Pete's drug stash. So Pete proved to be the drug dealer we knew of, but otherwise an opportunistic braggart, implicating his poor dad in much more than he deserved to be drawn into.

After the raid, District Attorney Moore called my lawyer's office to advise that this case seemed doomed from the start. The attorney he spoke to at Thompson's office once worked for Moore as a Deputy DA, so Moore was more forthcoming than he'd typically be. He acknowledged that he should have gone with his gut instinct, that the Ron Coury he'd known for many years, coupled with the vouching and full support of Metro Undersheriff Eric Cooper, should have guided him the other way.

But there at Winners the night of the Nielson house raid, we all knew it was finally over. No Pete, no accuser, no case. His credibility as my sole accuser was trashed and he himself now had criminal charges to face. Despite the unbelievable levels of manipulation, corruption, and machinations designed to ruin me, the case against us would never make it to trial. And so we toasted.

Whatever became of Pete? He was convicted on drug-trafficking charges and sent to prison for a nice long ride.

Bottom line: I was a free man again. Free, that is, to continue my quest for expanded gaming at Winners and the fight against Stan Gunster and his Opportunity henchmen.

But I soon learned it wouldn't be over quite yet. The Nevada Gaming Commission had other plans for me. Their own investigators are empowered to protect the integrity of the state's most critical industry. Pete's arrest and conviction on drug charges didn't mean I hadn't done what he'd accused me of. That was the Commission's concern; they ordered a full investigation into the Nielson allegations to determine whether I was worthy to remain a Nevada gaming license holder. If what Nielson claimed was true, I'd be stripped of my gaming license.

The gaming authorities are extremely thorough when they undertake an investigation on a licensee or a candidate for a license. Despite the fact that I'd been living in Vegas for 20 years, two agents were assigned to my case. They visited my old neighborhood and interviewed friends and former neighbors in Brooklyn. They closely examined me and my life for the last 40 years, from New York to Las Vegas.

Months later, they concluded their investigation. At a hearing to determine my worthiness to remain a gaming licensee, I was cleared and given a clean bill of health by the Gaming Commission. However, they did issue a stern warning that if I ever again uncovered a thief in one of my businesses, I wasn't to handle it internally. Their orders were clear. Call the police! That's what they're there for. I agreed and it was time to get back to business. I was more than ready to get on with my life and the various businesses Dan and I had started.

CHAPTER 18

The Antagonist Returns

With the Nielson matter behind us and a couple of years of profitable operations at Winners, we were ready to ask the Opportunity City Council for the casino use permit we were denied in 1988. Their elaborate efforts to bury us with Nielson's bogus felony charges having failed, they knew we'd be back for the permit and were prepared to sue in order to prevail. Our tenacity and persistence were proven and I hoped we could dispense with the games and be treated fairly as a property developer and casino operator.

A supper club adjacent to Winners, Sabrina's, had received approval for nonrestricted gaming. Another gaming operation just a half-mile away, Simon's Casino & Brewing Co., had received approval as well.

In the early '90s, Opportunity's local ordinance called it "limited gaming"—up to 199 slots and nine live table games, which included a sports book. As our public space was limited and I didn't plan to expand our footprint, this was fine with me. I could never fit anywhere close to the upper limit of gaming machines, tables and a sports book in Winners anyway.

By now, former City Committee member and local activist Stan Gunster had become the city councilman in Winners' ward. Furthermore, I'd learned that he had an interest in a graphics business. It wasn't a direct competitor of Suburban Graphics, but it was in the same line of work. Still, I went out of my way to meet not only with Gunster, but his colleagues on the Council, in order to explain what we were hoping to do and why we were doing it, giving them every chance to review our plans, ask questions and discuss concerns. Each meeting was one-on-one with the Council members.

My meeting with Gunster went well, or so it seemed. He heard me out, reviewed the design plans, and said he'd been to Winners and that it was an excellent fit in the neighborhood. He appreciated the time and money that went into developing so much more than a local tavern for the community he represented and said he had no problem supporting my request to add gaming to our existing facility. Then, as our face-to-face ended, he shook my hand. But the warm feeling up my spine that I left with wasn't what it seemed to be. Instead, it was the blood running down my back from the proverbial knife he stabbed me with as I exited his office.

In what should have been a major warning sign, one of the councilmembers said to me, "This is a big project for you. It just so happens that I own a nursery and sell palm trees to large commercial sites for fifteen thousand dollars each. They'd make a nice addition to your landscaping. How many would you like?"

Certainly suspicious, but not yet fully understanding the tainted game I was involved in, I simply replied, "Thanks, but I don't really need any fifteen-thousand-dollar palm trees in my little flower bed along the curb."

In the subsequent investigations we launched, we discovered that this slimeball of a public servant had a history of offering similarly priced trees to other developers who came seeking his vote for their project.

Of course, this information wasn't easy to come by. Several years later when George Day, a TV crime reporter from KXYZ-TV, a national network affiliate, conducted an eye-opening investigative series on Opportunity civic corruption, Day reported that in all their investigative team's past investigations, including union irregularities and even the Las Vegas mob, they'd never encountered more resistance to talking on the record than with development applicants in the City of Opportunity.

Other than the guy who tried to shake me down for palm trees, when I met with other councilmembers, they invariably responded, "Did you meet with Councilman Gunster? This is in his ward."

I replied that I had and he was very supportive. "He committed to supporting us and I hope we can count on your vote as well." In my naiveté, I still had faith in the integrity of the system. We were led to believe we would be approved.

As you may recall, we'd also hired Milano the "fixer"—the lobbyist and go-to guy if you needed something in Opportunity. You'd go see Mark and explain your issue, to which he'd invariably respond, "With a retainer of twenty thousand dollars, it'll get done." I guessed that he spread some money around (legal political contributions, of course, ahem) to circumvent any potential problems.

But I had good reason to be suspicious and the feeling was confirmed when, days before our hearing, Milano resigned as our attorney. "We're going to lose," was his excuse. That was it. We'd have his "legal opinion," but no intervention with the Council on our behalf.

The day of the hearing approached and my partner Dan and I got ready. In such hearings, it's the burden of the applicant to demonstrate that his project won't be a detriment to the health and welfare of the community. So from our hearing before the Opportunity Planning Board in 1988, I knew we'd have to address every valid concern that anyone from the Council or community might have regarding traffic, parking, noise, crime, and the big one, property values.

In my estimation, the decisions of governing bodies were fairly arbitrary, so approvals or denials were often determined more by relationships between applicants and legislators than facts. Here, we lacked any reliable relationships, so it would be a coin toss. Also, I didn't know what their impression or opinion of the true impact a business like Winners might have on property values, so I decided to find out definitively.

I hired a real estate appraiser named Jerry Knight and said, "People always come to these meetings and say a certain development is going to hurt their property values, yet I've never seen anyone come in with hard evidence to prove or refute it. I want you to do a study. Find locations that have nonrestricted gaming around the valley, identify what the annual appreciation rate of homes was before the gaming property opened, and show how it changed after the property opened. Gaming will either help it or hurt it, but let's find out based on facts and figures, so we don't have to do battle against guesses and unfounded assumptions."

Ambushed at the Hearing

Jerry appeared before the Council with large display boards that demonstrated in real hard numbers, one property after another, the before-and-after impact of gaming. The analysis showed that gaming didn't have a negative impact on one single home. In fact, it proved beyond a doubt that the introduction of nonrestricted gaming in a community had a positive impact on home values. Clearly, making recreational gaming available in a convenient location to homes, along with the social benefits of the accompanying amenities such as restaurants, lounges, movie theaters, meeting rooms, hotel rooms, etc., had all provided a positive contribution to the entire community.

In his questioning, Gunster started to reveal his true colors. "The area you're discussing in one example went right to the valley's Northwest Mall and reflects commercial property, so that's not very accurate with regard to homes, isn't that right?"

Jerry calmly replied, "No sir. Our study is limited exclusively to residential properties. We took great care only to reference residential properties in each of the four areas around the valley that we analyzed."

Jerry continued, "I've heard people present here complain about how, if approved, nonrestricted gaming will hurt their property values. It won't. These comparative property examples are evidence of my conclusions. It will improve the value of their homes and investments."

A Realtor who identified herself as Judith Klein countered Jerry's study. "I actively work this community and we've recently had three listings expire in the adjacent Ashby Heights condominium community, because buyers are afraid of Winners being here and possibly expanding. They're directly adjacent to the shopping center Winners is in. This application, if approved, will continue to hurt these homeowners' property values."

At this point my attorney, Alan Cromwell, stood and said, "I'd like to cross-examine this witness."

Gunster turned to the City Attorney and asked, "Can Mr. Coury's attorney do that?"

"No," came her quick and unequivocal response.

My attorney maintained his composure. "All due respect, I have the Nevada code right here if you'd like to review it. It clearly states that attorneys have the right in all quasi-judicial proceedings, of which this Council meeting is one, to cross-examine witnesses providing testimony to the Council."

The mayor balefully stared at him. "You're not going to cross-examine anyone, but I appreciate the law lesson."

I then took the microphone and said, "I've been a Realtor in this valley since 1976, which represents nearly twenty years of experience. I have the current Multiple Listing Service printout for the Ashby Heights community from as recently as this afternoon. In the twelve-month period preceding today's date, there has been only one expired listing. The reason it expired without selling is readily apparent—it was overpriced by thirty thousand dollars. Here are the comparable listings and sales to support my conclusions. I note my, uh, colleague Ms. Klein didn't bother to provide any support for the blatant lie she just stated on the record. Let's put her under oath, under penalty of perjury, and ask her to say it again! I'll swear, under oath, that what I'm representing today is truthful and factually based. Will she?" I pointed to Ms. Klein who, just like the bullies of the world, melted into her seat.

Opportunity Mayor Daley was quick to stop my speech and demands, instructing me to conclude my statement and not harass the good citizens of her community.

Good citizens, indeed. I'd attended the Sabrina's and Simon's hearings. The gadflies at those hearings had been silent and both establishments had sailed through the hearing process without one negative comment from the same community Winners was in. In fact, Sabrina's bordered on single-family homes, directly over their rear wall. No buffer! Of course, they were both represented by Mark Milano.

In the 1988 hearing, people testified that bars were noisy. This time around, Jerry Knight killed the objection before it could be raised. He stated, "My associate here stood at the Winners' property line and I stood just over the wall at the Ashby Heights condo community. We each held up a tape player. He screamed at the top of his lungs. I have the tapes here if you want to hear them. You can't hear a thing. Even if Winners generated noise, there's so much distance from their property line to the residential area that it wouldn't be heard. But the fact is, it's not noisy. It's a family restaurant and they've been open for two years with no issues whatsoever. We checked the Opportunity Police Department's call records as part of our analysis and there's simply nothing of consequence related to this property."

We presented a neighborhood survey that Infidata, an independent research company, had conducted. Their analysis showed that the local residents overwhelmingly supported an existing property on Main Street expanding its gaming if it brought gourmet meals at affordable prices. Gunster immediately challenged the report. He asked if residents had been told that the property in question was Winners.

"Of course not," replied the Infidata representative. "That wouldn't be appropriate. There are professional standards for conducting studies and we strictly adhered to them."

Tom Lock and Simon Deadman, two economics professors and the heads of the Center for Business and Economic Research from UNLV, also testified. Deadman, a noted author also serving on the President's Council on Gaming, added that gaming truly provided many advantages to neighborhoods and local governments in the form of social benefits, taxes, and employment. "We've analyzed Infidata's study and it followed all the criteria customary for a valid impartial study," said Lock. "Also, we've conducted our own study and it supports the data that they've gathered and presented here."

Gunster grumbled, "I bet if you told them it was Winners, they wouldn't have been so supportive."

Yet again, Gunster's statement revealed the mission to stop our project and just our project. I turned to Dan and under my breath asked, "What's going on? This isn't the guy I lobbied."

I then told the Council, "I attended the homeowner's association meeting at the Ashby Heights condo community before this hearing. I had blueprints to show them—an entire presentation. I would have told them, 'Here's my building layout for those of you who have never been in it. Some of you mistakenly think I want to expand into a full hotel property. That has never been the case. I have no intention to purchase the adjacent vacant property. I just want to put more machines in the existing building. It's not an application to expand. Can I show you my plans? What it will look like if I add some machines?'"

Nothing I said or tried to present had mattered to the association members, most of whom were rude and unwavering. They didn't want to see or hear anything from me. "But I can report to you," I continued to address the Council, "an impartial Board, *this very council*, reviewing a legitimate business-use permit application on an already properly zoned site has agreed previously that an application like ours is entitled to this permit. I did everything expected of an applicant and more—certainly much more than you received or requested from Sabrina's or Simon's when you unhesitatingly approved their requests for limited gaming, less than three thousand feet away from my property."

At this point, Kim, an employee of ours who was attending the hearing, approached us with a bombshell that finally revealed exactly what a low-life Gunster was.

"Ron, do you want to know why Gunster is being such a jerk? Remember when you and Dan approved me diversifying from just doing slot glass to other areas of work? This is the payback."

"In what way?"

"We recently started getting a lot of smaller printing jobs away from his company. This has just been coming together for us, so I haven't had a chance to brief you on my success with it."

I couldn't believe what I was hearing; it just didn't make sense. Gunster's firm used top-of-the-line state-of-the-art equipment designed for very high-end booklet and brochure-type jobs. We had nothing to do with that niche of the market and couldn't be less interested. We'd just moved into the lower-budget more utilitarian market that, apparently, Gunster also viewed as his sole turf. And now, in what I believe was a total conflict of interest and abuse of power, he seemed to be retaliating by steamrolling over our gaming project.

Determining the motives of a few participants in a series of seemingly innocuous events that created a nuclear-like explosion in my world would be the question that would ring in my ears for years to come. It all begged the question, could a city activist and eventual councilman exert influence within the City Attorney's office and their Police Department to limit competition in his private business interests? The likelihood my opinions might be accurate were bolstered by the lucrative nature of the Las Vegas Valley printing business and were certainly heightened when it included the unique and cash-rich industry of operating gaming machines and tables. Would a cooperative team of city henchmen play an active role in bolstering unfounded criminal charges against an honest businessman's expansion plans to help out one of their own? Could it extend to do away with me as a corporate business applicant by whatever means they determined necessary? Little else existed to convince me otherwise. The story would play out in the most unforeseeable of outcomes.

Since Winners was in Gunster's ward, the other councilmembers, believing he knew what his constituents wanted, were prepared to follow his lead. We later learned that his objections were even more underhanded and self-serving than we'd imagined possible. But at the moment, this was egregious enough.

CHAPTER 19

The Circus Continues

Dan Hughes re-approached the podium and voiced our objection as soon as Kim told us of it. "Councilman Gunster competes with our company, Suburban Graphics, in certain aspects of print media. We believe that he should have disclosed this and should hereafter abstain from these proceedings."

Gunster immediately went on the attack. "I can't think of one job I ever bid on against you. Can you name even one?"

Of course, the information was so new to him that he had no way of knowing what jobs we'd won when his company was a competing bidder. Companies submitted bids and rarely knew who else was bidding, so Dan had no answer to Gunster's question.

Dan replied to the Council and City Attorney, "I don't know if that's true or not; I've just learned of this. But I think it's important to note that there's a likelihood it exists, thus the error should be on the side of caution that a serious conflict of interest is present here and to avoid even the appearance of impropriety, Mr. Gunster should abstain."

The whole thing suddenly seemed obvious. The reason for all Gunster's vitriol on a simple use permit application and animosity toward us and every speaker we presented had to be that if we were successful enough at Suburban Graphics or at Winners, we could conceivably invest in the kind of equipment his company used and compete with him on an even higher level than we did now. My mind boggled at all the ways he could limit our growth potential through hundreds of thousands of dollars in legal and hearing fees, lost gaming revenues, even railroading us into prison. Should this snake in the grass be a regulator and decider of fact in our use permit application? Wasn't it clear that he shouldn't participate further in our hearing? Of course it was. But not to the city's legal counsel.

Gunster turned to his obviously complicit City Attorney, Brenda Beals, another "public servant" whom I'd soon learn was equally ethically questionable and would stop at nothing to hurt us. He asked if she saw a conflict and, of course, she urged him to continue. We would later learn he also had plans to build three nonrestricted gaming locations of his own, but never disclosed this clear-cut conflict at the time either. Any area of his conflict of interest should have precluded him from participating in our hearing. Nonetheless, he moved for denial of our application. And just like that, we were blindsided with a motion for denial of our use permit and a unanimous vote followed in support of that motion.

At this point, all illusion of fair play had been stripped away and Dan and I finally knew, without a doubt, what we were dealing with. The Nevada State Ethics Commission subsequently concurred with our position on Gunster's conflict. They ruled he should have disclosed what would become his multiple business conflicts with us and abstained from our use permit and any subsequent hearings. Whoever said you can't fight City Hall must have spent some time in the Opportunity governmental environment of the '80s and '90s.

"We're headed to court," I told Dan. "Let's keep operating Winners with what we have and prepare to fight another day. We'll go to court asking a judge to find their ruling arbitrary and capricious, reversing the denial and granting us what's rightfully ours."

Surely, between the record we built, their past approvals of our competitors, and our clean track record operating a quality establishment, an honest court would see through all this muck and the open unfairness in how we'd been treated.

Fifteen machines would have to support our operation for the time being and after all we'd been through at Winners, I wasn't about to fold. We'd spent nearly $2 million, three times what we might have had we simply built a standard 15-machine tavern. So we pressed the pedal down and started the process with the district court.

A Possible Solution

I also paid a return call on Councilman Gunster.

"Stan, when we met, you indicated you had no problem with our project and yet at the hearing, you made it clear that you were completely against it. It's certainly your right to oppose a project, but why not just tell me up front that you opposed ours and let me properly prepare for the hearing, knowing what I'm in for?"

"I don't know what you're talking about," he said, treating me like a meal he hadn't ordered. "I never said I was going to support your project. There's nothing I can do to keep you from jumping to a mistaken conclusion."

He smiled at me, knowing full well that every word out of his mouth was false.

"You don't have to be for every project. You don't even have to be for my project," I said, looking him in the eyes. "Just don't lie to me. And that's exactly what you've done."

He considered his answer for a moment and then, through the same smug smile, hissed, "What are you going to do about it?"

The unspoken answer in my eyes was, "Plenty."

Gunster was about to find out that I'd make a much better friend than an enemy. I'd deal with him again, down the line. And that was okay, because at least now I better understood my opponent and as the saying goes, "Forewarned is forearmed." In the meantime, I knew I had to go to work to get my approval elsewhere.

As time passed, Matt Moore, who'd admitted that the Pete Nielson case stunk, retired as District Attorney. That created the opening for me to retain him and have him represent me personally.

My history with Matt was interesting in both a good and bad way.

When he first ran for District Attorney, the Suburban Lounge West was already a busy and popular local spot in Vegas. Between working at the Tropicana casino and owning the Suburban West, I'd met a host of amazing people, including Matt; famed UNLV basketball coach Jerry Tarkanian; G. Gordon Liddy; Robert Maheu, Howard Hughes's former right-hand man and go-to guy; former Nevada Governor Mike O'Callaghan; and many celebrities, such as fellow former Brooklynite and actor Brian Keith, Kenny Rogers, Gail Martin (singer and daughter of Dean Martin), Jerry Vale, Rodney Dangerfield, Louis Prima and Sam Butera, Farah Fawcett, Muhammed Ali, and Telly Savalas, to name just a few.

As a fledgling politician, stopping in at the Suburban Lounge on a busy night was a must for Matt Moore. In the still-small desert community, all political hopefuls had to visit with groups of voters in popular neighborhood gathering spots. Matt told me after winning the election that he enjoyed making campaign stops at my place and that introductions I'd made helped him get elected. It was, accordingly, a bit of a shock to me that in 1989, he approved filing charges against me based on Nielson's false claims at Winners. But as he told me privately, he was in a tough spot with the heavy political and police pressure Opportunity was imposing at the time. In his words, he believed I'd prove my innocence. Well, he was right, and now, with our new application for nonrestricted gaming, I could use his influence and popularity to my advantage.

When he tried to lobby the city on my behalf, he returned one day with shocking news. He said City Attorney Brenda Beals had told the City Council that I'd threatened her and her children. It was presumably in her office with no witnesses. I assured Matt that it was completely fabricated and wanted to prove it. He suggested I take a polygraph. I agreed and he arranged it with the polygraph company that Metro Police and the District Attorney's office used.

I took the polygraph, passed it with flying colors, and the company issued a certified report indicating the results. Matt delivered it to each councilmember. Might they reconsider the use permit request now? Approve me and we could avoid District Court? Obviously, Gunster was against us for personal reasons, but the rest of the Council? They could approve our use permit with a four-to-one vote and we could move forward.

Matt returned to tell me that the polygraph results had no effect. City Attorney Beals played the victim role to the hilt and the Council was unwavering, the facts be damned. I concluded both she and Gunster would stop at nothing to hurt us.

What they didn't know was how close they could have come to paying the ultimate price for their many heinous acts.

My uncle, Joe Charles, had attended the Winners City Council hearing and witnessed the treatment we received. He was also aware of the city's earlier efforts to dispose of us through the trumped-up Nielson criminal charges. A heavy cigarette smoker all his life, he'd recently received news from his doctors that cancer had invaded his body and he had about three months to live. His tough Brooklyn roots were apparent, having grown up with Uncle Louie, our neighbor who'd offered his unique brand of help with my Presidential Limo problems years earlier. They ran around in the same mob circles all their lives and had the same solutions to certain problems. They also had the same love of friends and family that was displayed time and again when someone they cared for was in trouble.

One day, Uncle Joe came to see me. He said that with only three months left to live, he wanted to repay me for the countless times I'd helped him out of various financial squeezes. He stated his offer bluntly, as was his way. "Ronnie, write down the names of these pricks in Opportunity who've been fucking with you. I'll whack them in one afternoon and never spend a day in prison. I got three months to live and I'll never go to trial, even if they catch me."

I was immensely appreciative that he came to me before taking matters into his own hands and I had to think fast to get his proposition off the table.

"Uncle Joe," I replied, "I can't let you do that. First of all, I don't want any part of something like that and while you may think Gunster and his cohorts deserve it for all they've put us through, what if your doctors are wrong? What if you live five or ten more years? I'd feel terrible to see you spend those last years locked up. The punishment doesn't fit the crime. No, let me beat them on my own legal terms. But I can't thank you enough for the offer!"

As it turned out, I was right. Not only was Uncle Joe's street justice the wrong thing to do, but he was a fighter and lived a few more years until his passing in 1996. Only through this book will those Opportunity bastards learn how close they came to an early grave.

CHAPTER 20

The New Castaways

In 1988, as we were planning Winners, I learned of a City of Las Vegas tavern location on North Decatur Boulevard and Vegas Drive, northwest of downtown. In the city of Las Vegas, nearly all taverns were limited to operating a maximum of 15 slot machines. A handful of locations were approved to operate 35 machines. These unique permits were no longer issued, but if back in the day, someone had gotten one and kept paying the renewal fees to the city, the location was grandfathered, even though nothing had ever been built on the site. This was exactly the scenario I'd found.

A guy named Billy Carlson owned the lot. He'd kept the gaming approval current and was looking to sell the property. I did an informal demographics study on the site. It was surrounded by apartments and many nearby single-family homes. The adjacent apartments meant a high density of ideal tavern customers within walking distance. Apartment occupants ate and drank out more often than the typical single-family homeowner and had few other big-dollar monthly financial obligations. Many were construction workers, making great money in the building boom of the 1990s, and tending to stop off at a place like ours for drinks, meals and video poker. From my initial research, this could be the best location Dan and I ever developed. We could buy, design, develop and operate the Decatur site just like we were planning at Winners.

Billy Carlson wanted $175,000, a fast escrow, and all cash. However, we faced an ongoing problem—lack of liquidity.

At the time, a couple of new companies were entering the slot-route business and competing with the longstanding route operations. In our terrific capitalistic system, more competition drives creativity, motivating people to think outside the box in order to make things happen. New route companies needed to find ways to get the older companies' customers to give them a try; otherwise, though they had lots of machines, they had nowhere to place them to earn revenue.

I met with the owner of one of those new route companies, Lou Magnani, who was wealthy and motivated. Lou knew us from Suburban Graphics, where we'd done some design work for machines he was creating. Plus, Dan and I had a great reputation as operators of the two Suburbans and were known around town as a couple of honest guys. When we met, I showed him our elaborate plans for Winners and told him it would be opening in a few months. He loved what we were doing there and wanted in on the location. I told him it was too late, as we'd already contracted with United Coin, the same company that operated our machines at both Suburbans.

I anticipated his disappointment and had worked it into my pitch. "Here's the thing, Lou. I have a new nonrestricted place on the drawing boards. If we make a deal with you for this location, I'll give you a shot to bid my other three places when our current contracts expire."

Lou was enticed. "So what are you looking for?"

That was the question I was waiting for. "Well, we'll need to be creative to allow me to save face with leaving United Coin, which has been very good to me these past years. We need to do something they'd never do."

"Like what?"

"A large amount of front money. You help me close this deal with

167

upfront cash and I'll sign with you and get it built. As soon as the doors open, your thirty-five slots are operating in my new place."

"How much are you proposing?" Lou asked.

I felt it best to explain how we'd use the money before shocking him with a number. "We need to pay this guy cash for his land. We've already given him a deposit and opened escrow, so no one else can take this deal away from us. The lot costs a hundred seventy-five grand, all cash at close. We're going to name it either the Suburban North or the Castaways Casino, a great name with Las Vegas history."

The original Castaways was right on the Strip, very successful and popular, but it was razed along with the Silver Slipper to make room for a Steve Wynn project, The Mirage.

I showed Lou the drawings and he loved what he was seeing and hearing. Time to close this deal.

I said, "You front me two hundred thousand. Give me the cash now in exchange for my signature on your participation agreement. I'll close escrow and with the land free and clear, my bank will finance the build-out of the building."

"At what split?" Lou asked, intrigued.

"That's easy," I said, "I've earned an eighty-five–fifteen split with United Coin at my three locations over the years. You'll need to match it. We'll both do very well."

Lou pondered, but not for too long. "You have a deal," he said smiling. "I'll give you the two hundred grand and my lawyers will get you a contract on the deal." (The "split" is how much of the revenue from gaming machines goes to the business owner, and how much goes to the slot route operator.)

That was great news for Dan and me. A perfect outcome.

Within a day, we had documents signed, the check was in my hand, and we closed escrow. Billy Carlson was very pleased with our fast and problem-free performance. Doing what you say you're going to do, standing behind your word, and not taking any cheap shots at people are always important in business, especially in a small town like Las Vegas. Once you've built a solid reputation, people know it and the opportunities come a lot more easily.

Nielson Haunts Me

Still, a problem developed just as everything seemed so perfect. At the time, the criminal charges from the Nielson matter hadn't been resolved, so we couldn't expect approval from Gaming for the new location until we got that crap settled, and we didn't know how long that would take. We did know that it would be longer than Lou would give us; he wanted the Decatur site opened yesterday to begin seeing a return on his $200,000 investment. I couldn't blame him. It was time to think outside the box again.

I offered to find a different operator and give Lou the chance to back out. He wanted the location, but not if we weren't the operators. So now he wanted his $200,000 back, except we'd spent most of it closing the land deal. Thanks to a good relationship with him and our reputation, Lou agreed to a payback over time. We did that and made every payment exactly as agreed.

I still needed someone licensable to operate the bar while we were dealing with the criminal charges in Opportunity, so I spread the word among the various slot-route companies that I had a 35-machine location to lease out. Route operators were often approached by newcomers to the business. The instant success of video poker not only changed the business model of taverns from food-and-beverage purveyors to gaming locations, but it made operators quite wealthy, and quickly. That got the attention of people from outside the industry. Having friends in management of those slot companies helped my cause; they turned me on to prospective bar buyers I might be interested in selling to, just as I handed them people who approached me over the years when I wasn't interested in selling. Friends helping friends, yet again! A key to overcoming obstacles!

One route-company manager came to my office one day with two guys, Larry Furst and Ed Ashrawy. They'd just moved to Las Vegas from Atlantic City, after working in top positions for Donald Trump. They claimed credit for Trump's initial success in his New Jersey gaming enterprises. Was it true?

Oh, how often I'd seen some of my lower-level employees begin to believe that only their efforts were responsible for any successes I'd achieved in a venture. No risk on their part. No role in the vision and process to make a thought become reality.

Whether the tale these two gentlemen from Atlantic City told me was accurate or not, it wasn't my job to verify. I did confirm that they held high-ranking positions with the Trump gaming operations, but how instrumental were they in the resulting success in Atlantic City? I didn't know or care. If they could fund the acquisition, it solved my most imminent problem. Maybe they were no different than Dan and me in the early years, willing to put it all on the line to have a shot at being successful entrepreneurs. Only time would tell if they had what it took. My purpose was to find a tenant willing to pay our price for a turn-key operation and collect rent and whatever other contract terms we ended up negotiating. That was my only acceptable option until the Nielson allegations were laid to rest.

They didn't have all the money we required as a down payment, so I told Larry and Ed, "Dan and I offered my brother an opportunity to be a partner in a future place, but we haven't built a new location yet to fulfill that promise. If you want to take him on as a partner, he could be a big asset; he's run our places for years and knows the business inside and out.

"If you make him a twenty percent partner, I'll ease up on the down payment we required. The balance would be paid monthly over ten years under the terms of a consulting agreement."

Actually, we'd use their $100,000 down, reduced to $80,000 with Artie's involvement, toward reimbursing us for the $40,000 liquor license we had to pay up front to the City of Las Vegas. Larry and Ed were essentially getting in for $40,000 down.

They agreed and wanted to draw on the goodwill of the Suburban name, rather than the historical significance of Castaways, so they called the place Suburban Sports Lounge. That was fine with us.

In turn-keying the place for them, we completely outfitted it with cooking equipment, plates, silverware, and the opening food-and-beverage inventory. It was a great deal for them and a good deal for us, especially the timing. And we could help them survive and thrive in a variety of ways, particularly if they fell on bad luck through no fault of their own.

Our gaming attorney, Tony Cabot, urged me to put suggestions in writing to develop a record of the ongoing consulting I'd be providing. This was necessary to defend the arrangement if ever challenged and to protect us if they ever claimed non-performance under the consulting-agreement terms that substituted for the actual purchase of the business.

Quite honestly, in any sale to a buyer who paid us off over time, my advice would have been readily available to contribute to the likelihood of success and our uninterrupted flow of income. So formalizing a consulting agreement to ensure 10 years of payments wasn't that different from what I'd have done informally anyway. They could take my advice in situations that developed, or not. It would be their choice and their decisions would account for whatever level of success they achieved. Just as things should be.

In addition, having the experience of Artie as an on-site partner on a day-to-day basis would be very helpful to Larry and Ed. If they agreed to take him on as a partner, we'd fulfill our promise of equity to Artie and they'd gain a valuable asset, which I strongly felt they were going to need.

"But you should meet Artie," I continued, "to make sure you all like one another. If you want to do it, fine. If not, raise the additional money, pay me what I originally required, and the place is yours—one hundred percent."

They agreed to meet Artie and see how it went. Artie is a great guy, smart and personable—terrific with employees and customers alike, while also having learned the behind-the-scenes operations directly from me. He was a great catch for the right people who came to the table with no experience. Running a Las Vegas gaming bar with a restaurant is a lot different than holding a management position in an Atlantic City hotel-casino.

As I expected, their meeting with Artie went fine and they agreed to the partnership split.

The Early Results Are Strong

My plan was clear and ideal for a start-up for two new guys. We hired the opening crew, including attractive bartenders and servers. We weren't being sexist. The vast majority of our customer base would be male and simply liked to hang out at places where there were good-looking women—it was just good business. Two of our best, Michelle and Kelly, had worked for us previously at Suburban West. Both preferred this new site, closer to home for them. They were friendly and experienced and, not surprisingly, they attracted construction workers by the dozens.

Larry and Ed had fire in their bellies and that was the first thing they needed to take a shot like this. Hell, it was only about a decade earlier that I was that guy, taking my own shot in the bar business.

All seemed perfect for them to excel, right? Suburban Sports Lounge opened to terrific business. Crowds of drinkers, diners and gamblers filled the place on every shift. The first couple of months validated our design and staffing. Profits flowed in immediately.

Each week, I sent them a detailed written description of the events from my site visits and our discussions, fully authenticating all the advice I'd provided. The record of my performance would survive any legal challenge; it also provided a lot of solid advice to increase their likelihood and level of success.

Their payments to us were made in a timely fashion, except for a couple of anticipated hiccups. In the Las Vegas bar business, sometimes cash flow takes a dramatic dive when your slots hit a bad streak. You can end up with little or no hold (winnings) when a couple of big jackpots hit. If they called when a payment was due and they needed a few days to come up with the money, though we were under no obligation to do so, as a friendly gesture, I gave them an extension and waived the late fees.

Well, no good deed goes unpunished.

Everything I set up and did to help them succeed relied on one key factor, which I couldn't imagine would fail to occur: They'd need to actually heed advice from Artie, Dan and me!

One thing I couldn't have foreseen was that after observing the kind of money the bartenders made from tips, both for drinks and from jackpot winners, these guys' greed emerged. Both had middle-aged wives who were nice enough, but in no way could compete as bartenders with the skilled young women we had working there. Without notice, Ed and Larry hired their wives as bartenders on the prime shifts.

Distraught, Artie called me. "Ron, I just got to work and learned they let go of Michelle and Kelly. They've put their wives on the day and swing shifts. Aside from other factors, they don't have the experience to make and serve drinks at the pace this place requires. This isn't what our customers are looking for."

I contacted Larry and Ed and arranged a meeting. It was quite a delicate matter to raise and I did my best to address it as diplomatically as I could. "Guys, that's not a good move. Those girls you fired bring in the customers. If you want to put your wives to work, let them serve food; they can make good tips there. Or pay them to cook and give them a higher than normal salary. Hell, you can even pay them to stay home; this place can afford to do that. But don't put them behind the bar on the busy shifts. I'm not trying to offend anybody, but we hand-picked Michelle and Kelly for a reason. Many of your customers followed them here from the Suburban West. They come in every day, cash their paychecks, and leave a good part of it in your registers. That's how loyal this following is!"

"Thanks for the advice, Ron, but we don't need it. We also don't feel we'll be needing any more consulting, so you can stop writing us those weekly updates."

Larry and Ed had apparently learned enough about the business in a couple of months to ignore decades worth of collective experience.

Of course, I wrote one more report. I memorialized their wishes and informed them that at their request, I'd no longer generate weekly status updates. Instead, I'd remain on call, in case they needed to discuss any business developments with me. The terms of the consulting agreement would remain in full force and effect; all payments were expected on time, which would avoid the significant late fees and penalties we'd (thankfully) written into the deal.

Artie's 20 percent ownership had earned him little to nothing in profits above his salary, because Larry and Ed manipulated the monthly expenses, paying themselves and their wives at rates that wiped out any profits. Therefore, Art's 20 percent of nothing was nothing. He tried talking to them about the declining business, what he felt the causes were, and the unique bookkeeping they employed, artificially increasing expenses to minimize visible profits.

A short time later, they told Artie they didn't want or need him either. "You're a partner," they said. "We signed that deal. But we didn't promise you a job. As a partner, if there are future profits, we'll send you your share, but there's no salary here for you anymore."

I was busy in my office at Suburban Graphics when Artie walked in, dejected. He'd been so excited at the prospect of being an owner, only to have it pulled out from under him by two inexperienced guys with a separate agenda.

"You know what?" I told him. "If that's how they want to play, then that's how we'll play. Look at it this way. If they miss a beat, I'll put them in default and if they can't come up with all the money due, we'll own the place again and you'll be right back in there as a twenty-percent partner."

Karma rings true sometimes. As a result of their naiveté and arrogance, not surprisingly, Ed and Larry started having trouble paying their bills. I assessed the substantial late fees our agreement permitted, then sent certified letters with notices of default.

One day, they came to my office and said, "We just can't do it. We're not generating enough revenue. What can we do to get out of the deal? We'll give you the keys."

They could have had it all, but they got greedy and wanted to do things their way. I learned a long time ago, if you don't know what you're doing, listen long and hard to the people who do.

So just like that, we got the property back, changed the name from Suburban Sports Lounge to the Castaways Casino, and would re-open with a nautical theme. However, we had to get another nonrestricted gaming license from the city and state.

Fraudulence Is Far-Reaching

Along with Stan Gunster, Paul Ruggiero was an Opportunity councilman. Serving on the Council is a part-time job and Paul's full-time job was as a civilian investigator in the Special Investigations Bureau (SIB) at the Las Vegas Metropolitan Police Department, working on privileged license applications for the City of Las Vegas.

Dan and I submitted the typical paperwork for the Castaways licensing. At this point, we'd opened enough locations to be quite familiar with the process.

Metro SIB Investigator Powell Kearney, who worked in a very small office alongside Paul Ruggiero, was assigned to our case. Although Pete Nielson went to prison, I believe from the bottom of my heart that Ruggiero was still doing the bidding of Stan Gunster. I don't know if he believed I was a bad guy who'd gotten away with something in the now-resolved Winners case or he was just continuing the back-scratching for his fellow Council buddy, but Kearney's treatment of us as applicants for gaming and liquor licenses was disgusting. I believed then, as I believe now, that Gunster had corrupted dimwitted Ruggiero to betray his oath as an officer and share lies about us with his officemate—lies that had been proven to be lies, resulting in all our criminal records being sealed.

The sealing process, when successful, is intended to clear someone's good name, allowing him to thereafter swear, under oath if need be, that he was never arrested or charged—in my case, that our entire legal mess and the alleged events never took place at all. If Ruggiero didn't have immunity from prosecution in the performance of his duties, we might have successfully sued him personally, but that was an added battle to contemplate another day. Believe it or not, years later, Ruggiero actually became the mayor of Opportunity! A slimeball in charge? Judge for yourself.

When you're headed toward a hearing with the Las Vegas City Council for a gaming property, after filing your application, you're interviewed by SIB. You have a chance as an applicant to review the report that will go to the Council, ask your own questions, and answer any further ones the council might have. Having been cleared by the District Attorney, the Gaming Commission, and the court that signed off on sealing my records, Dan and I arrived for our meeting, anticipating a smooth interview.

Wrong.

Detective Kearney, a big burly Irishman, said, "You know I work with Paul Ruggiero, so I know a lot about you guys."

Our antennae immediately went up. "What can we answer for you?"

"Nothing," came Kearney's terse response. "I've completed my report for the Las Vegas City Council."

So we read the report that he submitted to the Council and mayor of Las Vegas, a dozen pages recommending denial of our licensing for the Castaways, citing the accusations made against us in Opportunity, while making no reference to the fact that we were completely exonerated. It didn't matter that Nielson was behind bars; it was easy for this jerk to imply that we were unfit for a privileged license.

Knowing that the city almost always followed whatever Metro recommended, we were furious. After months of being closed during renovations, Dan and I had the Decatur location ready to open, completely remodeled, with people on the payroll. The whole thing should have been a mere formality.

"Wow," I said. "Between you and Paul Ruggiero, you've torpedoed my whole project. Can I get a copy of this report?"

"No."

"Why not? There's a copy machine right there." I motioned across the office.

"You can't use it."

"Okay," I said. "I hope you've got nothing else to do today."

He squinted at me, unsure what I was up to. "Why?"

"Because we're going to hand-write a copy." I turned to Dan. "You start with page six. I'll start with page one."

We pulled out two legal pads and painstakingly copied what he'd typed, making him sit there while we wrote every goddamned word. When we finished, I took our work upstairs to Ruggiero's and Kearney's boss, my old friend Eric Cooper. "Eric, you know what I've been through in Opportunity and you know we're about to open this place on Decatur."

"Yeah, how's that going?"

"At the moment, not so well." I handed him the pages from the legal pad, which he immediately began reading. "This is what your Detective Kearney, with Paul Ruggiero's help, is submitting to the City Council."

Eric was fuming. "Ron, I've never gotten in the middle of an investigator's report to the Council, but this is dead wrong." He picked up the phone and immediately called Las Vegas Mayor Shirley Potter and every member of the Vegas City Council. "Mayor, I'm going to put this in a letter, but I want you to be aware that I've known Ron Coury for almost twenty years," he said. "He runs taverns that are head and shoulders above other places in town and my investigator is submitting a report to you recommending a denial. I disagree with it one hundred percent. I know about the incident he's referring to and I want you to know that Ron has been cleared. I have no idea what my investigator is up to, but he's wrong." True to his word, Eric followed up with letters reasserting these facts to every single council member he'd called.

A short time later, my gaming attorney Tony Cabot and I made the rounds at City Hall, another common practice before a public hearing. We visited Mayor Potter and the council members individually. Each of them referred to Eric's call and subsequent letter, as well as Kearney's report. The undersheriff refuting, in full, the contents of one of his own detective's report for an applicant's unsuitability for a gaming license? They told me nothing of the sort had ever happened before.

Mayor Potter told us, "I have no problem with you guys."

Bud Coleman, a councilman friend and fellow tavern owner, said, "I wish you'd actually kicked that piece of shit's ass." I think he was referring to Nielson, but maybe he meant Ruggiero, or even Kearney, all of whom deserved a good ass-kicking.

Bob Holden, Mayor Pro Tempore, a man I also considered a dear friend, told us, "You're fine with me."

However, Kerry Kettleman, the councilman in whose ward the Castaways was located, sang a different tune. At the hearing he said, "Madam Mayor, we have this report from Metro. It's very disturbing."

In a heartbeat, Bob Holden chimed in, "We also have that letter from the undersheriff, which disputes the veracity of the report."

This caught Kettleman off guard. Fumbling, he said, "I was going to make a motion we follow Metro's recommendation, but it sounds like you don't agree. So what about a twelve-month limited approval?"

"Not so fast," Holden said. "Why would we make the applicant do this again in twelve months, incurring further legal fees? We can call him in for a hearing if he ever does anything we don't like at this location. I move for approval."

Kettleman started to sputter and object, but before he could do any more damage, Bud Coleman seconded the motion.

Mayor Potter said, "I'm going to call for a vote."

We won approval and the Castaways Casino opened to great success and brisk steady business. Bartenders Michelle and Kelly were back, as were all their regular customers.

Again, friends doing the right thing for friends. It's a testament to the importance of friendship and loyalty during tough times.

CHAPTER 21

Weed and Seed

In 1994, our son Joey was already driving and our daughter Angie was in her early teens when Joan came to me and said, "The kids don't need me like they used to and I don't have much to do other than taking care of the house. If I go out and get a job, I'll earn minimum wage, which wouldn't change our lives in any way, given the successes you've had. What I really love is raising kids. Since I can't have another child, what would you think about adopting?"

Joan had had a hysterectomy around 10 years earlier, so adoption was a sensible alternative. We did a lot of reading and research about it and found an attorney specializing in adoptions. Ishi Kunin, a friend to this day, still practices family law in Las Vegas. Ishi paired us up with a birth mother who didn't want to have an abortion but couldn't financially support another child. When she had the baby in December 1995, we brought Tommy home. There were a number of technical difficulties along the way, but with Ishi's help, everything worked out well. Tom's arrival made it the finest Christmas our family could have hoped for.

Almost immediately, I bought a house around the corner from where we lived and on the same lake, so it'd be easy for my parents to visit us, because my mom never drove. She could simply walk around the corner anytime she wanted to see the baby and visit Joan, who was 42 at the time.

To me, it says a lot about Joan, who recognized that her greatest skill was raising children and maintaining a family.

The minute we got Tommy home, he was ours and an instant member of our family. Today, so many children need a home and if anyone who reads this is considering adoption, but is unsure about bonding and attachments, I'm here to tell you: I have never, not for a single moment, felt any different about Tommy than I have about Joey and Angie, both of whom Joan had through natural birth. The joy we experienced bringing Tommy home and growing our family, coupled with the opening of the Castaways and having years of legal problems behind us, was all wonderful. I was feeling like all the bad luck one guy could encounter in business was finally behind me and great things in our lives were multiplying. And then . . .

Shootout at the Castaways!

For a couple of years, the Castaways went gangbusters. Then, the Fiesta Hotel and Casino (1994) and the Texas Station Hotel and Casino (1995) opened—both right down the street. Both were big operations that catered to locals and put a serious damper on the bar businesses around them, including ours. We struggled to reclaim our customer base, came up with some successful promotions, and managed to recover some revenue we lost to the competition.

Then in 1996, the FBI and the police department joined forces and formed what was known as the Weed and Seed Team. The team's mission was to identify and "weed out" bad guys from various areas of town. It was a good plan. Unfortunately, they were working an undercover drug sting, trying to nail a big-time dealer, and for reasons that will forever remain a mystery to me, without asking or notifying us in advance, they used our parking lot at the Castaways to meet and bring him down.

As the money changed hands, the suspect was in his car, backed up against our rear-lot block wall. Two undercover units pulled in from both sides in front of him. The problem was, they didn't pull in tightly enough and when they tried to arrest the guy, he floored his accelerator, hitting two federal agents, as others pulled their weapons and started firing. It was the Wild West once again, guns blazing and bullets flying everywhere. The drug dealer had just enough space to squeeze through and get away.

So just as the Castaways was getting back on its feet from the new competition, stories on all the newscasts led with: "Shootout at the Castaways!" "Drug deal gone bad at the Castaways!" "FBI agents injured in gun battle at Castaways!" All of this was accompanied by images of our lot taped off and cones marking where every bullet shell had landed. If you watched the news, you'd think a drug deal and shootout went down inside our bar!

I immediately sent a press release to every news outlet to predictable results—no clarification on their stories. Any hope I had about changing the narrative came to an abrupt end a short time later when I was playing baccarat at Caesars Palace. A pit boss I knew well said, "You know, Ron, my wife and I used to come to the Castaways all the time, but since we saw on the news what happened, we're afraid to go back."

The story wouldn't go away. The manhunt to catch this guy was the lead every night. Our business went right into the toilet. My attorney said, "Ron, you know Metro and the FBI have loss-management divisions and you're clearly a victim here. You can quantify that you've lost half a million this year in net revenue. Go get made whole."

I went to see Sheriff Heller, who said, "The FBI really runs the show, but nothing's stopping you from submitting the form to loss management."

My next stop was to see the FBI's Special Agent in Charge, Jerry Ryan. Once he heard the reason for my appointment, he brought in his Deputy Attorney General. I patiently explained what happened, to which his response was, "People like you really offend me."

Confused and disappointed, I said, "What type of people are you talking about?"

"We risk our lives every day to make your life better and safe," he said sanctimoniously. "I'm talking about the kind of people who would try to see financial gain from a deal where two of my agents were injured." The fact that the agents hadn't been shot, just bumped out of the way by a car and neither seriously hurt, didn't seem to be a consideration to him.

"Look," I said, "I'm a big supporter of law enforcement. I'm not looking for trouble or any gain, but you guys picked my parking lot without my knowledge or approval." I pushed a stack of financial records across the desk to them. "Here are the numbers. What happened devastated our business and we haven't been able to recover. These records confirm that. I waited a long time before coming to see you, hoping the news would fade and my customers would start coming back. But our reputation as a 'drug-infested shootout bar' has continued to be a stigma, even after all this time. I'm not here looking for an easy buck or a payout for doing nothing. You can see for yourself the way this whole thing has destroyed our business and I am just trying to get close to even."

"You can submit a request," Ryan finally said. "The woman who handles these things will get you a form." Then he took a long pause. "But you've been to this agency for help before, haven't you?"

"Are you talking about the investigation into the corruption in Opportunity that your predecessor Rick Hackman began last year?"

Rick was the former FBI Special Agent in Charge who also served with me and Eric Cooper as Board members for the Marine Corps Support Council. A state senator friend of mine had written the FBI, requesting an investigation into the corruptive elements I and others had encountered in Opportunity. Agent Hackman opened an investigation and, for all I knew, it was ongoing. The FBI does not comment on the status of any investigations, but a news article in the *Las Vegas Sun* in February 1997 confirmed through the senator's office that he had requested an investigation, after I and other developer constituents of his were encountering shakedowns in Opportunity. Hackman told me they'd opened a file, I was called in for an interview with two of their agents, and now Ryan's implication was an indication the investigation was continuing.

"Yes sir, I looked forward to a federal prosecution of those in the City of Opportunity's 'golden circle of influence' once your agency confirmed what had happened to myself and other developers."

Ryan continued, "That's right. It just seems kind of funny to me that you want our help on the one hand, then have the other hand out for money."

Despite my anger, I remained calm and professional. "Sir, with all due respect, the corruption that's going on in Opportunity is so wrong, you should go after the guilty and get to the bottom of it. It has nothing to do with this Castaways situation we're discussing. I was doing nothing but conducting business at my bar when your people picked my parking lot for this operation and the ensuing fiasco. Why didn't you use a park or public property? Why did you use private property? I've been injured and I'm just asking for some restitution to help me keep the doors open. Not a gain, just to possibly be back where I was if the FBI had never set a sting up in my parking lot."

"Interesting," was his only response.

Not long after we met, he proceeded to personally kill the federal investigation that was going on against the Opportunity gang.

Dan and I were both shell-shocked, but we never filed the damages claim. We just bit the bullet without a fight. In the meantime, we were stuck with a bar where people were afraid they'd get hurt if they stepped inside.

As life would have it, however, the name associated with our economic downturn also resulted in an unforeseen opportunity.

What's in a Name?

The nearby Showboat Hotel and Casino had a problem. Everyone knew the Showboat as a longstanding fixture in town; it opened in 1954. But when some local investors bought the property, the seller, a large corporation with other casino properties around the country with the same brand, limited the time span that the buyer could use the name. That deadline was approaching.

I was quite surprised when their attorney contacted me about buying the name of our bar. Selling it was doable; for a new name, we'd just change our signs and menus—all for the right price, of course. I had no idea what to charge them, but I heard from a friend that he believed Steve Wynn paid around $90,000 for the "Mirage" name from an old motel on the south Strip. I thought I'd try to sell ours for more. I gave it a couple of days and set a meeting with the attorney.

We met at a local restaurant for lunch. We knew many of the same people, both of us having been in Las Vegas for a long time. Eventually, we got down to discussing the deal. I gave a short presentation about the anticipated costs of a change—the hard costs of signs and menus, the soft costs of the goodwill of a popular tavern, and the royal pain in the ass it would be. Then I told him that it was a take it or leave it deal and delivered the terms: $420,000 total, with $20,000 down and $20,000 a year for 20 years. Wherever I could set up an annuity, I did. Artie, Dan, and I would do very well under this deal.

The attorney was visibly surprised at the amount. He explained that the reality-TV show *Survivor* had recently premiered to exceptional reviews and a large audience. The Showboat investors intended to redecorate their public spaces in an entire Survivor-Castaway theme. He told me he was authorized to offer $50,000.

I didn't miss a beat. "Thank you for meeting me and I'm sure we'll see each other again," I said, getting up to leave.

"Can I call the partners to see if they'd like to make a counter offer?"

"I don't see why not, as long as the partners are all together and if a decision is imminent," I responded. Knowing that the three owners were standing by, I concluded that their desire for our name was definitely high.

Their attorney stepped away from the table and made the call. Not unexpectedly, he returned with a counter offer of $75,000 cash, all up front. I thanked him, told him that my proposal was firm, and if they didn't want the Castaways name, that was just fine with me.

He made another call and returned with a handshake, indicating that we had a deal—my full asking price and the terms I proposed. Dan and Artie would be delighted.

After the name was sold, we changed the name of our place to the Alibi Casino.

In the ensuing years, the Alibi earned decently, but never made it back to the kind of money we'd been generating before the parking-lot incident. When the recession hit in 2008, construction work ceased and seemingly overnight, a huge portion of our customer base was forced out of town. There's little you can do when your remaining customer base just doesn't have disposable income. Things got so tight that Dan and I even waived the rent the bar was paying us as its owner-landlords.

With no economic relief in sight and no profits for the Alibi in the foreseeable future, selling the place seemed to be the best option.

We eventually turned the Alibi over to an up-and-coming chain of gaming companies called King Enterprises. I met with their Vegas manager and offered to hand over the place for $0 going in. It wasn't like I could justify any kind of sales price with zero net revenues to show for the last two years. On the other hand, we wanted a premium rental return with annual cost-of-living increases. The manager extended his hand and said, "Deal!" We shook and the King Enterprises people were gems to work with. The paperwork was drawn up and rent commenced two months later. To this day, they pay on time every month. A decent conclusion to a roller-coaster history for the property.

CHAPTER 22

Breaking Glass

Way back in 1986, Dan and I started a company called Glass Supply.

After running Suburban Graphics for two years, we had bid on and were awarded a very large job to change over the front glass panels for all the Las Vegas Hilton's slot machines—hundreds of them! The Hilton had just completed a major casino remodel and wanted their slots to match the theme and colors of the new design. But then we learned that no local glass companies inventoried enough glass sheets with our required thickness and quality. Dan met with the Hilton people and explained the situation, asking for an extension on the deadline. They were obviously disappointed, but when he explained that every print competitor in town faced the same constraint, they agreed to give us the extra time.

Dan and I were relieved to hold on to the largest amount of work Suburban Graphics had seen to date, but Dan said, "We can't ever let this happen again. We need more control over the lifeblood of what we do." He had the brilliant idea of opening our own glass shop.

The real money for us was in sales at Suburban Graphics. But with our own glass company selling to our graphics company and other customers, Glass Supply could succeed as a new business. At the time, our art director at Suburban Graphics, Peggy, was married to Jay, a local glass cutter. Dan met with him and struck a deal in which Jay would own half the business as owner-operator and Dan and I would own the other half as silent partners. Our reasoning was that other printing companies competed with Suburban Graphics and if any of them won a print contract that we didn't, we could still sell them the raw glass, thereby getting a little piece of the action. The outside business would also tell us who was getting which jobs. Our print competitors wouldn't buy from Glass Supply if it was known that Dan and I were owners, so we stayed under the radar. If anyone ever asked, Jay could simply say he sold glass to us at Suburban Graphics as he did to most of our competitors.

Dan's idea was a natural and proved to be even more strategic. As Suburban was the leader in sales volume in our market, people would think, "Wow, if Jay is selling to Suburban, the biggest shop in town, we know he can meet the quality requirements and deadline demands," which were often tight and inflexible, whether the end customer was a slot manufacturer or casino.

Exactly that happened and before long, Glass Supply was selling glass to nearly all of our graphics competitors. Our product line grew to include all types of glass and mirror sales, shaping, beveling, and insulated window-unit fabrication. But now Jay had a decision to make: keep his share of the profits or sink them back in to grow the business. Dan and I were fine with either decision. Dan's only directive to Jay was, "Just make sure we get what we need for printing at Suburban Graphics." Jay reinvested and Glass Supply got so big that we had to expand our leased space twice to meet sales demands.

Just two blocks away from Suburban Graphics was a large glass shop in a 15,000-square-foot building on two-thirds of an acre. With a built-in ceiling crane for off-loading heavy crates of glass from eighteen-wheelers, plus two large roll-up doors on each end of the building, a heavy-duty forklift, glass racks and cutting equipment already in place, it was ideal for Glass Supply. It was also right in my wheelhouse as a working Realtor.

I met the owner, Hector Sanchez, and proposed a sale with a modest down payment. I'd waive the commissions, something no other broker bringing him a deal would do. That alone meant a lot to him, because whatever I proposed as a down payment wouldn't be negated by the seller commission. Hector knew of Glass Supply from our short time in the glass business, respected the good reputation we'd developed, and wanted a fast and clean deal. We agreed on all the numbers, signed the documents, and closed escrow in record time. And just like that, Glass Supply had a 15,000-square-foot home.

Sadly, several years later, Jay was in a serious car accident and couldn't handle the physical challenges of Glass Supply. By this time, Suburban Graphics had grown to a more than $10-million-a-year business.

Bob Valentin, a one-man air conditioning service company, was one of our early customers at our first bar, the Suburban West. He was a good all-around handyman and became a trusted friend. One day Dan said to me, "Bob might be a good choice for replacing Jay as a general manager at Glass Supply. It could help him and us at the same time."

We met with Bob and explained how we'd set up things to run. "We'll tell people you bought it from Jay and you're the new owner," we said, "and we'll stay in the background."

We shook hands and for a couple of years, Bob ran Glass Supply, performing well enough that neither Dan nor I ever had to walk in the door. We held all our meetings in our offices up the street at Suburban Graphics.

Suburban Travel

In 1995, at the ripe old age of 43, I started working less and traveling more and thought, "Why not open a travel agency?"

This was before the widespread use of Expedia, Hotwire, Orbitz and the rest of the online travel consolidators. And in those days, if you had an International Association of Travel Agents (IATA) card, you got free airline upgrades to first class, better rooms in hotels, and free familiarization, or "fam," trips all over the world. The major hospitality and transportation industries knew that happy travel agents meant referrals and more business.

Glass Supply had a lot of unused front-office space in which we could easily house a three-person travel business. The time that we didn't want people to know we owned Glass Supply had passed. Our print sales were now international and we were doing well enough that we no longer cared if our competitors knew they were buying their raw glass from us.

As was my custom with any new business I was starting, I went into Suburban Travel every day. While I was in the building, I met regularly with Glass Supply's General Manager, Bob Valentin. At one point, Glass Supply numbers had declined and I was moderately concerned about future profits and business viability. Bob believed our recent dismal-looking profit and loss statements were due to increased competition after two national glass suppliers had set up shops in Las Vegas. Dan and I figured that we could scale down, give up the original broadscale business concept, have fewer employees and related costs, and Glass Supply would simply sell to Suburban Graphics and the occasional competing slot-glass provider. Slot-glass profit margins were excellent, but other products we sold to the retail glass industry and contractors were far less profitable. So I was in and out of all areas of

Glass Supply throughout the day, while also going in to Suburban Travel. It became common knowledge to the Glass Supply employees that Dan and I were the true owners.

One afternoon as I entered the Suburban Travel space, a young counter employee of Glass Supply named David Duran approached me. I'd gotten to know him a little through my daily presence on-site. Looking around somewhat nervously, David asked, "Sir, can I come talk to you after work? Will you be down the street at Suburban Graphics?"

I said, "Sure." Clearly, he wanted to speak with me in private.

Yet Another Drug Problem

That evening, David appeared in my office at Suburban Graphics. After some introductory small talk, I asked him what was on his mind.

"Well," he said, "up until recently, me and everyone at Glass Supply thought Bob was the owner of the place."

"That's what you were supposed to think," I replied. "We had our reasons."

"No doubt, but there's things going on you should know about."

"Oh yeah? Like what?"

"Bob has a major coke problem."

Wow! I hadn't seen that coming.

"Thing is, with certain cash customers, Bob tells us, 'Don't write them up on a traditional invoice. Write them up on this other paper-work. Collect the cash and bring it to me.' I knew it wasn't right, but I figured if he wanted me to handle transactions in a way he could feed his habit, it wasn't really any of my business. But learning you're a part owner with Dan, well . . . if the money's going to him with your knowl-edge, it's not that serious. But if it isn't . . ."

193

"David, I don't know anything about what Bob's up to. That's not how I do business."

He nodded solemnly. "I didn't think so. The way you come in and greet us, and the general way you carry yourself, I just respect how you operate. I thought I should bring this to your attention."

"I appreciate you coming to me," I said. "And I could use a little more of your help. I need to be able to prove what's going on."

"I can give you a list of those customers and I can give you some estimates of what they buy. What else can I do?"

"Would you be willing to wear a wire? I'd like you to engage Bob in some conversations and get me proof that he's as implicated as you say. Otherwise, if we confront him, he could claim this is something *you're* doing and just trying to pin it on him."

"But Mr. Coury, I'd never . . ."

I motioned for him to stop. "I'm not saying you would, David. I'm just telling you what we need to be on guard against and prepare for. We're discussing a serious criminal matter."

"Yes, I understand. Whatever you want me to do, I'll do it."

I set David up with surveillance equipment I owned and he began recording his conversations with Bob.

Why did I have surveillance equipment readily at hand?

After my nightmare experience with Nielson in 1989, I began recording meetings with employees and others if loans were discussed, money owed was returned, and for virtually every other potentially serious matter I was involved in without a third-party witness.

Remember, I was still under a direct order from the Gaming Commission not to try to handle such things as thieving employees on my own. If anything like that should ever go wrong, I was to call the police. No "self-help," as they called it.

Every night David and I met to review the recordings he'd made that day. It was a stunning and disappointing process, as the guy I heard on the tapes bore absolutely no resemblance to the one I considered a friend, handed the keys to a business, and essentially made a profit-sharing manager.

"They'll never know. Screw them," I heard Bob tell David on the recording.

"What if they find out?" countered David, trying to get Bob to reveal more incriminating information.

"I'll torch this building so they can't prove anything against me," he barked.

With that, I knew I had enough to go to the cops.

"Wait," said David. "There's more. One of our customers, Smitty's Glass, owes us a lot of money. I know you've been telling Bob his unpaid receivables are so high that the company can barely pay the bills and you and Dan don't want to dump any more money into the operation."

David was exactly right. Bob always countered with excuses about breakage and business being slow and since I considered him trustworthy, I took his word at face value.

"Our numbers keep getting worse as a result of Bob's stealing and he's been feeling the pressure," David continued. "He wanted Smitty's Glass to pay the thirty thousand they owe to get you off his back. He asked me to take care of it."

From the uneasy way that David said this, I knew I didn't like the way the conversation was heading. "What did you do?"

"Well, Bob told me to do it by any means necessary and he knew me and my circle of friends, so he knew how far I'd go to carry out his order. I got a couple of my gangster friends together and we kicked in the door of his house and threw a beating on him and his adult son, who works with him," David said. "It got pretty hostile there."

I couldn't believe my ears. "We're talking about the owners of Smitty's Glass?" I asked, shocked!

"Yeah."

This was getting worse by the second. "Where do they live?"

"Opportunity."

Goddamn it! I thought.

"We roughed them up and told them we want the money you owe Glass Supply paid or we'll be back! Of course, they said they didn't have it, so we ransacked the house, stole some shit and left them tied up in the bathtub."

For a moment, I wasn't sure where to begin. "David, this is *not* how I do business. And now that I know this, I have to go to the police. But it will be better for you if you go into Opportunity right now and come clean. I appreciate what you were trying to do for me by recording Bob, but we can't ignore this. It's far bigger than embezzlement. The cops probably know about it already! They just haven't shown up yet."

"Okay. I'll do whatever you say."

"That's right, you will. As in right now."

To David's credit, he went straight in and they directed him to the esteemed public servant we caught lying in his written reports and again at our preliminary hearing, none other than Detective Ted Banich.

Am I the Only One Who Has To Play by the Rules?

David told Banich everything and when I heard about it later, I sure as hell knew what Banich was thinking. In my opinion, he'd already called his co-conspirators in Opportunity politics and said, "We've got Coury this time." I could picture Stan Gunster, Brenda Beals, and a few other ethically questionable, small-town bullies celebrating at the thought that their bulldog with a badge was hot on my trail. Yet again.

"State records show that Ron Coury and Dan Hughes own this property and company," said Banich.

"Yes, sir, that's true," replied David.

David said Banich's expression was pure ice. "We were coming out there next week to talk to you guys. As you might imagine, the owner of Smitty's came in right after this incident. You're looking at major felonies here." And then came the kicker. "But if you tell us that Ron Coury ordered the home invasion, you'll get a pass—full immunity, free and clear."

"But he didn't order it," David said. "I didn't even know he owned the company at the time."

"Be that as it may," Banich said low and slow, "point the finger at Coury and you walk away free from any criminal prosecution. Don't help me and I'll make it my personal mission to see you wind up in prison for the majority of what's left of your living days."

"I can't do that," said David. "I'm not going to lie. Mr. Coury had nothing to do with this. I'm sure of it!"

When David came back and reported all that happened, I was truly moved. His honesty and loyalty rang true, despite the assured prosecution, conviction and prison time he was facing. "For now, I've got to deal with Bob," I said. "But David, you did the right thing. When they move to prosecute you, I won't forget this. That, I promise you."

David thanked me, knowing he'd screwed up by following Bob's orders.

Next, I contacted the Las Vegas police financial-crimes division and told them, "I've got a manager who's embezzling. I've got him on tape talking about torching my building if he gets discovered and I need someone to come see me and deal with him."

The detective there seemed more interested in getting me off the phone than seeing that justice was done. And here I was, trying to play by the rules. "We don't send detectives out for that kind of thing. Just confront this guy yourself."

Now maybe, under normal circumstances, that would be fine. The detective didn't know all that had happened to me before this.

I called my gaming attorney, who was beside me at the Gaming Commission hearing when I got my marching orders on how to conduct business with thefts in the future. "Tony, I don't know what to do. The police want me to just confront Bob and that's exactly what the Gaming Commission ordered me never to do again."

He quickly gave me a name, Pat Burke! "This guy is the Chief of Enforcement at the Gaming Control Board. He was at all your Winners hearings and will know the position you're now in. He's a good guy and will help you. They have their own agents who carry badges and guns. Talk to him."

None of the problems at Glass Supply were a gaming matter, but I was a gaming licensee. Anything I did in life, gaming-related or not, fell under the Control Board's scrutiny. This may sound a little extreme, but the Nevada Gaming Code holds all gaming licensees to a higher standard—and not just in the operation of our gaming business, but in all we do. The Board may deem "any activity on the part of any licensee" that reflected badly on gaming to be grounds for disciplinary action.

Amazing! Right? But that's the law if you chose to participate in the privilege of gaming in Nevada. So how I dealt with Bob wasn't an option for me.

I called Pat, the Chief of Gaming Enforcement, who clearly remembered me from my Winners hearings. "I've caught my general manager at a non-gaming business embezzling. I have indisputable recorded proof and a witness. As the Commission ordered, I tried to involve the police, who told me to confront this guy, Bob, myself. The problem has escalated to the point where I have him on tape, describing how he'll burn down my building and destroy all the evidence if I learn of his scheme. There's too much at risk now to let another day go by without stopping him."

"Mr. Coury, I totally understand the position you're in. We'll help you. I'm going to send an agent over. Invite Bob into your office for the conversation. The agent will be outside your office door. I don't want Bob to know he's there, because I want him to speak freely. Just leave your door open. When Bob is in and sitting down and facing you, my man will be in the doorway."

A year later, I'd hire a security company to install what they called "bullet cameras" and microphones in my office. But for this day, the technology was simpler. I put an old-style (but state-of-the-art at the time) video camera inside a beer box with a hole cut in it and pointed it at the chair where Bob would be sitting.

The Gaming Agent, Randy Dorfman, arrived early. He examined the office layout and said he'd position himself in the adjacent office. Once Bob entered my office, he'd come out and stand just outside my door—invisible to us, but only feet away and able to hear and witness all that was said. Between the video camera and the gaming agent, no one would successfully claim I did or said anything that I didn't!

I wanted to ensure that Bob came over, so I used an additional ploy. Weeks earlier, prior to learning of his thefts, I'd offered him a 28-foot Sea Ray boat I owned and wasn't using. He stored it at the Glass Supply back lot—fenced and secured. I called and told him I had someone who wanted to buy it for a nice price. By now, I knew he was on the dash for cash, needing money wherever he could find it for more coke. I told him they'd pay $15,000 for it, but wanted it today so they could tow it home to San Diego. I said I'd split the money with him if he brought it over to my building. He jumped at the chance.

Bob arrived, all smiles and lighthearted. I had my handyman and friend, Jimmy, standing by with his truck. Once Bob unloaded the trailer from his truck and entered the building, Jimmy would hook it up to his truck and take it to a safe location until I knew how this all ultimately played out. The stage was set.

"I'm gonna get right to it, Bob," I said as soon as he sat down, knowing the camera was rolling and Agent Dorfman could hear everything. "I know you've been stealing from us and I know how you've been doing it."

Bob immediately launched into a denial so seemingly heartfelt that if I hadn't known what was going on, I might have believed him. I played excerpts of some of the most damning tapes, all implicating him without a chance of any doubt.

When Bob knew I wasn't buying his story, he was convinced that the game was up. "So what happens next?" he asked. "I go to jail?"

"Not necessarily. I'll need you to sign a note that you'll pay us back. After what happened to me at Winners, my attorney advises that I have to inform the police of what occurred, but he also said if we settle our differences civilly, the authorities aren't likely to get involved. If you don't want to settle this privately, then yes, I'll hand you over to the cops today and let justice take its course."

Shaking, but with some signs of relief, Bob agreed to sign.

When he was done, I called out, "Agent Dorfman?" He entered and for a flash, Bob was shaken and confused. "Bob, this gentleman isn't here to take you in. He's a gaming agent, here for my protection and as a witness. He's just going to escort you out of the building, so you can't later claim that I laid my hands on you or coerced you in any way."

Bob thanked me profusely, then left the building without incident.

The next time I heard from Bob was a couple of weeks later, when he contacted me by phone. "I'm not paying you back," he said. "My attorney says I don't have to."

"Bob, if you don't, I'll press charges," I replied calmly.

"Go ahead."

Bob didn't know that I'd videotaped the entire meeting and confession. The recordings that David had made further sealed his fate. If pressed, I was confident our evidence would result in a conviction.

Friends in High Places—Again

I contacted former DA Matt Moore, explained what had transpired at Glass Supply, and said, "With my former general manager refusing to honor the deal we made, Dan and I want to press charges. I don't want this getting settled and dismissed and I don't want it going to the bottom of any assistant district attorney's work pile, waiting years for a prosecution. I'd like to hire you to steer this through your former office. Will you take this case as my advocate? Stay on them and see it through?"

"It's just money, right? He hasn't done anything physical yet?" Matt replied. "Go with a civil suit and we'll get you a judgment."

"Matt, we took this guy in. We treated him like family. I gave him a percentage of the profits as a bonus and a partnership in a boat I owned. His thank-you to me was a thumb in my eye. A civil judgment is too little for what's happened here."

I wanted this to go the criminal prosecution route. After his conviction, either the judge would order restitution or we'd sue civilly and win a judgment. Matt grew convinced that I was right and together, we took the package of evidence over to the DA's office.

Matt was deeply respected at his former digs. When we walked in, we were treated like royalty. It was also a great case, all put together for them. They'd file the charges and a warrant for Bob's arrest would be issued. It would be done in a matter of days.

A week later, Matt called and said a warrant had been issued.

"Great. When do they pick him up?"

"Well, they don't, not unless he's a violent criminal. The warrant is in the system. If he ever gets pulled over running a red light or the police encounter him in some other way, they'll see the warrant on the scope in their cruiser and they'll bring him in."

Months went by, nothing happened, and I started thinking Bob had to be the best driver in the world. People I knew around town were telling me he was out and about, bar hopping and feeling untouchable. Clearly, since nothing happened to him and not knowing a warrant was waiting, he surely believed he was in the clear. In the meantime, he was telling everyone that I was lying, he never stole anything, and that basically, I was an asshole ruining his reputation for no good reason.

Frustrated beyond words, I called a Metro patrol sergeant, Randy Sutton, who worked the sector where Bob lived. As a longtime friend, I'd socialized with him often over lunch or dinner. Knowing all I'd been through with Opportunity and Pete Nielson, Randy was angered by Bob's betrayal of my trust and friendship.

"Randy, how about you send a couple of your guys over and execute the warrant?" I asked. "Is that breaking any rules?"

"Not if there's a warrant it isn't."

Just what I wanted to hear. "Christmas weekend is coming up. Let's do it right beforehand. Staffing at court will be very light, right? He'll spend a few days in jail waiting for a judge to come to work, won't he?"

A chuckle on the other end of the line. "Most likely, unless he knows someone!"

I gave Randy Bob's full name and Social Security number. "If his pickup is in the driveway, he'll be home. Don't knock on the door and tip anyone off, unless his truck is there."

"I'm on it, buddy," Randy said. "I'll call you when it's done and tell you how it went."

Later, Randy called me with a blow-by-blow account. He sent over two cops in one patrol car. A knock at the door and there was Bob. "Mr. Valentin, would you please step outside?"

"Why? What's this about?"

"Sir, we have a warrant for your arrest."

At this point, Randy told me that Bob started screaming at the top of his lungs. "Who does Ron Coury think he is?!"

Even on the way to the station, Bob was still apparently fuming. "Fucking Ron Coury can't get away with this!"

The two officers had no idea who he was talking about; they were just doing what their sergeant told them to do. Though the image was entertaining to visualize, I was somewhat saddened that this was happening at all, as I'd lost what I had believed to be a dear friend.

Matt stayed on it with the assistant DA assigned to our case and the trial date came quickly. At the trial, Bob and his lawyer claimed it was all an accounting error, Bob was an innocent victim, and I was overreacting and actually coerced him to confess.

But then, Matt and I produced the videotape of the meeting and the audiotapes of Bob and David discussing his thieving schemes in detail. Added to that, Agent Dorfman had witnessed the meeting and David, who'd yet to be prosecuted for the home invasion, was there as well. In an instant decision by the bench, Bob was convicted of embezzlement and received a five-year suspended sentence. If he stayed out of trouble, he could remain a free man. Full restitution was court-ordered.

In the end, I was glad things worked out the way they did. Bob refinanced his house and paid Dan and me back the entire balance of the money he'd stolen.

As for David, he retained a prominent local attorney, a family friend, but even he couldn't erase the fact that David was guilty as charged. He was prosecuted and convicted. Despite his inappropriate and possibly illegal efforts, Detective Banich never persuaded David to lie. And true to my word, I stood by David. When he was sentenced to 15 years in Nevada state prison, I wasn't about to leave him hanging.

I called my old buddy Eric Cooper yet again. By then, he'd retired from the Las Vegas Police Department and, with his wife, moved to northern Nevada. I'd never had a reason to learn anything about the prison system, the Parole Board, or any other criminality-related people or departments. Faced with David's current situation, I sought Eric's knowledge and advice. Amazingly, I learned he served, of all things, on the Nevada Parole Board. He knew all about my Glass Supply embezzlement developments from our regular talks over the phone. But David's sentencing was news to him.

"Eric," I said, "I need to help this kid out. Opportunity tried to screw me again and he did right by me. I've got to do whatever I can to help him."

"Do you know who's on the Parole Board with me, Ron?" he asked.

"Who?"

"Norm Ziola."

My old buddy who had my back with the slot-machine slugger and who'd helped get me my Honorary Deputy Sheriff's badge! "I'll be damned!"

Eric and Norm lobbied for the needed votes and got David out of prison in under a year. It was a small miracle. David was elated and has since followed my guidance and mentorship to the letter, now operating successful businesses of his own in both Las Vegas and San Antonio, Texas.

CHAPTER 23

Snake Hunting

Though we were in the process of taking Opportunity to court for a judicial review of the denial of our nonrestricted gaming license, that day never came.

Instead, in 1992, the city proposed a settlement, allowing Winners to have 40 slot machines, a couple dozen more than the 15 we were allowed on our restricted license, but far fewer than the 199 we were applying for. In our discussions, city officials claimed they intended to severely limit gaming in the Ashby Heights area and that our 40 slot machines would be more than twice as many as they'd allow for everyone who came after us. We also knew that litigation would take years and we hoped to get the full allotment of machines in Winners to help pay our mounting costs.

So even though we'd built a record that we could take to court and likely prevail, when the settlement offer came, we accepted it.

However, the playing field we were on was even more tilted against us than at the first hearing. By now, Sabrina's had opened with 199 machines, right up the hill from Winners. Simon's Casino & Brewing Co., across the street from Sabrina's, was in full swing with 199 machines, eight live table games and a sports book. The Bonanza, a full-blown high-rise hotel-casino complex, was just down the street in the opposite direction. Many other applicants who had yet to build their places had approvals to operate all that gaming, even though they'd never made any substantive presentations to the Council. Last but not least, guess who else had applied for three nonrestricted gaming locations in Opportunity and had them approved without anywhere near the presentation we made to the City Council of which he was a member? His three places were approved on what amounted to a consent agenda, approving multiple items in one swift vote. Good ol' Stan Gunster was represented by Attorney Mark Milano. Sounds rather incestuous, doesn't it?

Indeed, Dan and I attended the City Council meeting where these applications sailed through the approval process. We were there to settle the city's counterproposal to our original application for the nonrestricted use permit for Winners.

But the barracudas weren't done with us yet.

More Blatant Shenanigans

At the 11th hour, as we were signing the settlement agreement, we found that the City Attorney's office had thrown in extra language we hadn't previously agreed to. In addition to limiting us to 40 machines, the settlement unexpectedly stipulated, "Coury and Hughes cannot ever again come before the City of Opportunity for additional gaming. This use permit goes with Coury and Hughes. If they ever sell, that new applicant will then have to come forward for a use permit."

Though stunned, I was burned out from the investigative and legal expenses of clearing my name in the Nielson debacle, not to mention all the accompanying bills to make a comprehensive presentation at our hearing. I just wanted to stop spending and start earning. Dan was in full agreement. We signed the settlement and waited for the scheduled meeting where the Council would formally adopt the settlement.

Around the same time, many changes were taking place in state and local laws regarding nonrestricted gaming, which made it even more important to get the whole thing over with. Bowing to pressure from the Nevada Resort Association, the state legislature had enacted a law that limited any business other than hotel-casinos to 15 slots. Only applications filed with the Gaming Control Board prior to July 1, 1992, would be honored.

If we were a 40-machine operation, we'd be forever grandfathered as a licensed nonrestricted-gaming location. On the flip side, if we continued the fight in court and lost, we'd be forever precluded from reapplying for more gaming, which the new law disallowed. Had we known we'd be destined to operate a 15-machine location, we could have built a small tavern for less than half of what we'd spent on Winners. Accepting this 40-machine limit prior to the enactment of the new state law was the best strategy available to us, no matter how unfair it truly was.

On June 25, 1992, just six days before the new law went into effect, we were on the agenda before the Opportunity City Council to have our settlement agreement adopted. As Dan and I sat waiting for our item to be called, we watched in disbelief as our old "friend" Mark Milano, representing multiple new locations, successfully secured approvals for Gunster's three places and a few others to operate up to 199 machines and nine live table games. There wasn't one word from a single professional witness, nor any opposition from a single member of the community. Milano merely stated that this would be good for the city, creating jobs and generating tax revenue, and the Council approved them all.

Obviously, we'd been misled into believing our 40 machines would be unique and that gaming would be severely limited throughout all of the Ashby Heights area of Opportunity. But if we tried to back out now, there was no telling how that would affect us, with the new law being enacted six days later. Ah . . . the foot of Gunster, on my throat, again.

Adding insult to injury, Gunster was the lone vote to deny our settlement agreement! Despite his nefarious personal agenda, we received the approval to operate 40 slots, grandfathered under the new law and presumably able to fight another day. Down the road, we'd deal with the last-minute condition that we never again ask for more gaming. Now it was time to make this 40-machine deal happen and start generating increased gaming revenues.

Our approval didn't come without some last-minute jabs from the Council. The mayor, Virginia Daley, babbled about how applicants who didn't agree with Council decisions shouldn't sue the Council, and future applicants shouldn't believe that suing the Council would be in their best interest, despite her willingness to settle our specific matter.

Councilman Paul Ruggiero also went on record as they were preparing to vote on "ordinance-exception" language, allowing the Council to waive hotel-room requirements for nonrestricted gaming under "certain conditions"—meaning, of course, for their friends. He actually stated that they were writing this waiver for "certain applicants," but wondered aloud what the Council would do if others (as he stared down at me) tried to benefit from it as well.

This Council was so unjust and clearly unconcerned about how transparent their intentions were, it turned my stomach. But I assured Dan that this settlement was the best thing for us long term; one day there would be a different Council and what was occurring here wouldn't stand.

We operated our 40 machines for a couple of years, but had serious competition from the flood of places offering greater gaming diversity. We desperately needed to get a date for Council reconsideration of our settlement agreement. Even if we were denied, we could take that to court for a review of their selective treatment of us. But not a single Council member was willing to put us on the agenda.

It was tough to compete with new places that had so many more gaming options. Previously, on any given Friday, we'd cash $150,000 in paychecks, primarily from construction workers who preferred to cash their checks with us rather than at a bank. But as the big boys opened their hotel-casino down the street and all the competitors around us targeted blue-collar workers, it decimated our business. "Cash your paycheck with us," their ads proclaimed, "and get a free token to play our million-dollar slot machine!" or some such pie-in-the-sky promotion. We couldn't compete with an offer of $1 million in cash, no matter how remote the chance of winning might be. When the Bonanza Hotel and Casino opened, not long after we did, our Friday check cashing of $150,000 dropped to $30,000. It was hard to watch how this city was affecting us with their corrupt and preferential ways.

Armed with these facts, we visited Opportunity City Council members, one at a time. Our statement was simple and direct: "When we made that deal to settle at forty machines, your staff told us you were going to restrict gaming in our area. Not only haven't you restricted it, you've done exactly the opposite and we're having trouble competing with all the places that you've licensed and approved for more gaming than we have. This is extremely unfair!"

I'm sure by now you can imagine what the responses were. "Sorry, we made a deal. You said you wouldn't ask for more."

I met with my lawyer. "Let's take them to court. This is totally out of line."

"Ron," he said, "the way it works is, you can't just run to court. In order for me to have something to put in a petition for judicial review, you need them to put it on an agenda and deny you."

"So I'm handcuffed?" I asked. "The fact that I can't get on an agenda to get denied keeps me from ever being considered?"

"Unfortunately, that's how it works."

Finally, the solution came to me. It was so clear. "We need a new Council member, someone who'll be fair and impartial," I said. "And it just so happens that my old 'pal' Stan Gunster is running for re-election."

Game On!

I spoke with many of my customers who lived in the area and learned that Arnold Stafford and Dorothy Jones were filing for election, both running to replace Gunster. I reached out to each of them and wasn't surprised to learn they'd heard about me and my battles with the city. In lockstep with Gunster, Councilman Chuck Becher was another die-hard opponent of mine, against whom a young and eager newbie to politics, Bonnie Hessman, had filed to run—just the kind of new representation we'd hoped for. I met with and liked Bonnie, so our support went to her, along with Arnold, and Dorothy.

All three candidates agreed that I hadn't been treated fairly and said they'd appreciate my support. However, being honest and morally minded (imagine that, in Opportunity), they told me they couldn't make any guarantees about what they'd do if elected, because it would be unethical. There couldn't be even the vaguest semblance of quid pro quo.

"I'm not looking for guarantees," I told them. "This Council has already told me, 'Don't ever come talk to us again.' We need people on this Council who'll treat all applicants fairly. So I'll do what I can for you."

With that, we contributed to all three of their campaigns. But I wasn't done with that snake Gunster, not by a long shot.

I had my investigator look into him. I knew what I knew about him, but I didn't know what I didn't know. We learned some interesting new things I could use and launched a multi-month "Vote No for Stan" campaign. We never endorsed anyone; we didn't care if you voted for Arnold Stafford, or Dorothy Jones, or any other new candidate, as long as the name wasn't Gunster.

At the time, KJUL radio, 104.3 FM, could be heard anywhere in the valley, playing easy-listening music like Bobby Darin, Frank Sinatra, Nat King Cole, and the like. It was the station with the most listeners who were likely voters. I became friendly with Teddy Weinstock, a Suburban West customer and a manager at KJUL, and made him a simple proposition.

"Whenever Stan Gunster runs a spot, I want you to run one of mine right after it. Every time. I'm not giving you a budget; I'm not telling you what I will or won't spend. You charge me for as many spots as you run." I doubt Weinstock had ever heard anything like that before.

The first ad I had recorded sounded like an urgent news announcement, with no music, just an authoritative no-nonsense female journalist intoning:

"Attention Opportunity voters. Stan Gunster is running for re-election in Opportunity. It is time for a change in Opportunity. Stan Gunster has failed to file an annual financial disclosure. Stan Gunster has failed to list all the corporations he is involved with. With one corporation Stan Gunster failed to list, he claims it has done no business. To the contrary, the Review Journal reports that this company's annual sales were projected at one and a half to two million dollars. What Stan Gunster has done violates Nevada state law. Stan Gunster also failed to ever list his land investment company, controlling numerous Opportunity properties. This also violates Nevada state law. Stan Gunster, what you've done is obvious. The facts are public record and are being investigated. That's why it's time for a change in Opportunity. Opportunity voters, please vote on

May second for the candidate of your choice. Let's say no to Stan Gunster. Paid for by Dan Hughes."

And we were just getting warmed up. A second one went like this:

"Attention Opportunity voters. Stan Gunster is running for re-election in Opportunity. It is time for a change in Opportunity. For about a year, Stan Gunster has driven a mint condition, 1950s-era, Chevy classic with dealer license plates. It appears this vehicle is owned by an auto dealer who appeared before Stan Gunster and the Opportunity City Council to develop a major auto mall in Opportunity. Stan Gunster is not a car dealer. Stan Gunster claims the use of this vehicle was a test drive. I am sure that all of us would love to test drive the car of our choice for a year. It would be great if the average citizen could avoid paying car insurance and registration fees rather than just an elected official. Stan Gunster, what you've done is obvious and that's why it's time for a change in Opportunity. Opportunity voters, please vote on May second for the candidate of your choice. Let's say no to Stan Gunster. Paid for by Dan Hughes."

As Stan produced a new ad, I'd get a copy of it from Teddy and write one that responded to his cries sounding like, "Please vote for me!" and "Don't believe these false ads about me, I'm the victim!" Every ad I ran right after his was a direct reply to what his latest ad stated.

"Opportunity Councilman Stan Gunster is a master at sidestepping and dodging the truth. Everything he has done wrong is always someone else's fault. Sure, we made Stan Gunster vote on property development near his, without disclosing his personal interests. We made Stan Gunster do design work at his graphics company for developers appearing before him, and never disclosing his hidden relationship with them. And, I suppose, we made him drive that classic automobile with dealer license plates for up to a year after voting on the dealer's auto mall. Of course, we made him avoid vehicle insurance and registration fees while driving with dealer plates. I guess we made him omit vital corporate relationships on his

annual financial disclosures. The fact that the law requires these disclosures be accurate means nothing. We made him do it all. Sure we did, Stan. It's all our fault. Just say no to Stan Gunster on May second. Enough is enough. Paid for by Ron Coury."

And a fourth stated: *"Opportunity Councilman Stan Gunster continues blaming everyone else for his record. Sure, Stan Gunster voted to deny a legitimate existing business application for more slot machines. What Stan Gunster hasn't told you is, on June 16, 1992, he was approved for three liquor and gaming locations in Opportunity. Then on June 25, 1992, just nine days later, he voted to deny someone else the same use permit without disclosing his own plans to compete in Opportunity in the liquor and gaming business. Wouldn't it be great if we all could plan a business and use our power as a Councilman to limit competition? These items are public record and available to anyone to verify. Any hint of corruption in government and abuse of power should be investigated and exposed. Stan Gunster's acts are being exposed and investigated. Just say no to Stan Gunster on May second. Paid for by Ron Coury."*

Bringing down Stan Gunster for all his injustices was one of my most satisfying efforts. Every hour he spent deflecting real or perceived threats was an hour he wasn't being effective as a candidate. I drove him crazy with what I'd gathered from my spies, private investigators, friends and even his own associates. People love to talk, especially when they think they know something you don't. Everything I learned, I tried to use at the right time, in the right way, to drive this snake under the nearest rock.

For example, it would have been easy for me to get an attractive young woman to join his campaign in the perfect position to tell me what he was up to, where he'd be and when, what he and the campaign team were thinking. I did just that and anything I learned proved to be very useful.

I also hired a video-production crew with broadcast-quality cameras with the CBS logo on both sides, sporting official-looking CBS "60

Minutes" caps, to show up at one of his campaign speeches, for what appeared to be a taping for their Sunday-evening show. Their appearance at Gunster's rally totally stunned him and turned him into a babbling fool in front of prospective supporters. Watching him duck the cameras and reporter as he exited his event is an image I'll never forget. It portrayed him looking so guilty of something, as onlookers witnessed his rapid exit, that it surely cost him supporters and votes.

If the community at large knew more about what was occurring, I might gain support from voters, so raising community awareness could help in many ways. Anything that might cause people to seek out details, vote for a change, and maybe voice opinions to elected officials in my favor could help. So I sent direct-mail flyers to every household in Opportunity and ran full-page ads in the *Opportunity Home News* every week, citing new incendiary facts. To counter his erroneous accusations that Dan and I were outsiders, one flyer listed the dozens of charities we contributed to.

I also purchased advertising for large roadside billboards situated on major thoroughfares leading out of the City of Opportunity.

> *YOU ARE NOW LEAVING THE CITY OF OPPORTU-*
> *NITY, WHERE THE WISHES OF THE FEW DICTATE THE*
> *FUTURE OF THE MANY,*
> *WINNERS TAVERN*

Another read:

> *YOU ARE NOW LEAVING OPPORTUNITY, WELCOME*
> *TO THE UNITED STATES OF AMERICA!*
> *WINNERS TAVERN*

Also:

OPPORTUNITY DESERVES HONESTY IN GOVERN-
MENT. VOTE NO FOR GUNSTER ON MAY 2nd!
WINNERS TAVERN

Rumors I fed to his camp regarding improprieties I was told he'd engaged in worked their way up the ladder, directly to him. He was now worried about things that would never develop in actuality. That, and all my radio spots, billboards, and other media efforts contributed to throwing him off kilter as his image seemed constantly under attack.

With all this simmering and election day approaching, I went to get a photo of the classic auto that Gunster had been "test-driving" for so many months in its parking space in front of his business. As I was taking the picture, who should emerge from the building but Stan himself! Visibly agitated and looking exhausted, he approached me. "After all you've done to me, what now?"

"Not much. I just want the voters to have a clear image of this great car you've been test-driving for nearly a year. This picture will be prominently positioned in the next edition of the Opportunity Home News."

He looked defeated.

"You know, Stan, I had no idea we were in direct competition. You never told me about it. You never disclosed that you wouldn't support anything I did, because you thought we were taking business from you. Instead, you shook my hand and said you loved my project, then sandbagged me at the hearing and attacked each of my witnesses. That's a betrayal that goes beyond a simple disagreement. I take what you've done personally."

"When is it going to stop?"

I smiled. "Right now, if you like—downtown at Johnny Tocco's

Boxing Gym. I'll rent one hour of ring time; you sign a waiver and climb in the ring with me. We'll go bare knuckles, just you and me. If you can walk out of that ring with me down for the count, I'll stop everything—all the campaign efforts I'm spearheading. But to get there, you have to give me the chance to kick your punk ass and not get in trouble for it. Agree to that and win, it all ends—radio, direct mail, everything."

I doubted he'd take me up on it, but I was hopeful and had to give him the chance. Predictably, he just shook his head and walked away.

So the battle continued until Election Day, the day when Stan Gunster, the fair-haired boy of Opportunity, the incumbent shoo-in to defeat his upstart opponents, lost his Council seat to Arnold Stafford. In fact, we swept the field that election day. Bonnie Hessman also defeated incumbent Chuck Becher. I now felt I had a chance at two "Yes" votes and would just need a third. A new mayor, Michael Fazio, was also elected. A visit to the new Mayor was in my future in the hopes he might be my third supporter on the Council.

Gunster had won some early rounds against me, but as an old friend, G. Gordon Liddy, once famously said, "In the battle of wits, sir, you are unarmed!" Gunster was unarmed and something beyond that. Later, a *Las Vegas Review-Journal* reporter spoke with a professor at UNLV who talked about how what happened between the City of Opportunity and me had changed the face of local politics. He cited the fact that one businessman who was wronged and willing to go after the person responsible cost a sitting councilmember an election.

In the final irony, somehow Suburban Graphics wound up on Gunster's company's mailing list and, each year, we received a Christmas card. In the spirit of the season, I started sending a card in return, with a special heartfelt message for Stan.

"Dear Stan: If you ever think of running again, I have plenty of dirt I didn't use the last time around. I will never forget. Bring it on.

Best,

Ron"

Believe it or not, one year I heard back from him in the form of a certified letter that read simply, "Please stop sending us cards."

One More Unexpected Hurdle

I met with our new councilman representing Winners' geographic ward, Arnold Stafford. After providing him the rundown of my entire history with the past Councils, I asked him to place us on their agenda for a reconsideration hearing of our settlement agreement. All I wanted was the same type of license they'd granted to my two nearest competitors. Councilman Stafford agreed and as my ward representative, it was entirely appropriate that he be the one who placed the matter on the agenda for a hearing.

Trying to lobby for the three Council votes and avoid court, with the time approaching for our next round of use permit hearings, I invited Mayor Fazio to meet me at Winners, so he could see the inside of the establishment and determine for himself that it was a quality place—more than just another tavern—and a real asset to the community. I also invited a reporter, Jay Parmann, an employee of former Nevada Governor Mike O'Callaghan, to join us. Mike was also a columnist for the *Las Vegas News* newspaper. He'd written two editorials questioning Opportunity's treatment of me and urging the powers in place to start treating me more fairly. Jay was running Mike's well-read local community newspaper, the *Opportunity Home News*. Mike and I were fellow board members on the Marine Corps Support Council of Southern Nevada, as well as longtime friends. In addition to knowing me, Jay was a resident of Opportunity and quite interested in what was going on in his city. After our original Council denial and the oddities surrounding the hearing, like any good newsman, Jay suspected that something wasn't right and wanted to learn more. He knew his employer was already a friend and supporter of my cause.

After greeting Mayor Fazio, I got right down to business. "Michael, contrary to false rumors spread by my detractors, I'm not looking to expand the size of this building," I said, motioning to our surroundings. "All I want to do is put more gaming within these four walls. In exchange, the community gets a nice place to relax and eat a meal worth forty dollars for half that amount. I understand that not everybody is a fan of community-based gaming and in that case, they can just drive by and let me run my business like every other enterprise they choose not to patronize."

Fazio didn't hesitate after we toured the entire building. "I love it! This is great! My wife and I will come here. Really good job, Ron." We shook hands and I felt like I was one step closer to an approval—until Mayor Michael Fazio did exactly what Gunster had done the first time around. He badgered every witness I called. He told everyone in attendance that this kind of operation had no place in the community. The vote went against us. Again!

After the meeting, Jay and I went to see Fazio in his office.

"Mr. Mayor," I said, struggling to keep my demeanor calm and cool. "What happened? You said you fully supported my plans for Winners and now this. I'm confused, to say the least."

Like his pal Gunster, Fazio gave me the self-satisfied smirk of a person who acted like he was above the laws of the state or even those of common decency. "I never said that."

I glanced at Jay. "That's interesting. Because Jay was with me and he remembers hearing exactly what I did."

"Well, I guess both you guys need hearing aids, because I never said any such thing."

He thought he had me beaten.

"Okay, Mikey, if that's how you want to play it. Don't get me wrong. I'd respect you if you just disagreed with my project and said so from the start. That's your right. But I want you to remember this day, Mr. Mayor, because the time will come when you'll regret it. I make a much better friend than an enemy."

"Is that a threat?"

"No, it isn't a threat. But it is a promise. That's why I want you to remember that sometime in the future, you'll have a really bad day. And somewhere, somehow, I'll be at the bottom of it."

That day came sooner than Mayor Fazio could ever have imagined.

One night, he was having drinks in the exclusive House of Blues Foundation Room atop Mandalay Bay, fully comped no doubt. As I later heard, he was partying hard, drunk, and getting overly friendly with several women there, touching them inappropriately and against their wishes. I guess because he held a powerful position, he thought he could do whatever he wanted and get away with it.

What he didn't know was that a good friend of mine was a high-ranking corporate executive at Mandalay Bay. My friend also resided in Opportunity, was aware of the ongoing political shenanigans, and was disgusted at the level of corruption and favoritism. I was home one night when his phone call came.

"Hey, Ron, how's it going?"

"Still battling our Opportunity friends. You know me, never stopping 'til the fight is won. How about you?"

"Good. And I just did you a favor that's going to make your day tomorrow."

"Really? How'd you do that?"

"Just make sure you read the morning newspaper."

With a laugh, he left it at that, except for a promise that tomorrow would be a very good day.

And it was indeed. Come morning, I was up early and went to the driveway to bring in the paper. There it was, plastered on the front page:

OPPORTUNITY MAYOR MICHAEL FAZIO
ARRESTED AT MANDALAY BAY

Due to his behavior in the Foundation Room, Mandalay Bay security was called in. Back then and probably even today, if a high-profile politician or celebrity messed up in a Las Vegas hotel or casino, more often than not, security kept it quiet and internal, knowing that if they didn't involve the police, they'd have a favor in their back pocket. It's probably a good practice. However, my buddy knew full well how Fazio had screwed me, so instead of keeping it all in-house, he called Metro and asked the police to pursue it to the fullest.

Then came the really sweet part.

Still believing, apparently, that he was above the law, Fazio threw fuel on the fire by physically attacking the responding police officer, not a smart move under any circumstances. Sure enough, there was Fazio's criminal mug shot that morning, staring out balefully from beneath a banner headline that couldn't have been more humiliating if I'd written it myself.

And it was about to get even better. A private investigator I'd hired uncovered more dirt on the mayor. Apparently, his salary was being garnished for non-payment of debts, a little tidbit that got leaked to our local network TV news affiliate and wound up on the evening news. I didn't need to be named as a source. It was more than enough for me to see good ol' boy Fazio experiencing the payback I promised.

Naturally, with his arrest and the embarrassment of having his salary garnished, Fazio announced, shortly after, that he wouldn't be seeking re-election. His reason? The usual you hear from a disgraced public official. He wanted to spend more time with his family. He couldn't even come up with an original excuse! He might or might not have imagined it was me behind it, but if he ever reads this book, he'll know that my promise to him was fulfilled.

In the meantime, his term wouldn't expire soon enough for me.

CHAPTER 24

The Corruption Continues

Getting Gunster out of the way felt great, but with all the competition, the kick in the gut from Mayor Fazio sent us right back to District Court. Thankfully, getting on an agenda and being denied had its upside. Our 3-2 Council loss gave us the chance for judicial review in the Clark County court system. We were assigned a judge in the civil division and after hearing all the arguments from both sides, she was clearly moved. She ordered Opportunity's outside counsel, Jordan Lebowitz, to have the Council put us on an agenda and give us "a full and fair hearing." That was music to our ears—finally, a clear message from a court that the Council hadn't treated us fairly and had better do so immediately. A hearing date was set and we were filled with optimism.

We appeared before the Council, ready to make yet another comprehensive presentation, when the dishonorable Mayor Fazio, whose term in office hadn't yet expired, stopped me. He said there was no need to make a presentation; the Council knew all it needed to know.

I responded that the court ordered a full and fair hearing and shutting me down before I spoke would be looked on unfavorably by the judge.

I glanced over at Lebowitz, who had personally received the order from the court. He was silent, looking a bit confused. Nonetheless, he let the mayor go on with his instruction that I turn all my paperwork over to the City Clerk and dispense with the presentation.

Prior to the hearing, I'd met privately with Councilman Henry Gilliam and felt it went well. He'd previously joined the Gunster bandwagon against us but now seemed like he was reconsidering the matter. I entered the hearing with indications that Gilliam might consider us favorably, so we could win with three votes from Gilliam, Stafford, and Hessman and not have to return to court.

After Fazio shut down my presentation, another of what I believed to be Gunster's minions stepped up to the public podium.

Hearing that Gilliam was wavering, this supposedly upstanding Opportunity resident questioned the councilman's ethics in participating further, since he served on the Opportunity Boys and Girls Club Board of Directors, a charity Dan and I had contributed to. He wondered, aloud of course, if this might be a conflict of interest.

Gilliam turned to City Attorney Beals and asked her if he had to abstain. She'd also heard that his vote for supporting us was a possibility. Despite Gilliam telling her he earned no income as a volunteer board member and that our support for the charity didn't benefit him in any way, Beals told him she wasn't "comfortable" advising him on the matter and that he should seek a ruling from the State Ethics Commission, which would take months to obtain. She knew just what she was doing.

Without a legal opinion from his own City Attorney and a challenge from the community, Gilliam felt he had to abstain. The two new councilmembers, Stafford and Hessman, voted for approval. Ruggiero and Fazio voted against. The motion failed in a 2-2 tie. Of course, months later, the Ethics Commission ruled that Gilliam had no conflict and should have voted and, they added, that the City Attorney should have advised him so. But at that point, it was already back to court for us.

Here Comes the Judge

Given the unfair treatment we'd received, it was possible, even likely, that the judge would now actually grant us the use permit, which was within her power. This judge was an attractive female jurist, known publicly for enjoying high-risk sports activities. In a motorcycle-racing mishap, she lost her right leg below the knee and even though she walked with the aid of a prosthetic, few would ever take notice of her handicap. Living in town for over 40 years, I'd grown to know much about our longtime residents and always felt bad for her injury and the resulting impairment she'd face for the rest of her life. My admiration for her, however, ended when her true colors were revealed.

In the interim, between being snubbed by the Council and our next appearance in court, one Saturday morning I was in the steam room at Caesars Palace Spa. I was there nearly every Saturday for a massage and a quiet morning of rest. A local general contractor, also a regular at the spa, came into the steam room, sat next to me, and said, "You have a big case coming up in my friend's courtroom. It means a lot to you, doesn't it?" I didn't know it but he told me that they had grown up in the same neighborhood and were good friends their entire life.

"You bet it does. We've been fighting the City of Opportunity for years."

"Well, she knows I know you and asked me to tell you that you're a sure winner for fifty thousand dollars!"

I responded, "There's no way I'd commit a federal crime paying off a judge after playing by the rules for so many years. I could've probably bribed my way to approvals long ago, but I'm not breaking the law for anyone. Tell the judge to do the right thing and I'll be a friend forever."

"Okay, kid, it's up to you."

And that was that. He never mentioned it again, nor did I. I thought about approaching the FBI, but after my previous experience there with Jerry Ryan, I wasn't too optimistic that they'd care about someone soliciting a judicial bribe from me. Besides, I wondered if the contractor really did represent the judge, or if he might be taking some sort of shot at me.

I told my attorney about the bribe attempt. He said I did the right thing, but didn't feel we should say any more about it.

On the appointed day, in came the judge. My attorney told her how the Council ignored her order for a full and fair hearing, then voted again to deny our request.

The judge ruled from the bench that day—in favor of Opportunity. That's right, she ruled against us! Her summary judgment ruling meant the case was thrown out as having no merit, with no triable issues of fact! How could that be? She'd previously ordered that we get a full and fair hearing from the Council. How could there have been triable facts before and none now? I can give you 50,000 reasons, that's how!

Off we went, appealing to the Nevada Supreme Court. Represented by our law firm's best litigation attorney, Todd Touton, the plight of Winners was well presented to the justices.

By now, the genie had been long out of the bottle and there was no putting it back. With a huge operation like the Bonanza Hotel and Casino just down the street and Sabrina's and Simon's on our other side, I had a major concern about *ever* making serious money at Winners. We'd spent a ton battling the city and keeping our other businesses afloat, while all our competitors had more gaming than we did and were doing great. Our only chance of ever making real money at Winners might be through a sale, not operations.

In the time it took to get before the Supreme Court, Fazio's term expired and he was out as mayor. The newly elected mayor of Opportunity was a seemingly quality guy named Paul Stewart. All my recon on him indicated he wasn't part of the old-school crew. He and I had a good rapport and I candidly asked him one day, "Can we just get out of the court system and give Winners the use permit we've always been entitled to? I think we might have the votes with you and a new Council in place."

Paul replied that he was familiar with the history and was willing to work toward a resolution, but the city had spent so much money in legal fees over the years to get to this point, there'd be an uproar if he curtailed it now. He wanted to see how the Nevada Supreme Court ruled and then we'd talk. So we waited.

In 1999, 11 years after we purchased the parcel of land for Winners, the Supreme Court ruled. Their decision, among other things, found:

". . . We conclude that there exists a genuine issue of material fact as to whether gaming conditions in the Opportunity area have fundamentally changed since the signing of the settlement agreement so that the forty-machine restriction may constitute an inequitable and oppressive restriction on appellants' use of their property and confers no benefit upon respondents."

The justices were remanding it back to the District Court. I didn't relish the thought of going before that judge again. Not without paying her $50,000 in tribute. But with a favorable Supreme Court ruling published, it was time to see if Mayor Stewart was a man of his word. I called him. I said the Supreme Court had ruled and it was in our favor. Could both we and the city avoid any more legal fees and just settle this without going to court again?

Mayor Stewart agreed and said the court's ruling would be exactly what he needed to put this on an agenda. He did just that and we were granted an approval with a 5-0 vote for a limited gaming-use permit for up to 100 machines and five live games. This was less than the limited-gaming maximum of 199 machines, but I was the one to suggest these limits to the mayor, so it looked like he'd negotiated something away from us as he floated the settlement idea among the Council members. It could help him save face if needed and didn't hurt us, as we didn't have space for more gaming than that and never would. More than a decade had passed since our first planning hearing and it was finally done!

Kissing Opportunity Goodbye

Now we had a gaming bar we could sell at a nice profit. We could also operate it, of course, though it would only be machines and a sports book. I wanted to keep the value of the five live tables we were allowed as a bargaining chip for which a buyer would pay big dollars in a future sale. The tables had a lot of intrinsic value, but if I added them at this late date and they failed financially, I couldn't sell the bright future of live table gaming to potential buyers.

And frankly, after such a long beef with Opportunity, I wasn't eager to stay there. The best play was probably getting a premium price for our nonrestricted gaming-use permit and the fine facility we'd built, sell Winners, and go somewhere where we'd be appreciated.

However, I did make one significant addition to our gaming operation as we searched for the right buyer. With so many local sports books nearby, getting a northern Nevada–based sports book, from the Reno/Lake Tahoe area, to put a betting counter in a southern Nevada location might make sense, as their betting lines were sometimes different from those of our competitors.

I soon made a deal with a northern Nevada sports book operator, Cal-Neva, to put in a satellite sports book at Winners and it worked exactly as I hoped it would. All I did was get rent from them, no percentage of the action, but it definitely boosted our traffic. Guys popped in to see the lines and make a bet or two if they liked the numbers. While they were there they'd often buy a burger or beer, or play a slot machine.

Winners had a waitress who'd started with us at Suburban East. Jackie Sofia was a sharp, college-educated woman and happened to be my general manager Bob's sister-in-law. We'd originally opened Winners with my brother and Bob managing, but Artie, Bob, and James, the manager at Suburban East, were anxious to do their own thing. As Dan and I sold off the two Suburban Lounges, we helped them set up their own janitorial and maintenance business, BAJA Enterprises, an acronym for Bob, Artie, James, and (James's brother) Anthony. Anthony owned a plumbing company and they were all handy in their own way, so it had great potential to succeed. Dan and I helped them out with starting capital and by steering some corporate clients, friends of ours, their way.

That done, I promoted Jackie to general manager. She understood my general business philosophy: There's no substitute for doing something right and on deadline. She also shared my belief that just because there's a deadline doesn't mean you rush or do things half-assed. My philosophy was and is, if you come up short and try to tell me you didn't have the time to do it correctly, what made you think you had the time to do it over again? Doing it over always takes longer.

Jackie was a terrific GM and while things would never be what I originally envisioned for Winners back when we had nearly no competition on Main Street, we continued doing decent business, with lots of action on the machines and a packed dining room. Jackie even had the idea to promote the family aspect of our dining facility. She set up a big trunk, like a pirate's treasure chest, filled with inexpensive toys. Kids loved it right away. We began selling more meals and more drinks to moms and dads, and one parent often sat with the kids in the dining room, while the other played video poker for half an hour. We implemented a "Free Cab Home" policy, for anyone who'd had too much to drink. I opened an account with Vegas Taxi and was billed monthly for cab rides for customers. We still had the 120 beers from around the world and the Beer Battalion contest, where customers who sampled all the beers we offered won a custom-embroidered Beer Battalion jacket.

All told, we were nicely profitable, had a unique gaming license that generated superb revenues, plus the option to add more machines and table games for added value. We were perfectly postured for a profitable acquisition deal.

I put out the word among my many friends in the slot-route industry. Before long, I was approached by the Alan Investment Corp. from Arkansas, headed by a man aptly named Alan, who was looking for a nonrestricted gaming location.

As we began to hammer out a deal, I asked, "Do you want to buy the real estate or do you want to lease it? I value the real estate at $2.75 million, or you could lease the property for $20,000 per month."

"No," said Alan, "that's too high; we're just going to lease it."

I was more than happy with his answer, as we preferred renting it. Throughout my career, I'd made a habit of acquiring residential properties every couple of years, whenever I could pull together a down payment. Along with the commercial properties Dan and I owned, we'd each developed nice portfolios. There's nothing like owning your own property. We enjoyed selling businesses and then renting the real estate to the buyer, setting up an annuity for ourselves.

We structured the Winners deal so the rent would go up a few points every year, which helped protect us against inflation. Also, all repairs and ancillary operating costs were the tenant's obligation. A sweet deal for us—so sweet, in fact, that a couple of years later, Alan approached us about purchasing the property outright.

After years of leasing, they eventually bought the property from us. Of course, we sought and received optimal pricing for it.

CHAPTER 25

Pranks for the Memories & No One Hits a Home Run Every Time

I've been sharing a lot about my businesses and some of the scrapes I've been in, but I don't want to give the wrong impression. Despite the challenges I faced along the way, I've had a hell of a good time and shared more laughs with my friends than I can remember. Here are a couple of the more memorable examples.

A group of my New York friends and I once went on a Caribbean cruise. Every morning we all met for breakfast, then went and took it easy by the pool. Around 4 p.m., we headed to the spa for a massage or steam. Passengers either paid a flat fee to have unlimited access to the spa or a daily rate of $15.

One of my friends on the cruise, Steve Bistany, is a man of many endearing qualities. He's soft-hearted, gentle, and has a fun-loving demeanor, but he's also constantly looking for a deal. Rather than pay to access the spa each day, Steve waited until the receptionist wasn't looking and slipped through for free. Mission accomplished, he'd join us in the hot tub and proudly declare, "Got in for nothing. Didn't pay a cent." After hearing it over and over, I saw an opportunity to have some fun with him.

I secretly secured some of the cruise company letterhead and an envelope. Then, sitting down at one of the guest computers and using the printer, I crafted a letter from the spa director to Steve, demanding payment or risking ejection from the cruise at the next port of call. I incorporated a writing style that I thought might support its authorship by a British gal in management.

> *Mr. Bistany,*
>
> *You've been identified as a guest who has cheated Princess Cruises through repeated, unauthorized, and unpaid access into our spa facility area. Our surveillance records and accompanying information render it clearly evident that you've done this four times during the current cruise itinerary. In this act of theft, you have violated not only Princess Cruise's policy, but British Maritime Law and all such actions are cause for ejection at the next port of call. Unless resolved by you tomorrow, you will be escorted by security officers from the ship at the next island stop, your luggage will be left at the pier and you will be deposited there to arrange your own passage home. This will be all at your sole expense, with no credit due or forthcoming from Princess Cruises for the unused remainder of your cruise. Kindly present yourself at the spa desk tomorrow at 5:00 p.m. and ask for me. This matter must be rectified to avoid the undesirable alternatives described above.*
>
> > *Sincerely,*
> > *Ms. Samantha Whitingly, Spa Director*

That night, I arrived early for dinner, located the maître d', and gave him the sealed letter, along with a $50 tip, with instructions to deliver it to Steve at his table. I took my seat and shortly, out of the corner of my eye, I saw the maître d' hand the envelope to him at the table where he was seated a short distance from mine. He opened and read it, then started looking like he was about to become physically ill as he gazed around the dining room, no doubt hoping some of us would be watching him and laughing, so he'd know it was all a gag. No such luck for Steve.

After dinner, we all headed to one of the lounges for a cocktail. Steve walked in, clearly quite upset. "Cuz, I gotta talk to you."

"What's up, Steve?" I'd never worked harder in my life to keep a straight face.

He handed me the letter. As I read it, he began to practically hyperventilate. "Jesus Christ. Why did I do this? I should have just paid the fifteen bucks, goddamn it. Now I have to go down there and beg for forgiveness."

I saw the opportunity to sink the hook even further. "Hang on a second. You're telling me they delivered this to you at dinner? In front of your friends? They couldn't bring it to your cabin and deal with it privately?" I paused a beat. "Instead of begging forgiveness, you should show some righteous indignation. I think *they* owe *you* an apology!" I turned to our friend Rocco, who was also in on the gag. "What do you think?"

"Absolutely. He walks in there with his tail between his legs, they might decide to make an example out of him."

"You guys are right," steamed Steve. "Screw them! I'm a customer. I've lost a bundle in their casino every night. This is no way to handle something like this."

The next day couldn't come quickly enough.

At the appointed hour, we positioned ourselves along the back wall of the spa, so we could see the front desk through the tinted glass. Steve marched up right on schedule, a wronged man demanding justice. The clerk picked up the phone and the spa director, a very proper woman, appeared. Steve whipped out the letter and let her have it.

Thoroughly confused, the director took the letter, scanned it, then handed it back, shaking her head and pointing assertively to the register, undoubtedly now demanding payment. Steve got a look on his face, which we know and love him for; he knew he'd just confessed his entire crime to someone who knew nothing about it, but was in authority. Then he glanced through the window.

We were all there, laughing so hard that, well, with all the water around, it's likely some spillage occurred. Seinfeld fans know the term, "NEWMAN!" when something like this happens. As he saw us, pointed, and smiled, his expression tacitly exclaimed, "COURY!" To his credit, his response was brief when he paid his way in. "You fuckin' guys. That was a good one."

Unfortunately for Steve, that was far from the only time he was on the receiving end of one of these pranks.

For about 15 years, the same group of friends and our families vacationed in Myrtle Beach, South Carolina, at a beautiful oceanfront complex called the Kingston Plantation, where condos rented for as much as $500 a day. Budget-minded Steve found a $59-a-night room at a nearby Holiday Inn Express. Who could blame him? He was solo, hanging with us by the ocean every day, and could use any of our condos to change clothes or shower. Why spend hundreds just to sleep?

His room included a free breakfast buffet, but it ended at 9 a.m. and day after day, Steve slept right through it, as our group was out late every night.

Whenever he joined us at the beach, he'd grumble, "Dammit, I missed the free breakfast again!" On our next-to-last day, he announced, "I'm getting that breakfast tomorrow. I'm setting my alarm for eight just to be sure."

The following morning after another late night, I called his room early, affecting my best Southern accent. "Mr. Bistany, this is the front desk. Because of heavy volume this morning, we're extending the break-fast buffet by one hour, to ten a.m."

Grateful for another hour of sleep, he hit the snooze button. Making sure he'd have plenty of time to eat, he showed up at 9:30.

"What are you doing?" he demanded of an employee who was clearing off a table. "Breakfast is available until ten. Didn't you just call my room and tell me that?"

The buffet manager intervened. "I'm sorry, sir, the buffet always closes at nine a.m. sharp. We never extend it."

"As soon as the guy looked at me and said that," Steve later told me with a shake of his head, "I knew it was COURY!"

Along with the cruises, beach vacations, and practical jokes with my old friends came the failure of ventures and losses my partners and I sustained. Naturally, not all my business startups were successful, and I've had as many swings and misses as any serial entrepreneur and niche finder.

The Art Shop

The year Joan and I were married, 1975, a new style of framing pictures or keepsakes was introduced and known as decoupage. Decoupage was made by mixing together two clear liquid substances called Envirotex. Once combined and stirred, it dried clear and was as hard as plastic over whatever you poured it on. Fine art, photos, rings—virtually any objects or paper products were visible, but protected from damage or aging. The artwork was suitable to be hung as decoration in a home or business.

Decoupage seemed like a great business opportunity for Dan and me. We rented space in Commercial Center, which at the time was one of the largest and busiest shopping centers in town. We called our new business The Art Shop. I worked nights dealing, so doing 9-5 at the shop was easy. I handled custom decoupage production orders and other necessities in the back, while Joan manned the front counter. We also inventoried various pieces of art for sale and provided custom framing that we subbed out to a nearby framer, who wholesaled to us and we resold the frames at retail. A number of artists and hobby folks around town brought their work in for us to sell on consignment. Our little 2,000-square-foot store looked pretty good when it was full of displayed items. If I didn't have a custom decoupage order to work on, I selected a print from our inventory and decoupaged it for retail sale in our display area. My dad, Dan, and I each invested $10,000 for a $30,000 total bankroll to make this dream happen.

But it wasn't to be. We tried radio and newspaper advertising, with little result. Expenses began to add up and sales remained soft. We couldn't drive enough dollars through the register to stay open, even though Joan and I never took a salary. After about nine months, we gave up and closed.

I was broke again with no savings. I told my bosses at the Tropicana I'd take any overtime shifts that came available. They accommodated my request and shortly thereafter, I worked 42 days in a row. From time to time, when people on the next shift called in sick and it was busier than expected, they let me work a double shift. With overtime pay and another shift of tokes, life was good and I again started saving.

By the next year, I could afford real estate school and became a Realtor by day and dealer at night.

PRANKS FOR THE MEMORIES

Bungee Fever

In 1992, Dan and I were approached by Scott Tillman, a former Nevada Gaming agent we were friendly with. He'd done a lot of research on a new, high-risk, but exciting sporting activity and was looking to form a partnership.

Since the first bungee jump in 1979, the sport had grown to more than $50 million per year in sales around the country. The bungee business was easily and accurately tracked and all the operations paid for liability insurance each month based on their prior month's activity. Most platforms for the jumps were on cranes that could move from place to place, though some operations were permanently mounted.

Down the street from our office, Dan and I owned a large vacant lot next to a two-story building we also owned, used for storage and leased to tenants. It stood just between the I-15 freeway to the west and the Las Vegas Strip a half-mile to the east. Great visibility to a lot of traffic for this new business!

We wanted to do it right, with no temporary cranes and using only custom-made cords manufactured for our specific jump heights, proper insurance and full licensing. We located a used construction tower crane in California, certified as fully operable by a reputable crane dealer. We flew down and examined it and everything looked good. We agreed on prices for modification to our specs, delivery, and erection and $130,000 later, we owned a tower crane. Bungee Fever Las Vegas would soon be operating.

It took months to get it moved properly and safely installed, but finally we were ready to open. Fate, however, had a different plan for us.

Our very first weekend, there were three bungee-related accidents across the country. In each, cords appeared to break. In truth, the cords used were improperly fastened together, unlike our custom-made one-piece cords, specifically designed for our jump heights. All were captured on video and aired on national and local news programs for a week. The coverage started with statements like, "Well, if you thought bungee jumping was safe, watch this report and think again." I faxed a press release to each local media outlet, pleading with them to report the facts: The accidents were all at temporary parking-lot operations; none were fixed structures like ours; the cords were rigged. We had proof of licensing, full insurance coverage, and certification by a nationally certificated training facility and equipment supplier. There were no rigged connections, only mountain-climbing-grade carabiners and custom-made cords, all tested at thousands of pounds of pressure strength. We were licensed and inspected by the city as a legitimate amusement ride. I invited media folks to come and see our operation.

My releases were ignored. The inaccurate and incomplete reporting continued, as did the ever-exciting action video of people falling and getting hurt. We hoped business would "bounce back," literally! But months later, we pulled the plug on the venture and lost north of $300,000.

CHAPTER 26

The Toughest Battle

In 2005, the incoming president of Costa Rica paid a visit to Las Vegas. He wanted to bring Costa Rica into the 21st century and had a keen interest in developing his country's real estate. He was looking to introduce real estate schools, testing for agent licensing, and a system of homeowners associations for the growing number of condo complexes and housing communities in Costa Rica. He also wanted to bring in casinos.

Nevada State Senator Mike Schneider, a buddy of mine since the 1970s, was responsible for coordinating the president's tour of Las Vegas. Mike knew I was an entrepreneur, always looking for new deals. He recommended me as a casino developer and operator, as well as a longtime Realtor.

Mike filled me in and I was immediately interested in personally setting up and operating the real estate schools and a management company to coordinate the various homeowners associations boards of directors, in addition to leasing the right site for a full-fledged casino attached to an existing hotel. I'd always wanted a big property, but I never had the bankroll to build one. The timing was perfect too. Dan and I had recently sold a number of our businesses and we were looking for the next big thing to get into. I bought a plane ticket to travel to Costa Rica with Mike and his brother, Steve, to get things started.

However, life had other plans. In November 2005, I went to Santa Barbara for my annual physical with Dr. James Murray, a practice I'd begun 20 years earlier on the recommendation of my buddy, Eric Cooper.

I was in great shape, weighing in at a steady and muscular 185 pounds at 53 years of age. I regularly ran three to five miles around the lake adjacent to my house, even in 100-plus-degree summer heat, and enjoyed full workouts and lifting weights so much that I built a full gym in my home. Still, my dad had fought cancer for more than two decades, beating colon cancer in the '60s, but eventually losing his battle to pancreatic cancer in 2002 and, as I mentioned earlier, he had brothers and sisters who'd died from the "Big C." Deep inside, I always felt cancer would find me. Early detection and treatment were my hopes for surviving it. In-depth annual physicals were important to me and seeing Dr. Murray was ideal. Each year, he coordinated a thorough three-day physical and when the results were in, he sat down and meticulously went over all the findings with me.

As usual, my physical began at an hour-long meeting with Dr. Murray. He asked me about what I'd been doing the past year and how I had been feeling. During our conversation in 2005, I mentioned one small oddity I'd observed. "When I eat or have a drink, it seems like I have to clear my throat a lot for the first hour or two. Does that mean anything?"

"Let's find out."

Among a battery of other tests, he ordered a barium swallow, which operates like a moving X-ray. You drink the barium-laced liquid and the specialist observes what's going on as the fluid passes through your throat and esophagus and into your stomach.

When I was done with all my exams, on day three, I headed back to Dr. Murray's office expecting to get what, for the preceding 20 years, had been glowing reports. However, this time there was a small glitch. The radiologist noted that during my swallow test, it appeared that the barium passed over a small bump at the base of my esophagus. The radiologist believed it was probably just a small particle of food stuck on the esophageal wall. He advised keeping an eye on it and following up with another test the following year. But because of Dr. Murray's thoroughness and familiarity with my family history (he'd diagnosed and treated my father's pancreatic cancer), he looked over the report and asked if I could stay in town for another day.

"Why?" I asked, growing a little concerned.

"Because if it's just a food particle, fine. But an esophageal tumor, if that's what it is, is so aggressive, it can end a person's life in less than six months. You won't be around in a year to do another swallow test as the radiologist suggested, if my concern is warranted. Stay a day, I'll get you on a surgeon's table this afternoon, and they'll biopsy it. We'll find out for sure what that bump is."

"Wow," I said. "I'm leaving for Costa Rica on Monday for what could be the biggest deal of my life. A friend has put me in a position that most people can only dream about!"

"That's fine, Ron, but we need to get this done first. You'll be home by Friday, plenty of time before your Costa Rica flight."

I had the procedure done that afternoon, which revealed it was a tumor. When I walked in for my appointment the following morning, Dr. Murray said in his thick Boston accent, "I didn't get the results yet; let me call."

He dialed the phone and it didn't take long before I could tell something was seriously amiss. My worst suspicions were confirmed when he slammed down the phone. "Goddamn it, *cancer!*"

He took a moment to regain his composure. "The surgeon who did the biopsy told me last night he didn't like how the lump looked. It was jagged, not smooth, a telltale indicator, but I didn't want to worry you until we got the pathology report. It's not good, Ron. This will grow fast, pierce your esophageal wall, and attack your stomach and other organs in a matter of months."

I answered with a voice so calm it surprised me. "Okay, we're going to war. What do we do now?"

"A surgeon at USC Medical Center in Los Angeles, Dr. Tom Demeester, specializes in surgery for esophageal cancer. He's the only guy for you. I'll get you in to see him next week. You're not going to Costa Rica."

It was all hard to accept, because other than the need to occasionally clear my throat, I felt fine. Hell, I felt invincible!

Dr. Murray explained that even if I qualified for the surgery, only eight percent of people diagnosed with esophageal cancer survive it. I'm not a particularly emotional person, but when Dr. Murray stepped out of his office, I looked out the window by his desk and said, "Well Dad, I guess I'll be seeing you soon." A somber yet pragmatic thought.

The Good News—and the Bad News

I went home and broke the news to everybody.

"Don't worry," I said, "this is just another battle I'm going to win." I didn't mention that it was yet to be determined whether I was even a candidate for this potentially life-saving surgery or if my fate was already sealed. No need for the whole family to worry at that point.

I went to USC Hospital and met with Dr. Demeester. "I need to run my own tests and endoscopy," he told me. After two days of exams, he said, "The good news is you're an excellent candidate for surgery."

I wondered if he could hear my sigh of relief.

"There's more good news. I know this cancer very well and I've never encountered a tumor this early in its development. I don't know how Dr. Murray found it so early, but you're lucky he did, because the sooner we get it, the better it is for you. You're in remarkable shape for a fifty-three-year-old man. My surgery takes anywhere from eight to twelve hours, so I prefer someone healthy and in excellent shape to endure that much time on the operating table.

"It's highly invasive. I have to remove a perimeter around the tumor, which tends to have cells growing almost invisibly in the esophagus, nearby lymph nodes and upper stomach. We want the best chance of curing you and not just forestalling its progression. It means taking out the majority of your esophagus and a good part of your stomach, then connecting what's left between your throat and stomach. I will have to open you up from your jaw line to your belly button. Also, a six-inch incision across your back.

"Life is going to change for you in some big ways. You can never lie flat again, because without an esophagus, whatever's in your stomach will come right up to your windpipe and mouth. You'll have stomach acids in your mouth and you could potentially choke, drown, or inhale and aspirate the acid into your lungs. But if we're successful, you're going to live."

That we were even talking about life after the operation gave me hope.

He went on to explain that with a severely reduced stomach area, my meals would be very small. Instead of a typical stomach to process food and drop it to my intestine, what remained of my stomach—elongated to replace what was removed—would be a narrow tube. This thin channel in my upper chest area would act as my stomach forevermore. Food ingested in any quantity would stretch the already stretched organ, resulting in discomfort and pain.

Then he told me he was scheduling my surgery for December.

It was still November. "No offense," I said, "but I've had it in my head now for a week that I have a tumor growing in my body. I want it out yesterday! Is there any chance I could move up the list to do this sooner? I'll pay extra."

"Mr. Coury, I know this cancer; it's all I do. I need to assemble the right team for what could be more than a ten-hour surgery," he said. "A month won't change anything, so stop thinking that way. But to be honest, this will be the toughest thing you've ever been through. With a relatively low survival rate, you should go home and get your affairs in order."

Friends for Life!

I returned home with a couple of weeks until the surgery. It was time enough to think about my life, my responsibilities, and what would happen if, God forbid, the surgery didn't go well. As anyone who's lost a loved one can tell you, one of the worst things is when, in the midst of your grief, you have to go to a mortuary, select a coffin, write an obituary and make all kinds of difficult decisions—not to mention the expense of it all. I'd done all this for my dad and I realized the last thing I wanted was to put my wife and kids through the same ordeal.

I went to Palm Mortuary and met with the woman who'd helped me make the arrangements for my father's burial. I said, "I could die during this surgery, or I might survive it. But no matter what happens, I don't want my family to have to deal with planning a funeral." With her assistance, I went through everything, paid for it all, and got it done and behind me.

One of the hardest parts was calling my many friends and telling them, "I got this news and I'm going in for surgery in early December. There's a pretty good chance I won't survive it. So I just want to say, I feel like I had a great run and I love you."

How many guys get to say goodbye? Most people were shocked, especially because I didn't look or act the least bit sick.

Don Tamburro, a great buddy and a real stand-up guy, was living in Texas at the time. Don, who'd done extremely well in the car business, and I had enjoyed a lot of good times together, vacationing in Myrtle Beach and traveling to different spots around the world on his private jet. Don's the kind of guy who'd do anything for a friend in need, day or night, rain or shine, no questions asked. Don called me one day just to say hello.

"I was just about to call you," I said. "I've got some pretty big news." After explaining my diagnosis and chances of survival, I continued. "It's unfortunate, but they caught it early and I'm hoping to beat it. But I just wanted you to know you've been a good friend these past few years, I've loved getting to know you and your family, and if I wake up and survive it, the ride continues. If not, well, this could be goodbye."

"Holy shit, Ron, I never saw this coming. I'm sending my pilot, Kinsey, out to fly you to L.A. for the surgery."

"You don't have to do that, Don. I'm flying into Burbank, it's under an hour flight, and I already bought a ticket on Southwest."

"No way. You're going to be on a plane with ninety people coughing and sneezing, you're going into the fight of your life and the last thing you need is to catch a flu bug before this surgery. You're flying on my plane—clean air guaranteed. It's not an option."

I couldn't have been more touched. "Wow, buddy, thank you. I don't know what to say." I will never forget his act of concern and love for a friend.

Paul Smith, a chiropractor buddy, was also there for me. Although we knew each other informally from Saturdays at the barbershop and the spa at Caesars, we became very close in 1995, after a drunk driver rear-ended me at a stoplight at more than 40 miles per hour. Years earlier, when I was in the Marines, I suffered a fractured neck. Even though it healed, the muscles around the injury remained tight—the vertebrae compressed on nerves and, on occasion, I found myself immobilized and in considerable pain. When the car accident exacerbated that old injury, I was in agony. After weeks of seeing different doctors, few options remained to me. There was nothing the doctors could do short of a triple-fusion surgery, which entailed opening me up and fusing a rib bone over my vertebrae to keep those bones from closing in on the nerves. It sounded like hell, but I figured I didn't really have any choice—until Paul convinced me to come see him.

"I've been doing this for thirty years. I've treated Don King, Mike Tyson, Larry Holmes, and many other celebrities. Give me five visits to treat you. If you're not feeling better, go have the surgery."

Okay, I thought, what do I have to lose?

I went to his see him and he worked on me for over an hour, and for the five following days as well. It was miraculous. I had better mobility than before the accident! From that point on, we grew very close as friends. I invited him to my home where we worked out together or walked around the lake. Paul is a very well-read professional and keeps up on all the latest medical literature. When I broke the news about my tumor, I said, "I'd really appreciate it if you could come with me to see Dr. Demeester and ask the questions that I don't think to ask."

"Of course, Ron, whatever you need. I'll be there every step of the way."

That was a great comfort to me at such a difficult time. Paul is a true friend in every way.

On My Way into Combat

As the date of my departure and surgery approached, I had a difficult conversation with Joan. "I don't want you or the kids coming to
California and the hospital. I'm literally going to war. If I was going to
Vietnam, you couldn't come with me. I love you and I'll miss you, but
the doctors have told me if I'm going to pull through this, it'll be long
and hard there and I'll need a lot of rest to recover."

"But honey . . ."

I'd anticipated her objections. "Please, I don't want any of you to
see me in the condition I'll be in or to feel like I need to help you all
through this. I'm asking you to please stay in Vegas and take care of the
household, the kids, my mom and Aunt Gloria." Tommy was young and
would need stability and reassurance. Joan understood.

Even though I knew how hard it was for her, she and the kids
respected my wishes. I'd need them plenty when and if I got home. As
Dr. Demeester said, the first year of recovery would be long and hard—
a feeding tube for up to three months and mostly in bed for the better
part of the year.

When the time came, Paul flew with me on Don's plane to L.A.
and true to his word, he was my advocate at every turn.

When I first arrived at the hospital, I had two goals. The first, obviously, was to survive. The second, which I shared with the doctors, was,
"My daughter is getting married in January. I really need you to get me
home for the ceremony." They acknowledged my request, but didn't
offer any guarantees.

Finally, the moment of truth arrived: December 5, 2005. As they
prepped me for surgery and began administering anesthesia, I realized
I'd never told them about my prior neck injury and to make sure they

kept my head and neck supported a certain way. The lights went out before I could mention it.

My friend and workout partner, Mark Beckerle, a Vegas cop, had driven to the USC Hospital the day before my surgery to see me. A spiritual type, Mark said he believed with all his heart that people undergoing surgery see a bright white light. If they walk to it, they go to heaven and die on the table. "Buddy," he said, "if you see a white light, *run the other way!*"

During my surgery, I did see just such a light. As if watching myself and all the doctors and nurses from above the operating table, I saw myself facing the light. Remembering Mark's cautionary words, I turned and did, in fact, run the other way. Was it real or a dream? Had Mark induced the vision? Did it happen when I was bleeding out from my spleen, which got pierced during the operation and needed emergency removal to stop the bleeding? I'll never know.

My next conscious thought came 12 hours later when, thank God, I woke up in post-op.

My first sensation was that my entire torso was numb; the epidural they'd given me to block the pain had yet to wear off. However, the epidural didn't cover my neck and my second sensation was that of excruciating neck pain.

The ICU nurse could see I was in agony. "What's wrong? You should still be numb from the surgery."

"It isn't that," I grimaced. "I have an old neck injury and they apparently placed me in odd positions during surgery without supporting my neck. Whatever you're giving me for pain, it's not helping."

Then I saw that Paul was in the room. "Paul, please give me an adjustment—something."

"I wish I could, Ron, but if I move you, it'll tear open the stitches along your jaw line and I don't think any of us want that."

"Is there anything you can do?"

Paul thought about it, then moved behind the head of my bed and did some manual traction to try to open up the vertebrae a little. It worked like a charm when he was pulling, but as soon as he let go or lightened up—bam!

The first night was brutal and the pain was really rough, but you won't hear me complain about it too much today. I was alive.

The next day, they wanted me up and walking around, which I was able to do. However, things turned bad pretty quickly. I was in ICU for several days after developing the dreaded staph infection, MRSA. If MRSA overwhelms a patient's immune system, severe and potentially fatal complications can occur. It's especially concerning, because it's largely resistant to antibiotics.

Next came blood clots in both of my legs.

Honest to God, it seemed like anything that could go wrong did. Even after the surgery, it was touch and go.

I had to sleep in an adjustable bed that enabled me to elevate my torso and avoid choking on stomach acid. I also had to try to avoid sliding down in my sleep, which inadvertently caused me to lie flat. As it turned out, waking abruptly with a mouthful of stomach acid, gasping for breath, and sucking that crap into my lungs would be my reality forever.

Finally, they moved me into a regular hospital room, where I remained for a month.

My brother Artie and our cousin Doug Charles, who lived in Southern California, came for a couple of days at a time, as did my good buddies who also lived in California: Gerry O'Shea, Brian Golie, and Doug Vind. They wanted to be around for moral support and when I was awake, they tried to lift my spirits. Dan, the great friend and partner that he is, stayed behind and tended to our business holdings, watching my back, as always.

Recovery

Even though my condition continued to improve, I could see that an early hope of making it home by Christmas wasn't in the cards.

When I left for surgery, Joe was 27 and Angela was 24 and on their own, but Tom was only 10. Joan had raised three wonderful, caring children, and our family replicated the way I grew up, trying to have dinners together, each of us catching up on the days' events. Large Sunday dinners included my immediate and extended family, as well as friends visiting Las Vegas. During my surgery and recovery time in the hospital, I missed my three kids and Joan more than words could ever say.

Meanwhile, Paul was at my bedside all day, every day, feverishly working on his laptop. I later learned he was writing thorough updates on my status and emailing them to the many friends I've been blessed with.

When Paul went home to be with his family, my pal Brian came to spend Christmas Eve with me. Brian got me in a wheelchair, rolled me outside, and for the first time in almost a month, I felt sun on my face. It's amazing how the little things become so important and memorable in times of trouble.

Brian went home to be with his mom, but Gerry, although he had two kids himself, came and spent all of Christmas Day with me. I'll never forget the moment I needed to get up and take what would be my first actual shower since surgery. I had to have help just to walk. Gerry, God love him said, "This will be the first time I ever took a shower with a guy."

December gave way to January and I really started to think I was on my way to a full recovery—until I awoke early one morning in a panic. I couldn't inhale. As soon as I took in even the smallest breath, it was as if someone had placed a plastic bag over my head. I had no idea what was happening and I couldn't even summon enough breath to ask a question.

The doctors determined that I had a pneumothorax, essentially, a collapsed lung. This occurs when air leaks into the space between your lung and chest wall, then this air pushes on the outside of the lung enough to make it collapse. Caused by my surgery, it was why I couldn't grab more than a split second of air. I needed yet another procedure, where they had to insert a tube to release the air surrounding my lung and suffocating me. What they didn't tell me was that they couldn't give me anything else for pain. I was on so many meds, I was maxed out. I could hear and *feel* them cutting my skin and pushing in the tube, a sensation I will *never* forget. As painful as it was, as soon as they got the tube where it needed to be, I could take a full breath and it was all worth it.

By the time I was cleared to return home in January, I still had a drain in my side, I was on a ton of medications, and the feeding tube remained in place. The doctors told me that when they connected what was left of my stomach to my throat, it was like sewing Jello together. For that reason, I couldn't attempt to swallow anything for months, because if anything should tear in the area where I was resectioned . . . well, that would be the end of that. Each day at home, Joan hung a feeding bag on a stand next to my bed and I got my nourishment.

Even though I was weak, uncomfortable, and nearly died several times, I'd accomplished my two goals. I was alive and damned if I wasn't in attendance at my daughter's wedding. It took all the strength I could muster, but I walked Angela down the aisle, albeit slowly, and she was the prettiest and happiest bride I'd ever seen.

A Semblance of Normalcy

Over the course of 2006, I gradually grew stronger and after repeated tests, I was finally allowed to start eating. As I'd been warned, my stomach was a narrow tube that dumped right into my intestines and when I started ingesting solid food, the pain was through the roof. If I ate only two chicken wings or two bites of a sandwich, I felt like I'd over-stuffed myself at Thanksgiving dinner. But I was thankful to resume a reasonable facsimile of a normal life. Finally.

I still had to get used to sleeping upright to avoid inhaling stomach acid. Ingesting these poisons into my lungs caused aspirational pneumonia. When this occurred, I had to treat it for a week or more with daily doctor visits to receive nebulizer treatments, shots to avoid infection, and to cough that stuff out of my lungs. After years passed and a half-dozen such incidents, a lung-function test revealed that my lungs were permanently damaged and worked at only 70 percent of normal capacity. Waking often throughout the night and adjusting my elevation or position became a fact of life and something I eventually came to accept.

Also, since the surgery, I undergo a Positron Emission Tomography or PET scan each year, which is, to date, the best cancer-screening test available. It clearly depicts images in the body and highlights possible problems. Between scans, every ache or pain would make me think, "Uh-oh, is that a tumor?" Thankfully, year after year the reports have come back, "NO CANCER!"

After the fifth PET scan, Dr. Demeester declared me cancer-free. While he urged annual scans to be on the safe side, he released me to my general practitioner and told me to get on with my life. He retired that year. I'll never forget him for the life-saving surgery he performed. Nor will I ever forget or be able to adequately thank Dr. Murray for finding the tumor so early.

I lost over 40 pounds during my month-long hospital stay, along with a great deal of muscle mass to atrophy. A few years after surgery, I'd gained back 15 of my lost pounds, but I was maxed out. These days, I can't eat enough to exceed the calories I burn through ordinary activity. The pain and eating several small meals per day just don't allow me to get back to where I was pre-surgery. However, my doctors tell me I'm healthy and lucky to be alive, so it's an adjustment I accept. "Get used to it. Let go of the desire to be what you were," I tell myself. "It's just the way it is." That's my reality now.

I worked out diligently all my life. It was useful as I ran my bars in the early years, never knowing when I might be in an altercation. It helped me be prepared if I saw an event requiring physical force to keep peace. Ultimately, tenacity and stamina carried me through the toughest battle imaginable.

As I learned more about esophageal cancer, I found out that approximately 13,500 Americans contract it annually and 12,500 are dead within a year, reflecting the eight percent survival rate the doctors had spoken of. I made it, and I'm certain that my excellent physical condition enabled me to come through nearly 12 hours of surgery.

So hear me when I say: Stay in good shape all your life. You never know when you might really need it! And remember, regular physicals and early detection really do save lives.

Tragically, early detection wasn't in the cards for my wife, Joan. Just one year after my surgery, she was diagnosed with advanced colon cancer. Despite our best efforts and multiple surgeries, chemotherapy, and radiation, this horrible disease took her from us just two years later, on December 28, 2009, at age 56.

I had been married for more than 30 years, with three wonderful children. It saddens me beyond words that Joan wouldn't live to be a part of the future lives of Joe, his wife, Rita, and their sons Rocco and

Duke, who now live in Scottsdale, Arizona; or Angela, her husband, Joe, and their sons Connor and Nathan, who live a mile from me in Las Vegas.

When Joan got sick, our son Tom was only 12. During her illness and for years after her passing, I was thrust into a new role as a single parent. Tom and I grew much closer and we lived like two bachelors, cooking, grocery shopping, and experiencing all that comes with running a home together through his teenage years.

My Aunt Gloria passed away in 2007 and my mom a year later, having survived my dad by six years.

After graduating from college, Tom and his girlfriend, Brittany, brought my fifth grandson into the world. In 2018, we welcomed Aiden Christopher Coury to our family.

CHAPTER 27

Selling Suburban Graphics

Suburban Graphics was a tremendous business for Dan and me. It was fun and highly profitable for two decades, but the way we sold it was quite a coup.

Every year, the Global Gaming Expo came to the Las Vegas Convention Center, and Suburban Graphics regularly exhibited there. It was an excellent venue to display our slot-glass designs and promote the advancements we made each year as a supplier to slot manufacturers and casinos. Dan and I also walked the convention floor, learning what was going on with competitors and what new games manufacturers were promoting. It was a tremendous opportunity to rub shoulders with decision-makers from hotels and the slot industry to promote our business. We invariably ended up with more work as a result of these shows.

Over the years, we increasingly observed monitor-based slot machines in the display areas. Rather than glass in the typical three-front framework of a machine, our product was being replaced by flat-screen LED monitors. We could see that soon, designs, colors, and entire games could be replaced from a slot-director's desk computer, rather than the old manner of slot-glass change-outs, the heart of our graphics business. When these new-generation machines first began appearing, they were exorbitantly expensive. But after a show one year, Dan said to me, "You know, it's just a matter of time before those prices come down, like transistor radios in the sixties and calculators in the seventies."

A huge part of our business relied on machine retrofits; changing the glass or the reel strips, when operators wanted to modify a game design or payout schedule. The machines themselves were built like tanks. They could last for decades. Hiring us to retrofit a group of existing machines was an attractive alternative to paying $10,000–$15,000 for each new machine.

Every alteration meant art and production work for us.

However, the writing was definitely on the wall. This monitor-based machine concept provided casinos with previously unheard-of options and ease of game-change opportunities. No new reels or glass meant no new business for us.

"When—not if—this LED thing takes off," Dan said, "our industry niche ceases to exist."

As forward-thinking businessmen, we'd diversified over the years to producing large display signs, vehicle wraps, and other types of work, but gaming device graphics still constituted 90 percent of our net. We also knew that when a new, better, and less expensive way of doing things comes along, old business models go right out the window. The new games were in the earliest stages of development and pricing was too high to be affordable, but believing they were destined to drop, we started thinking about an exit strategy. For now, our business was solid. Gross sales and net profits were excellent and made us a company prime for acquisition. Any major industry change would be many years away, but we weren't getting any younger and retirement was on our minds anyway.

It's a delicate matter to put your business up for sale. Handled badly, valuation is detrimentally affected. Employee loss generally follows rumors of a sale. Customers can pull business, looking out for themselves and developing new relationships with competing vendors. Our competitors could take advantage of the news—possibly exaggerate it a bit—and try to benefit as quickly as possible.

Back to Court and a Win-Win—For Us

Around this time, one of our employees, Adelaide Pritchard, wanted to leave Suburban Graphics to explore new opportunities. Dan and I were fond of Adelaide. She'd started as a receptionist and over time, we'd made her a sales representative, set her up with a few of her own customers, and paid her a commission in addition to her base salary. In her rise through the ranks, she learned our process, so she could bid jobs and delivery times, understanding how the complexity of any one project impacted the production schedule. She was essentially in business for herself and could earn as much or as little as her drive and performance dictated.

As a receptionist, Adelaide didn't need to sign a restrictive covenant agreement, but when we promoted her to sales rep, we required it, as we did with all employees who had access to proprietary information. Our longtime labor attorney, Howard Cole, prepared the document and as we soon discovered, they're called "non-competes" for good reason. As court rulings and Nevada laws changed, Howard would always update our covenant agreements to help ensure optimal enforceability.

At any rate, Adelaide announced one day that she was quitting and moving to Florida. Even though we were sorry to lose her, we wished her the best of luck.

Just a few weeks later, we learned she'd misled us. Not only hadn't she moved to Florida, but she'd gone to work for Lightning Graphics, a local competitor. We might not have known so quickly if one of our loyal customers hadn't shared an email with Dan that Adelaide had sent him, introducing herself as the new representative at Lightning Graphics and stating that as his former sales rep at Suburban Graphics, she knew our process, pricing, and terms and she could be highly competitive if his company gave her its business. Learning of this so quickly enabled us to apply near immediate damage control.

Dan sent Lightning Graphics the non-compete agreement Adelaide had signed, then called the owners to explain the situation. They didn't care what our agreement said and welcomed a lawsuit, believing we'd never prevail in court.

We then contacted Howard and he referred us back to his firm's litigation attorney, Todd Touton. Todd had done a stellar job for us before the Supreme Court in the Winners versus the City of Opportunity case back in the 1990s so I had great confidence in his litigation skills. He sent a more formal letter to Lightning Graphics, telling them Adelaide was violating the agreement she'd signed with us. The letter put them on official notice that employing her violated the terms of the agreement and that they—and she—needed to immediately cease and desist contacting our customers.

The Lightning Graphics response? They said non-competes were worthless. The company's principals were accustomed to operating in California, where such agreements were generally ruled unenforceable. But that wasn't the case in Nevada. Lightning Graphics' mainstay was creating big overhead displays at places like the Las Vegas Convention Center, but they desperately wanted to get into gaming graphics and figured the fastest and simplest way was to pilfer a competitor's employees. So we took Lightning Graphics and Adelaide to court.

Todd was nothing short of brilliant as he told the judge what had happened. After Adelaide gave her version of the story, the judge looked at her and said, "Young lady, by your own admission, these gentlemen at Suburban Graphics gave you every possible chance to succeed. You testified that you left them to make more money. You could have made all the money in commissions your sales would generate. But rather than staying with them and earning more money, you willfully and knowingly chose to ignore the covenant you signed in apparent good faith, then betrayed their trust by taking proprietary information about Suburban, including their bidding formula and customer list, and giving it all to your new employer. Then you had the nerve to actually reach out to one of Suburban's customers and pitch them with this letter I have as an exhibit. What have you got to say for yourself?"

Suddenly, Adelaide didn't have much to say.

"I'm ruling that Lightning Graphics cannot employ Ms. Pritchard for two years, as stated in the non-compete agreement," the judge announced. "Furthermore, neither she nor Lightning Graphics shall contact or do work for Suburban Graphics customers within that same two-year period. Violate my order and there will be sanctions against Lightning Graphics and its owners, whom, I note for the record, are seated here today. Fair notice, lady and gentlemen. Do not test this court or you will find yourselves on the wrong side of a large judgment and possibly a contempt order. I've heard what you're used to in California, but you're in Nevada now. We look out for our business people and you gentlemen have severely tested the limits of reason with your actions."

In addition to the order about their future actions, the judge also awarded us the return of the fees our lawyer charged to enforce the non-compete. When Lightning Graphics had to pay for our attorney as well as theirs, their miscalculation really had to sting.

Walking back to the law office with Todd, a couple blocks away from the courthouse, Dan and I shared how good it felt to see justice upheld. Then an exciting new thought occurred to me. "You know, if Lightning Graphics wants to get into gaming graphics so bad, why don't we see if they'll buy Suburban?"

Dan was skeptical they'd ever consider it, but I felt it was worth a try.

"Todd, you could contact their attorney and suggest, ever so casually, 'Your clients should make Dan and Ron an offer.' I've heard them talking about retiring.' If we contact them directly, they might suspect desperation and it'll hurt our negotiation on the price. But if you mention it in passing to their attorney, who knows? They might just nibble at the bait."

Todd agreed we had little to lose by trying. He'd call the attorney for the other side and plant the seed.

Lightning Graphics was owned by an equity-fund firm in New York that had acquired the company some years earlier, but kept the two brothers who'd started the business as employees. Todd executed my plan to the letter and sure enough, a short while later, Lightning Graphics came sniffing around, wondering if Dan and I really were thinking about retiring. We told them we were and after some negotiating, in 2008, we struck a deal.

Ultimately, they bought the business, initially leasing the real estate from us for a five-year term. Toward the end of that time period, they were still doing the large-format convention sign work, but as Dan had astutely predicted, prices on LED slots had plummeted. In the end, Lightning Graphics didn't renew our lease and relocated to a 90,000-square-foot facility. This left Dan and me with 48,000 square feet of perfectly good industrial space, which we leased to a medical marijuana growing operation that executed its option to purchase and now owns the property.

Quite a good deal for us to turn what might have become a dying business with a large unique piece of real estate into a profitable exit. Once again, some forward thinking, good planning and a little luck managed to turn lemons into lemonade.

CHAPTER 28

Car Adventures and Square Panda

Don Tamburro, my friend in Texas who generously provided his plane to take me to my surgery, relocated to Las Vegas in 2009. He and I spoke often about being retired, having few of the write-offs that operating our businesses formerly provided and wanting to earn again. Most important, we both felt like we still had one more round of empire building in us. We agreed it would be fun to do it together.

By this time, Dan and I had sold Suburban Graphics and Dan looked forward to retiring, flying his plane, enjoying his boat in San Diego, playing more golf and, in his words, never having so many employees again. He was burned out after managing a staff of more than 100 for almost 25 years.

Dan and I had accomplished great things for two guys leaving the Marines in 1973 with a few dollars between us. He was a terrific partner and we still owned all of our commercial properties together. What we accomplished together was only possible due to our combined vision, tenacious strategizing, diligence, and a fair share of good luck. But over our many years as partners in business, the contributions of all our employees must be acknowledged. Managing our affairs in the office under the watchful eye of our CFO, Jennifer Tarter, and with the help of my longtime and loyal assistants, Rox Ann Oldham, the former wife of my private investigator Mike Wysocki, and Jennifer Medeiros, who remains with me to this day, Dan and I had a great run. I would manage what was left of our joint holdings, so Dan was free to do as he wished in his well-deserved retirement.

Don Tamburro and I discussed what we might enjoy doing together. He expressed an interest in learning the liquor and gaming business in Las Vegas, so we explored that option first. A small hotel casino with a couple hundred rooms was up for sale. We toured it, beginning the typical due diligence process that we'd both grown accustomed to after years of business acquisitions, but it required too much remodeling. When nothing else was immediately available in our price range, we turned to other investment possibilities.

Real estate, like shopping centers and large office parks, was available, but none of the returns on investments attracted us.

One day toward the end of 2009, Don said he'd been contacted about an auto-dealership opportunity in Las Vegas. He asked what I thought about shifting our initial goal from me showing him the inner workings of the gaming business to him teaching me the car business.

A New Learning Curve

I didn't have to think long. I'd always enjoyed new and different challenges. He was a premier car dealer from all his past acquisitions and operations. I'd had the added benefit of seeing and touring his last three dealerships in Round Rock, Texas, when we returned from a Myrtle Beach vacation together. Along with showcasing Toyotas, Hondas, and Hyundais on a large piece of real estate he owned, he also operated a large collision center there. I was amazed at the organization and cleanliness of his entire operation. Knowing him as I did, I'd have expected nothing less.

The chance to learn the car business from Don was a no-brainer. I jumped at it. He and I shared a similar business philosophy. A decent businessman who made well-thought-out decisions, was good with customers, and was honest and savvy could operate almost any business. Once you ramped up on the specifics of an industry, you applied the same philosophies to the new business that you'd applied to all your others and success was highly probable.

I was also confident that I could contribute in any way Don envisioned. I'd been in Las Vegas for more than 35 years, had met thousands of people from my varied businesses, and believed that whenever they needed a vehicle they'd want to come and work with someone they already knew and trusted. A couple of well-placed press releases proved it true.

Our first venture in the Las Vegas automobile industry was Planet Hyundai, located on the high-traffic West Sahara Ave. corridor, a multi-street stream of long-standing car dealerships. It was a great location that had performed amazingly well during the economic boom of the 1990s, but after the crash of 2007–2009 slowed considerably. Don crunched the numbers and believed we could do something serious there. The price was right, as the business volume had diminished. It was also a fine real estate play, which we both had a great love for. We struck a deal with the seller to take over in March 2010.

When I shared the news with some friends and associates, the reaction was uniform: "Are you guys nuts?"

In 2010, the country was still crawling out of the deep and painful recession and Planet Hyundai had gone from being one of the best-performing Hyundai dealerships in the country, moving more than 400 new cars a month in its heyday, to selling less than 100 each month. It was a risk, but we took it on with our eyes open.

Also, a deal this big at that time was pretty meaningful news for a local media starved for positive economic indicators to report. We got some nice coverage in the local newspapers regarding the acquisition. I also found out that owning a car dealership is a fast track to popularity. People I hadn't heard from in 10 years came out of the woodwork, hoping I could help them get a fair deal on a vehicle. I received as many as five calls a week. I always assisted when I could and my personal network turned out to be a valuable resource for our business.

A lot of people dread the stress involved in buying a car, often with good reason. It's usually a long and tiring negotiation. You throw out a number and the salesperson disappears into a back room for a while, then comes back with another. You counter that and you're alone again for a while. Often, it's only when you've had enough and are walking out that you finally start to get anywhere. I thought I could help take the pain out of the process.

Based on my reputation, when people I brought into the dealership were given a price on the car they selected, they knew it was a good, haggle-free amount. The closing rate for customers who came through me was very high; they were comfortable with the deal and were treated extremely well by our team of employees. Knowing someone in an ownership position contributed to a different level of comfort than just walking in and getting picked off by the first hungry salesperson.

Another project Don asked me to handle was to improve Planet Hyundai's record with the Better Business Bureau. When we bought the dealership it had a terrible rating, as complaints filed by consumers were previously ignored. I established a rapport with our local BBB executive director and learned that we couldn't just start over with them, even with new ownership—not if we kept the same name. We'd have to work our way up to a better rating through performance results. Within a short time, thanks to good customer service and general business practices, we successfully upgraded the Planet Hyundai rating to an A+ and became an Accredited Member.

Shortly after taking over Planet Hyundai, Don's brother Dave, who'd worked for him for many years, left the Texas operation and joined us as a partner. Same with James Whelan, Don's long-time financial advisor, who came on board as our CFO and partner. We four made an excellent team, each with a unique skill set and ready to do great things together. We added to our operations teams, trained them in Don's time-tested and proven sales methods, and enjoyed excellent profits during the building years of 2010 and 2011. Then, with all staffing and training processes in place, the real ride began. Compared to the year-end numbers in 2012, we experienced a 26 percent rise in new car sales in 2013. Ensuring it wasn't just a fluke, we climbed another 25 percent in 2014. Planet Hyundai would rise to be among the five top-producing Hyundai dealerships in the nation.

Based on our belief in ourselves and the first year at Planet Hyundai, in 2011 we reopened the previously closed Centennial Hyundai dealership in northwest Las Vegas and built that up nicely. A couple of years later, we acquired Butts Motors, a Chevrolet, Cadillac, and Acura dealership in the town of Seaside, California, near Monterey. Because of our solid relationship with Hyundai, a new dealer opportunity presented itself. We discontinued the Acura brand and replaced it with Hyundai, operating as Peninsula Auto Group, with a vast selection of three brands on a large parcel of real estate.

In 2014, I came to know another car dealer named John Spano. Considering my fairly good relationship with him and nothing for sale amongst the close-knit group of Las Vegas dealership owners, Don asked me to see if Mr. Spano would consider selling us a business he owned in Henderson's Valley Auto Mall. It wasn't an easy negotiation for a variety of reasons, but with the help of Don and James, we finalized a deal to purchase the business and real estate in May 2015. We changed the name to Henderson Kia.

Shortly after acquiring the Kia store, we received an offer to sell Planet Hyundai and Centennial Hyundai for a terrific price. Don was ready to get out and it was an excellent gain for us.

Shortly thereafter, Don explained to me that he wanted to change his lifestyle and not work the remaining stores. He knew I'd invested based on his daily oversight. The great friend and partner that he is, he bought me out of the remaining operations as he decided how he wanted to exit the businesses. He and I continued as landlords of the $15 million, 11-acre Kia property.

Receiving that rent check every month was a healthy contribution to my monthly real estate income, but with the transition, I suddenly found myself out of business altogether for the first time since 1976. In nearly 40 years of starting, buying, and selling businesses, whenever some were sold, Dan and I always had a couple of going concerns to manage and generate profits. This sale, in October 2015, left me with no operating businesses. I had to decide, at age 63, what I wanted to do and the truth was, I just didn't know.

It Doesn't Take Long To Find Out

I'd grown to love playing Texas Hold'em poker, usually at Bellagio, sometimes at the Wynn, Mirage, or Aria. I've developed a terrific group of friends in the poker community and look forward to playing with them regularly. As I struggled with concerns about being rendered irrelevant in the business community, I played every day—for a couple of months, until retirement proved to be better in theory than in actual practice.

I found it simply wasn't enough for me to collect rental income and play poker. Retirement works for a lot of people, but for me, I'm hooked on being active in one or more business ventures. Sure, I still exercised nearly every day, had a loving girlfriend in Dawn O'Brien, and enjoyed spending time with my kids and grandkids.

But as with many relationships, Dawn and I grew to have different goals and interests and ended our relationship in 2017, while maintaining the highest level of respect for and civility toward each other.

Then, out of the blue, after months of enjoying alone time, I went to lunch with Stephanne Zimmerman, a true natural beauty—inside and out—and a highly successful CFO in town. We'd dated when Joan and I were divorced for a few years in the 1980s, but when I returned to my family and remarried Joan, my relationship with Stephanne ended with no ill feelings on either side. Some 30 years later, we went to lunch, then dinner, and are well on our way toward rekindling what once was. Time will tell where we end up. We've agreed to take it one day at a time and so far, each rendezvous is better than the last. Our love for one another has returned, and I feel like we are well on the way to an exciting new chapter in our lives.

And as for remaining active in business, I knew in 2015 that I wasn't done just yet. I wasn't interested in buying or starting a business at my age. Not alone! Instead, I wanted to align myself with a big ship and help steer it to greater success, such as sitting on boards of directors and consulting on major ventures. What I really wanted was what I'd always wanted—the challenge to grow something big into something bigger and more profitable.

So after being retired for a very short time, I spread the word that I was looking for something to sink my teeth into. Within months, I was considering several opportunities and by summer 2016, I found myself involved in some new and exciting projects.

I'm now on the board of a new company called Square Panda with retired tennis champion Andre Agassi, company founder and board chairman Tom Boeckle, fellow Board members Steve Miller, Frank Suryan, and former Board member, Doug Ammerman.

Tom and his twin brother Phil are co-founders of the highly successful PT's Pubs chain of taverns in Las Vegas. They contacted me to request that I join the Square Panda board of directors and help launch the product internationally. I attended a presentation by board member and company CEO Andy Butler. What I saw was enthralling.

Square Panda is a learning aid for children ages two through eight. It works in conjunction with a tablet computer and has vast potential to revolutionize how children learn to spell and read. It was initially available through our website and in select Barnes and Nobles stores. After a successful test period, we would be stocked in all 434 Barnes and Noble locations. Now we sell directly to parents via Amazon or our website. We're also introducing the program to school districts throughout the United States, already gaining entry into over 400 schools. We've made great strides in China and India, both of which are highly motivated to teach their children English at an early age. This could be the largest financial score of my career. Mark my words, Square Panda will soon be a household name.

I also accepted a position on the board of a local family-owned furniture retailer, Walker Furniture. We're expanding to other parts of Las Vegas and will grow what's already an extremely large and successful business into a giant in the local marketplace.

I'm a partner with Randy Sutton; national radio celebrity and columnist Wayne Allyn Root; and production-company owner Michael Yudin in a new TV show—a Vegas-based production that will follow police recruits through their academy training and into patrol cars for the first time, accompanied by their field-training officers. Viewers will follow recruits, bonding with those they've developed an affection for and seeing if their favorites actually succeed and become police officers.

It will also provide the nation with a candid view of what it takes to become a police officer, casting a positive light on policing, compared to what's too often depicted poorly by the media.

Randy has also asked me to partner with him on Celebrating Legacy, a groundbreaking social media concept that will, for the first time, provide people with opportunities to predetermine and describe the life experiences, messages, and feelings they wish to share with loved ones upon their passing and list who should be notified upon their death. It will also be an invaluable tool for future generations wishing to explore the heritage of their families. We're also founding the Wounded Blue Foundation. Unbeknownst to many people is an ever-growing problem of wounded and disabled police officers in America who were injured in the line of duty and have little in benefits and resources to support them when they can no longer work. Whether caused by vesting shortfalls or small-town agencies with limited budgets, far too many officers are in dire straits after an on-the-job injury disables them. The Wounded Blue Foundation mission will be to raise and distribute funds to worthy recipients.

Who would have guessed that some of the biggest deals of my life might come along at the exact moment I thought my days as an entrepreneur were nearing an end?

It has also been my honor to serve as a Board Member for the Las Vegas Metropolitan Police Department Foundation, which helps round out my work week by enabling me to show my support for and appreciation of our members of law enforcement. Don Tamburro and I donate $50,000 every year to a scholarship fund we founded in 2014 for the children of Metro officers. Formed in the memory of LVMPD Officers Alyn Beck and Igor Soldo, this Memorial Scholarship fund serves to honor the ultimate sacrifices these two officers made in the line of duty. Nearly 100 students apply annually and we award ten

$5,000 scholarships to deserving recipients, based on their transcripts, community service, and an essay in which they share the effects that being the child of a peace officer has had on them.

Another project, long in the planning phase, is this very book, the chance to describe some of the events that have occurred through the building or purchase of more than 20 businesses over the past 42 years. It's also an opportunity to describe the amazing friendships and finest business partners a man could ever hope for. Most are lucky to find one good business partner in their life. I've been blessed with many who are also close, trusted friends—more than I could ever have wished for.

Finally . . .

If I've learned one thing over the past six decades, it's that life is always waiting to surprise you. The only constant in life is change, and with change often comes controversy, sometimes even danger. You must be prepared to move forward in the face of whatever stands in the way of your goals and dreams. Another thing I've learned is to be quiet, if given the chance, and to listen. You can learn something from anyone regardless of their stage in life, position or worth. Summed up best on a refrigerator magnet I found many years ago, *"It's better to remain silent and be thought a fool than to speak up and remove all doubt!"* Most important, you must never cower to bullies or run from snakes in the grass who are waiting to undermine and destroy your every effort. Strive for success but, by all means, be alert and cautious along the way. One never knows what might be just around the corner.

To those of you who are finishing this book, may your ventures in life be less complicated than mine but, when necessary, may you have the fortitude and stamina to draw on the courage and tenacity that will enable you to prevail.

ACKNOWLEDGMENTS

There are many people beyond the incredible family and friends I have been blessed with who were integral in transforming my dream to write this book into reality.

Brian Rouff and Bob Burris helped me with the original draft, which, when transcribed from my oral recitations, exceeded 140,000 words. They not only helped put it all on paper, but were instrumental in reducing my narrative to a more traditional length of approximately 85,000 words.

Deke Castleman served as the official editor. He took a fine piece of writing and improved it substantially. I will be forever grateful for his cooperation, understanding, and patience as I introduced changes and additions—long after his initial edit.

Enormous gratitude goes to my first business partner, Dan Hughes, with whom I began my initial eight ventures. In addition, I'd like to express my eternal thanks to Don Tamburro, whose guidance took me to unimaginable heights in business and with whom I enjoyed a six-year run with more than a half-dozen car dealerships. I've been a friend and business partner with each of them—in separate ventures—for many memorable and incredible years.

Next, one of my oldest friends, Tom Kennedy. Knowing each other since kindergarten in Brooklyn, we maneuvered through grade school and high school together. He shared several of the early events in this book with me and later joined me in Las Vegas, witnessing many of the life-altering events of my adult years. Not only have his recollections reminded me of long-forgotten facts, but his writing skills provided the final editor's mark.

Jennifer Medeiros, my director of operations, oversees everything from my various real estate–based residential and commercial holdings and management through the seemingly endless analyses and implementation of new projects. She always steps up when called upon, watches my back, and ensures that those I interact with toe the line and honor their commitments. Little I've done over the last 20 years would have gone so seamlessly without Jenn by my side. Her loyalty and diligence are deeply appreciated and will never be forgotten.

While all three of my children played a role in motivating me to succeed and be a positive example to them in adulthood, my son, Tom Coury, made a major contribution by designing the cover of this book. His graphics skills made all those years of college tuition worthwhile. The love that he, Joe, and Angela have always shown me has made me a better person and father, for which they have my eternal love and respect.

And finally, no project like this could ever come together without excellent business support and legal representation. My gratitude extends to many companies and individuals. Thank you to everyone at Imagine Communications, and to Horizon Web Marketing's team, Carolyn Renaud, Matt Campbell, Ross Barefoot and Roy Nakamura. Also, thanks to David Wilk's Booktrix team, Barbara Aronica, Jeremy Townsend, and Kate Petrella, for producing this book to such a high standard.

My never-ending appreciation goes to several legal counselors whose advice and friendship are very dear to me. They include Donald Green, Richard "Rick" Wright, Steve Stein, Randall Jones, Doug Edwards, F. Robert (Bob) Stein, Howard Cole, Anthony Cabot, Jennifer Roberts, David Chesnoff, Don Martin and the late Chuck Thompson.

ACKNOWLEDGMENTS

Writing my first book has been an incredible experience for me. My final task for this project became obvious when I learned that a high percentage of books are now purchased as audiobooks. I realized then that I needed to determine who had the right voice for this one. I am honored that my life story is narrated by actor Michael Madsen, whose extraordinary voice is the sound of tenacity itself. My appreciation for Michael's talent and his many hours of work with me in the studio cannot be overstated.

The *Tenacity* audiobook, recorded at the Dog and Pony Show recording studio, exceeds my wildest expectations. I am grateful to John and Dawn McClain for their efforts in producing this outstanding audio version of my book.

INDEX